LABOR'S CONFLICT
Big business, workers and the politics of class

Once widely regarded as the workers' greatest hope for a better world, the ALP today would rather project itself as a responsible manager of Australian capitalism. *Labor's Conflict: Big Business, Workers and the Politics of Class* provides an insightful account of the transformations in the Party's policies, performance and structures since its formation.

Seasoned political analysts Tom Bramble and Rick Kuhn offer an incisive appraisal of the Party's successes and failures, betrayals and electoral triumphs in terms of its competing ties with bosses and workers.

The early chapters outline diverse approaches to understanding the nature of the Party and then assess the ALP's evolution in response to major social upheavals and events, from the strikes of the 1890s, through two World Wars, the Great Depression, and the post-war boom. The records of the Whitlam, Hawke, Keating, Rudd and Gillard governments are then dissected in detail. The compelling conclusion offers alternatives to the Australian Labor Party, for those interested in progressive change.

Tom Bramble is Senior Lecturer in Industrial Relations in the School of Business at the University of Queensland.

Rick Kuhn is Reader in Political Science in the School of Politics and International Relations at the Australian National University.

T0384599

LABOR'S CONFLICT

Big business, workers and the politics of class

TOM BRAMBLE AND RICK KUHN

CAMBRIDGE
UNIVERSITY PRESS

CAMBRIDGE UNIVERSITY PRESS
Cambridge, New York, Melbourne, Madrid, Cape Town, Singapore,
São Paulo, Delhi, Dubai, Tokyo, Mexico City

Cambridge University Press
477 Williamstown Road, Port Melbourne, VIC 3207, Australia

Published in the United States of America by Cambridge University Press, New York

www.cambridge.org
Information on this title: www.cambridge.org/9780521138048

© Tom Bramble, Rick Kuhn 2011

First published 2011

Cover design by Marc Martin, Small and Quiet Design
Typeset by Aptara Corp.
Printed in Australia by Ligare Pty Ltd

A catalogue record for this publication is available from the British Library

National Library of Australia Cataloguing in Publication data
  Bramble, Tom.
  Labor's conflict : big business, workers and the politics of class / Tom Bramble, Rick Kuhn.
  9780521138048 (pbk.)
  Includes bibliographical references.
  Australian Labor Party – History.
  Political parties – Australia History.
  Australia – Politics and government – History.
  Kuhn, Rick, 1955–
324.29407

ISBN 978-0-521-13804-8 Paperback

Contents

Preface   *page* vii

    Introduction   1

1 Labor's love's lost?   6

2 In the beginning: Labor's first quarter century   25

3 Between the wars   43

4 Hot war, cold war, split   55

5 Labor after 70 years   69

6 The Whitlam era   83

7 Economic rationalism under Hawke and Keating   104

8 Labor in the wilderness   126

9 The Rudd–Gillard government   143

10 The Labor Party today: what's left   168

Notes   194
Index   221

PREFACE

The authors of this book have been involved in radical politics for between 30 and 40 years, for most of that time as members of Marxist organisations, Socialist Alternative and its forerunners. Apart from a brief period in the early 1980s, when Rick was in the ALP, our relationships with the Labor Party have been from the outside. Because the ALP is a large and powerful organisation, historically associated with the left, it has affected the course and potential of all our political activities. This has taken different forms. As Labor has long been committed to managing Australian capitalism we have been highly critical of the Party. We opposed Labor governments in the late 1980s when they destroyed a militant trade union, the Builders' Labourers' Federation, and today we actively support campaigns against the Gillard government's treatment of asylum seekers, gays and lesbians, construction workers and Indigenous people. On the other hand, because Labor seeks to appeal to a working class voting base, and because a sizeable number of people believe that the Party is dedicated to achieving progressive social reform, we have also worked alongside ALP members and responded to initiatives of Labor leaders in various struggles against particular odious manifestations of the capitalist system. In recent years, these have included campaigns against WorkChoices, the invasion of Iraq and the Howard government's attacks on refugees. We took account of these different cir-cumstances as we worked alongside ALP members when they were drawn into struggle without sharing their illusions as to the core purpose of the Party.

An accurate understanding of the Labor Party and the logic of its devel-opment has been an important practical question for us. In this book we present our analysis of the ALP, drawn from historical and more recent evi-dence. We do so with the aim of explaining not only to those who have been repelled by the record of recent Labor governments why the Party behaves in the way that it does, but also to convince those who hold the sincere belief that Labor can serve as an avenue for progressive social change that their hopes are misplaced and that an alternative road is possible.

We are grateful to Ben Hillier and Jo Mettam, who provided assistance in our research. Many other people, with very diverse political views, provided us with information, insights and useful opinions. We would like to thank Liam Byrne, Diane Fieldes, Bob Gould, Mike Grewcock, Dick Gross, Sarah Ireland, Bill McCormick, Humphrey McQueen, Greg Patmore, John Percy, Sally Quilter, Eric Petersen, Stuart Rosewarne, Liz Ross, Andrew Scott, Scott Steel (Possum Comitatus), Frank Stilwell, Paul Strangio, Fleur Taylor, Joo-Cheong Tham and Norman Thompson. We are indebted to our readers, both the anonymous assessors provided by Cambridge University Press, and also those who we selected, Tom O'Lincoln and, in particular, Mick Armstrong, whose insights and guidance shaped our ideas. Without Mary Gorman's support and understanding, Rick would not have been able to participate in the project of explaining the contemporary Labor Party. Tom would like to thank Kaye Broadbent for her love and support during the writing of this book. We dedicate it to all those who share our desire for a world liberated from capitalism.

Introduction

'You're a joke! You're an absolute joke!' New South Wales Treasurer Michael Costa told delegates at the state Labor Party conference on 3 May 2008. He 'grinned and yelled at the crowd, and shook his fist in the air' in a 'Mussolini-like flurry'.[1] The conference then voted 702 to 107 to oppose his plans to sell off the New South Wales electricity industry.

This scene, and Costa's transformation from a young radical into a champion of neoliberalism, tells us a lot about the Australian Labor Party today.

Michael Costa was born in Newcastle in 1956, the son of Greek-Cypriot migrants who were manual workers.[2] His dad was a steelworker, then a railway guard; his mum was a process worker. Young Michael was politicised in the mid 1970s, in the context of intense conflicts, class confrontations and the dismissal of the Whitlam government. The level of strike action had peaked earlier in the decade, but remained high. Costa was embroiled in left wing politics from a young age. While still at high school he joined the Socialist Labour League (SLL), a Trotskyist organisation that advocated general strikes as the key to social change. He also became a member of the ALP. Later Costa switched his allegiance from the SLL to the Socialist Workers Party (SWP), a different Trotskyist organisation, with a more flexible political outlook.

Costa was dynamic, aggressive and bright. While a student at Wollongong University, he spent most of his time doing politics. He was the local organiser of the SWP's Socialist Youth Alliance and, with his allies, gained control of the Young Labor Association in the federal electorate of Hughes.

He had a run in with Peter Costello.[3] Then flirting with the Labor Party, Costello prevailed on his friend Michael Easson, the Young Labor leader, to expel the young firebrand from the ALP.

Costa returned to Sydney where, from 1979 to 1983, he was a rigger at Garden Island Naval Dockyard and an unpaid official of the Federated Ironworkers Association. While working, Costa also studied economics part time at Sydney University. For a while he was still associated with the SWP. Stuart Rosewarne, who taught one of his classes in radical political economy, remembers being confronted by Costa's 'particularly dogmatic take on the nature of capitalism'. He won three prizes for his third year results.[4]

After years of active membership, Costa left the SWP. But involvement with the far left had given him a series of skills – to organise, analyse and argue – that he was to use in his later union and political activity. In 1983 Costa took a job as an apprentice train driver. He was soon active in the Australian Federation of Locomotive Engineers (AFULE), becoming secretary of the Enfield Branch, and helped organise an opposition team for the union's elections in 1986. His ticket defeated the long established, left wing leadership of Bernie Willingale. Costa was elected president of the state branch of the union, a powerful but unpaid position. His success in union politics was accompanied by a rapid move to the right.

Michael Easson, by now Assistant Secretary of the Labor Council of New South Wales, spotted Costa's talent at a meeting of rail union officials. Easson, who had no memory of the Costello episode, recruited Costa back into the ALP where he lined up with the dominant right wing Centre Unity faction of the Party and rode on Easson's coat tails to greater heights. When Easson was elected secretary of the Labor Council in 1989, Costa was part of his right wing ticket and took a full time executive officer position.

Costa's drift to the right made him enemies, and not just on the ALP left. Soon after taking his post in the Labor Council, Costa threw a hand grenade at his comrades. Together with Mark Duffy, another Labor Council officer, Costa wrote a paper that criticised the Prices and Incomes Accord between the Hawke government and the ACTU. The two called for the dismantling of the traditional system of industrial arbitration, on which so many right wing trade union officials had built their careers, and forecast a grim future for the Party federally and in New South Wales. Duffy was sacked but Costa was allowed to stay. Together they expanded their paper into a book, *Labor, Prosperity and the Nineties*, which extravagantly praised the free market policies of the Hawke government. They called for a wages system that allowed bosses to cut pay if profits dipped. They urged greater competition between unions for members and advocated a looser relationship between unions and the Labor Party.[5] Remarkable views for full time trade union officials, but they did not prevent Costa from being preselected to stand for the then safe Liberal lower house seat of Strathfield in the 1991 state elections.

For some years, with the Liberals in power in New South Wales, Costa's political ambitions were thwarted. The Labor Council was for the most part ignored by the government, but when the Greiner government was defeated at the 1995 state elections by the ALP led by former Labor Council research officer Bob Carr, the Council was back in the thick of the action. In 1998 Costa was shoehorned into the secretary's position; he worked hard to maintain close relations with the Labor government.[6] At a time of labour shortages, Costa kept a lid on industrial strife at Olympic Games construction projects in Sydney. As a result of his generally supportive attitude to the government, he was appointed to a range of board positions within its gift, including at the New South Wales Grain Corporation, the Sydney Water Corporation, the State Rail Authority, the WorkCover Authority, Totalcare Industries, Pacific Power and Eraring Energy.

But it was not all sweetness and light between Costa and Carr. Costa opposed certain of the government's policies, such as contracting out public service functions, especially by the New South Wales railways. Yet, after being its managing director for several years, he sold one of the Labor Council's biggest assets, radio station 2KY, to the TAB. The unions also struck and demonstrated against the Carr government's cuts to workers' compensation entitlements in 2001. But, anxious not to strain relations with the government, Costa agreed to a compromise that suspended the union campaign while failing to deliver real concessions to workers. When the campaign reignited, he stood back. Costa was now winding down his involvement in union affairs and looking for new avenues for his talents.

In September 2001, following in the footsteps of his Labor Council predecessors, Costa was appointed to a sinecure in the New South Wales Legislative Council. In parliament, his career was spectacular. Less than 3 months after entering the upper house, and with the support of right wing shock jock Alan Jones, Costa was appointed police minister. His zero tolerance approach to policing was popular in the force and he defended police violence against demonstrators protesting against the World Trade Organization meeting in Sydney in 2002.[7] From police, Costa went on to other important ministries, including transport, economic reform and infrastructure, before being appointed to the plum position of treasurer in 2006. It was in this post, only a heartbeat from the premiership, that Costa finally came a cropper.

In the 1980s and 1990s, the Hawke and Keating governments had sold off the Commonwealth Bank and Qantas, along with other enterprises. The Carr government had sold the TAB. Now treasurer, and fired by his enthusiasm for the ideas of right wing economists Milton Friedman and Friedrich Hayek, Costa announced his plan to do the same to the New South Wales electricity industry. He was backed to the hilt by the media, Kevin Rudd's federal government and big business. But trade unions in the power industry and beyond, as well as a large majority of the electorate and ALP members, opposed this plan. There were strikes and demonstrations.[8] The bell tolled for Costa and his premier, Morris Iemma, when top right wing Party officials turned against them. So it was that Costa's proposal to sell off electricity crashed on the floor of the 2008 conference. Costa and Iemma attempted to press on with the sale regardless but they were by now dead men walking. The machine dumped both men later in the year. Soon afterwards, Costa quit his position in parliament. He then wrote a series of conservative opinion pieces for the *Australian* and *Daily Telegraph* and proved a popular speaker with business audiences.[9]

Michael Costa was not the first radical who entered the ALP with a desire to change the world and left active Party life a thorough going Tory. But the gap between his views as a young militant and his later outlook as a free market conservative was particularly wide. That a man who had a picture of Ronald Reagan on his office wall, was an open exponent of Thatcherite economics and was a climate change denialist to boot should hold high office in the ALP is indicative of major changes in the Party's outlook in recent decades. On the other hand, the career of this high flying Labor politician, who had very influential support, was spectacularly terminated by the trade union leaders and Party machine, demonstrating that, for all the changes in the ALP, it is still a very different animal to the Liberal Party. Costa's fall tells us something important about the connections with the working class and its trade unions that the Party retains to this day.

These two issues – the distancing of the Party from many of its traditional policies and its ever closer relationship with big business, and the maintenance of Labor's basic connections with the trade unions – are the main themes of this book. In Chapter 1 we consider in detail the nature of the ALP and rival interpretations of it. The bulk of the book is devoted to an examination of the party's changing relations with business, the trade unions and the working class more generally. We start with the formation of the Party during the defeats suffered by the working class in the great strikes and lockouts of the early 1890s, before moving on to the trauma of World War I and the torrid anti-conscription struggle. Labor's responses to the Great Depression form the centrepiece of Chapter 3, while Chapter 4 looks at Labor's second stint in federal office during a world war, the ensuing Cold War and the cathartic 1955 split. Chapter 5 provides an assessment of the nature of the Party after 70 years.

The second half of the book examines recent changes, starting with the election of Gough Whitlam as leader in 1967. Since then, and even more so from the period of the Hawke government, the ALP has become an organisation that in some ways would be quite unrecognisable to its founders; we trace this evolution in Chapters 6 to 9. In Chapter 10 we examine the changes that have occurred in the Party's material constitution since the early 1960s as well as some basic continuities. One feature of that continuity is Labor's consistent tendency in office to betray its working class supporters and to dash hopes of genuine social reform that have accompanied the election of Labor governments. We argue that this is a necessary consequence of Labor's ongoing commitment to capitalism. Chapter 10 closes, therefore, with a discussion of alternative strategies for social change.

Chapter 1

LABOR'S LOVE'S LOST?

Political parties have to adapt or die. If a party becomes fossilised while the rest of the world evolves it will lose support. As society changes, the size, characteristics and influence of groups that once formed the party's base may also begin to change. One hundred years ago, one-half of the Australian labour force, mainly blue collar workers, was employed in manufacturing and rural industries. As the rural workforce declined in the following decades, that proportion slipped a little, but the big surge in factory production during and after World War II saw it recover. The Australian Labor Party found its core of support among these workers.[1] Today, by contrast, manufacturing and rural industries employ only one in seven, so Labor must garner votes from outside its historic blue collar base if it is to win elections.[2] This shift throws up a big question: Is Labor still the party it once was or has it undergone a fundamental transformation? Debate has raged over this question for years. The answer depends on what you think the Labor Party is. This chapter identifies the essential character of the ALP – what makes Labor what it is – and also outlines several important debates about the nature of the Party.

A capitalist party?

For many modern Labor leaders, the character of their organisation is obvious. There is a continuous Labor tradition that embraces governments as diverse as those of Andrew Fisher, Jim Scullin, Gough Whitlam and Kevin Rudd. According to this view, the core of what makes Labor Labor is the Party's mission of civilising capitalism, which is counterposed to the more radical objective of abolishing it. In his first parliamentary speech as Labor leader in December 2006, Kevin Rudd invoked this tradition:

> Our movement for a century fought against Marxism, if you bother to read your history. We have had nothing to do with Marxism and madness. We have always seen our role as what we can do to civilise the market. That is where we come from as a tradition. Why do you think Keynes and the rest of them were called upon to try to save market capitalism from itself after the Great Depression? Because social democrats believed that you had to have constraints placed around the market, otherwise it becomes too destructive indeed.
>
> So, when it comes to our Labor values of equity, sustainability and compassion, we do not just believe that these in themselves are self-evident and worthy of being pursued; we also hold that they are values necessary to enhance the market itself.[3]

A few years before, Rudd identified the Party's tradition as a set of core values that 'have not changed'. These boiled down to support for a 'stronger Australia, a fairer Australia'.[4]

We agree with Kevin Rudd that Labor has from very early on been committed to making the Australian nation stronger, through policies that have combined the market and state regulation. But the nation and the market, while real features of Australian society, conceal and are underpinned by deeper structures, most importantly, the class relations of capitalism. It is precisely the Marxist perspective rejected by Rudd and the ALP that can reveal those structures and thus the fundamental character of the Labor Party. The following summary of the framework that we use in this book very briefly makes a series of controversial assertions about class relations. More detailed justifications for them can be found elsewhere.[5]

What do we mean by the 'class relations of capitalism'? Class is about the relationships among different groups of people involved in the process of creating social wealth. The way we gain our livelihoods, most importantly, the relations among the creators of social wealth and the controllers of productive assets who tell most of us what to do when we are at work, profoundly shapes our material interests and how we experience and think about the world. The working class, which provides the core of Labor's electoral base, is made up of those who, whether they do blue or white collar jobs, sell their ability to work – their 'labour power' – for a wage and have little or no formal control over what they and others do in the workplace. The owners and controllers of productive resources, the capitalists, purchase workers' labour power and, as a consequence, own what they produce. This wage labour relationship between workers and bosses is the core of capitalism. Only human labour creates new value; the other inputs into production only pass on the value already embodied in them to the final products. Capitalists' profits arise from the new value created by the labour of their employees and embodied in the commodities that come out of the production process. Profits are the result of the exploitation of wage labour, understood not primarily as moral judgement but as an analytical category. Understood in these terms, people's incomes are a consequence, rather than a defining feature, of their class.

The capitalist class includes the big shareholders and senior managers who control the productive resources of the private sector and the most senior politicians and public servants who control the resources of the state sector. They amount to a very small proportion of the population.

The working class has long been a majority of the Australian population. If we define workers as all employees except those in the occupations that involve substantial responsibility for controlling the labour of others, we find that the working class today comprises around 70 per cent of the labour force, a share that has declined only very slightly since the mid 1980s.[6] Then there are the intermediate classes of the traditional self-employed, including small manufacturers, farmers, shopkeepers, doctors, lawyers, accountants and publicans, and the modern middle classes of intermediate managers and professionals who have a great deal of autonomy in large institutions.

Because Australia is a capitalist society, national interests are, in effect, the interests of those who exercise effective power in the nation, that is, of the dominant social class. The Australian capitalist class rules by a variety of means. Within the workplace it rules despotically, unless reined in by strong trade unions. In the realm of ideas, through its role in the management of the mass media and educational institutions, the capitalist class rules more subtly. In economic matters, capitalists retain enormous power to control major investments, the flow of capital into and out of the country, the opening or closing of major enterprises, and the hiring and firing of millions of workers. They can and do use this power to influence government policy.

The capitalist class also rules through the machinery of the state, all the institutions of government in Australia. These include public service departments, municipal administrations, police and armed forces, court systems and prisons, as well as the relatively small parts that are elected: the federal, state and territory parliaments and local councils. The capitalist nature of the Australian state is guaranteed in several ways. First, there is a mingling of personnel. Senior state officials and private capitalists frequently have common backgrounds, attended the same elite private schools and participate in overlapping social networks. On retirement, top state personnel, these days including former Labor ministers, can expect lucrative jobs, board memberships or consultancies in the private sector. More importantly, the private sector and the state are interdependent. Most new value is created in the private sector, which relies on the state sector to maintain conditions for its profitability – a literate, healthy and disciplined workforce, efficient transport and communications infrastructure, a system of courts to protect property and resolve commercial disputes, and so forth. The state sector relies on taxes paid by workers and capitalists in the private sector for its sustenance. Thus the state depends on economic prosperity. This, in turn, rests on capitalist accumulation, that is, the process of reinvesting profits in improved machinery, equipment or technology, driven by competition among capitalists at home and abroad. Those in charge of both sectors draw their incomes from the exploitation of the working class and benefit from its continued subordination.

The internal bureaucratic and authoritarian hierarchies of the Australian state mirror those of corporations. The senior personnel of the state are paid very high salaries, and must always, if they are to retain their jobs, control their subordinates and, in the case of public service departments and government business enterprises, extract as much work out of them as they can. For this reason, and because their positions depend on capital accumulation, the top politicians, bureaucrats, generals and judges have an interest in maintaining the established social order. Indeed, a fundamental purpose of the police, armed forces and courts is to protect the interests of the capitalist class against the working class and foreign capitalist rivals by means of repression and military action. The heads of the state apparatus therefore tend to be conservative. This conservatism has created difficulties for the ALP, the party most identified with reform. The 20th century is replete with examples of Labor's reforms being frustrated by senior public servants, particularly in Treasury, the High Court and, of course, the governor-general and the New South Wales governor. During the 120 years of its existence Labor has adapted its reform program to what is acceptable to the capitalists and their state.

These economic and social relations have enormous ramifications for Labor's project of promoting the market and the national interest. As the economy is capitalist, Labor's pursuit of the national interest, regulation of markets, provision of infrastructure, promotion of economic growth, acceptance of the basic institutions of the Australian state and its role in advancing the national interest in relations with other countries, amount to a commitment to manage Australian capitalism.

The commitment of the ALP's leaders to promote the national interest also induces Labor governments to oppose and contain workers' militancy to ensure that labour power remains a commodity that can be profitably exploited. In periods of crisis, an inevitable feature of competitive capital accumulation and exploitation, Labor cooperates, readily or reluctantly, in depressing working class living standards to enable the capitalist system to recover. Its commitment to the Australian state and capital accumulation at home also mean that the ALP has pursued the national interest by military means in order to build Australia's influence through interventions in the southwest Pacific and southeast Asia, and the deployment of Australian forces in alliance with Britain, 'the mother country', and then the United States, 'the great and powerful friend'.

Although it may tinker at the edges of the system, the ALP defends a system characterised by profound inequalities in income and wealth. The desire to manage capitalism also means that Labor governments are in no position to challenge the root causes, in capitalist class relations, of oppression and alienation. Women's oppression, grounded in the structure of the family under capitalism, provides the capitalist class with the next generation of workers at cut price rates. Homophobia reinforces the illusion that heterosexual couples raising children is the only normal domestic arrangement. Racism, along with sexism and homophobia, can divide the working class and has the additional advantage for capitalists of creating the illusion of racial unity between bosses and workers on the grounds of their alleged mutual interests as, for example, 'whites'. Alienation, manifest in behaviour that is self-destructive, can be turned outward to hurt friends, loved ones or others – it is the consequence of the lack of control we experience because of exploitation and oppression. For prolonged periods, Labor has reinforced different forms of oppression, and continues to do so.

In its fundamental objectives, the ALP is no different from the Liberal and National parties or the Greens. They all accept the nation and the core feature of capitalism: the exploitation of labour by capital. They have all helped implement measures of state regulation of the market too. The ALP has tended to place a little more emphasis than the conservative parties on direct state action and the cooption of potential working class opponents, yet distinctions among the parties have not been a matter of fundamental goals but of policy style.

A workers' party?

Labor Party loyalists often invoke Prime Minister Ben Chifley's 1949 'light on the hill' metaphor for the Party's goals. It has lofty, even biblical, connotations:

> We have a great objective – the light on the hill – which we aim to reach by working for the betterment of mankind not only here but anywhere we may give a helping hand. If it were not for that, the Labor movement would not be worth fighting for.

The ambitions that motivated the ALP's helping hand were, however, rather modest:

> If the movement can make someone more comfortable, give to some father or mother a greater feeling of security for their children, a feeling that if a depression comes there will be work, that the government is striving hardest to do its best, then the Labor movement will be completely justified.[7]

This was more a flickering candle in a kitchen than a beacon atop a mountain. In its claims to ameliorate the conditions of the working class under capitalism, the ALP stands squarely in the earlier tradition of democratic liberalism in the Australian colonies, as both liberal and right wing Labor historians have pointed out.[8] Rudd's claim to 'fairness' was hardly unique; it is part of the common rhetoric of both major parties. Indeed, arch conservative John Howard was not averse to invoking the notion of a fair go in Australia, 'an egalitarian, fair minded country'.[9]

Labor is not, therefore, marked out by its commitment to fairness and social reform. But its relationship with the working class, primarily but not exclusively through the trade unions, is distinctive. From its earliest days, this connection set Labor apart from its opponents. The peak body of the urban union movement in New South Wales, the Trades and Labour Council, played a crucial role in the formation and electoral success of the New South Wales Labour Electoral Leagues in 1891. Most of the 35 new Labor members of the New South Wales Legislative Assembly and others who campaigned for Labor believed that the new Party represented workers in particular and would thoroughly change society.[10] Trade unions also created labour parties in the other Australian colonies. The links between the Labor Party and the working class go beyond its original connections with the unions. They have been apparent in the backgrounds of many politicians, the Party's members and core voters, and the continuing influence, formal and informal, of trade unions in the ALP. In these terms, there has been a very large contrast between the conservative parties and Labor.

The relationships between the working class and the ALP constitute Labor as a workers' party that reflects a particular form of working class consciousness. The daily experience of workers is one of exploitation, and this has had an ambiguous impact on their consciousness.[11] Exploitation and continued subordination to the boss can inculcate feelings of powerlessness, submission, adaptation to capitalist norms and a belief in the apparent imperatives of the system. But they can also breed a basic sense of class identification. At times, exploitation drives workers to fight and so, through the experience of collective struggle, they become more aware of their power and common interests. This class identification has been expressed in a host of ways. It has drawn workers together for the purposes of mutual defence and has distinguished the working class from other classes, most especially the capitalist class, in a relationship of mutual antagonism.

From the 1830s, workers' identification of their common interests led to the formation of trade unions in Australia. In the 1890s, the unions in turn set up the colonial Labor parties as the first political organisations of workers that were, or soon became, independent of middle and ruling class politicians. The creation of the unions and the new parties were important steps forward in the development of working class consciousness. But Labor took shape during a period when intense class struggles were defeated. While exploitation led to a desire for justice, workers' sense of their own powerlessness following their defeats encouraged the belief that they could not bring about social change through their own direct actions but had to rely on an arm of the state. The result was a strategy of parliamentary reform, which took institutional form in the ALP. Working class support for Labor has been reproduced by this mixed consciousness throughout the Party's history. The ALP has promoted the notion that workers should pursue change within the framework of the existing national political and legal systems.

Among workers who were conscious of their class interests a strong identification with the ALP as 'our party' rapidly emerged. It survived many betrayals of Party policy and attacks on workers by Labor governments. Just as devoted supporters continue to support their football club when it plays badly or loses, loyal Labor voters could not contemplate casting a ballot for a conservative team.

Neither in the 19th century nor more recently did Labor win support among class conscious workers because they were mesmerised by 'charismatic' ALP leaders such as William Holman, John Curtin, Bob Hawke or, less plausibly, Kevin Rudd, or because they were nostalgic for a mythical Golden Age of Labor. Their support grew out of their sense of powerlessness and class grievance generated by the material reality of working class life. The language of socialism, with its connotations of working class emancipation, appealed to them because it addressed their conditions of existence. Criticisms of inequality and exploitation in terms of class, or vaguer populist ideas, likewise made sense of their experiences. Populism was a powerful current within the ALP and identified a conflict between the broadly and loosely defined 'people' and a tiny minority, variously identified as the money power, monopolists or transnational corporations. The conspiracies and chicanery of this small group, rather than exploitation by the capitalist class as a whole, were responsible for the people's problems.[12]

For many decades, even right wing Labor politicians were prepared to mouth socialist phrases, by which they meant state ownership and regulation of the economy. In 1907, the future Labor prime minister Billy Hughes, for example, explained that socialism was a matter of increased state activity and it was being implemented even by the conservative parties.[13]

Conservative politicians helped perpetuate the illusion that the ALP was a socialist organisation and hence enhanced the Party's attractiveness to radical workers. The main evidence for Labor's commitment to socialism became the socialisation resolution of the 1921 federal conference, which promised not only state ownership but also the democratisation of production. But Labor's socialisation objective was a distant goal, rather than a policy for the next ALP government. It was, moreover, adopted opportunistically to help fend off left wing challenges to Labor's influence in the working class during the upsurge in militancy after World War I.[14]

After the Chifley Labor government's bank nationalisation legislation was overturned in 1948, the right wing of the Party invoked socialist rhetoric less often and eventually gave it away entirely. The left, on the other hand, kept the beacon alight for several more decades, harnessing militant workers to the ALP by invoking left populist ideas and socialism. In the period after World War II, the left generally meant by socialism a more thorough going program of state ownership and regulation than the right was prepared to countenance. At no time, though, has any more than a tiny minority of the ALP left desired socialism in Marxist terms, that is, working class self-emancipation. In the classical Marxist tradition, socialism is both a strategy and a goal: mass working class action to replace capitalism and its parliamentary institutions with a more radical form of democracy at all levels of society.

Although left and right were at daggers drawn during the 20th century, the right, which controlled the Party through most of its history, actually benefited from the activities of the left. With its promises of radical change, the left drew in generations of idealistic young workers and students and helped the ALP recover support after debacles and betrayals. By winning and sustaining the loyalty of militants to the Party, the left prevented them from struggling for a more radical program of social and political transformation, while the right, by demonstrating its firm control of the left, confirmed its value to the capitalist class as a force that could be trusted to run the state.

Labor's material constitution

The distinctiveness of the ALP's relationship with the working class can only be understood by taking a closer look at the structure of the Party. Early in the 20th century, Australian socialist Bob Winspear argued in his book *Economic Warfare* that

> To clearly understand politics and the beliefs of political parties, it is necessary to study the economic forces which influence them. We must study the material interests of the different political parties in the community.[15]

Winspear's approach, focusing on what we call Labor's material constitution – its relationships with different class forces in Australian society – was spot on. Later, the Russian revolutionary Vladimir Ilyich Lenin made the same point about the British Labour Party.

> [W]hether or not a party is really a political party of the workers does not depend solely upon a membership of workers but also upon the men that lead it, and the content of its actions and its political tactics. Only this latter determines whether we really have before us a political party of the proletariat.[16]

The class interests and hence politics of two powerful social groups in the structures of the ALP explain how it can combine a support base in the working class with a pro-capitalist program. Labor parliamentarians, Winspear observed, enjoyed working conditions, pay and social contacts that were very different from those of workers. Little has changed since. Labor politicians benefit personally from their distinctive role, receiving high salaries, perks, generous pensions and access to business opportunities after they leave office. They collaborate with senior public servants and representatives of other political parties and deal with business lobbies. They function as political mediators between the ALP's base in the working class and the capitalists, but are distant from direct struggles at the point of production.

In order to maximise electoral support by appealing to other social classes – not only owners of small businesses and farmers, but also capitalists – Labor's leaders water down policies that serve workers' interests. They appeal to 'the nation' and decry any notion that the ALP should serve the working class. John Curtin illustrated the point in the late 1930s: 'Labor is not a class movement; the Party belongs to the whole people'.[17] Far from Labor politicians representing the interests of the working class within the framework of capitalism, fighting to improve the lot of workers, as a social group they represent the interests of the capitalists within the labour movement and seek to sustain the cycle of capitalist profit making and investment.[18]

Before and after Winspear's *Economic Warfare*, it was evident that the parliamentarians' opportunist tendencies were a source of conflict within the ALP as they strove to establish greater autonomy from the trade unions, the other vital element in the Party's structure. Vere Gordon Childe's *How Labour Governs*, for example, dealt with the issue at length in 1923 drawing on his experiences in the Labor Party, including as private secretary to New South Wales Premier John Storey.[19] Efforts to control Labor politicians led to the introduction of procedures such as caucus discipline and, when the politicians refused to be so bound, to splits. But it was not just politicians on the gravy train who were responsible for the Party's pro-capitalist orientation; the trade union leaders, who dominated the ALP's committees and conferences for decades, were not exempt from conservatising pressures either.

Winspear also observed that trade union officials, by virtue of their position in society, gravitated towards conformism rather than radicalism. They used the 'working class as a stepping stone by which to lift themselves into a more comfortable and secure position'.[20] Consequently, Winspear wrote, 'the whole craft union movement has been marked by a succession of personal treacheries...'[21] An extensive international literature, reaching back to the late 19th century, complements Winspear's comments about the conservatising pressures on full time trade union officials. The starting point of many of these analyses is that the purpose of trade unions is to improve the terms on which labour power is exploited, not to overcome exploitation itself.[22] From their earliest days, trade unions began to internalise aspects of the society in which they were embedded. As they left their outlaw origins behind and were legalised, trade unions became part of the industrial relations machinery.[23] The job of full time trade union officials is to act as bargaining agents, to secure, within this machinery, the best wages and conditions for workers.[24] For them, the trade unions become an end in themselves, rather than means to an end.[25] In order to strike a deal they attempt to gain benefits for workers but also seek to moderate working class demands to levels capitalists find acceptable.

In addition to their role as bargaining agents, union leaders also enjoy various material advantages. As employees of their unions, officials are not exploited by a boss — they do not face the sack when a factory or office closes down. Most have significantly higher incomes and lead a relatively privileged lifestyle compared to the mass of their members.[26] The nature of their jobs means that union officials are not workers. Indeed, according to British Fabians Sidney and Beatrice Webb writing at the end of the 19th century, they form a 'separate governing class ... marked off by capacity, training and habit of life from the rank and file'.[27] These two factors have a large effect on their world view.

The parliamentarians and union officials are powerful, non-working class elements embedded in the heart of the Labor Party. They are distinct social groups that play distinct social roles. Through union structures and elections, and industrial action, workers are able to exert more direct, collective pressure on their union officials than they can on Labor politicians, who are insulated by the structures of the ALP and the electoral system. Because they take responsibility for actually running the state, Labor politicians are more integrated into the exercise of capitalist power than are union officials. Yet, despite their differences, Labor politicians and full-time union officials are performing the same high wire act, seeking to balance policies that perpetuate capitalism on one outstretched hand against actions to maintain working class support on the other. Both use their strategic positions in the Labor Party to further their interests as social groups, interests that are fundamentally pro-capitalist. Union leaders may criticise and discipline politicians, but they have never as a social layer fought to transform the Labor Party into an organisation that could challenge capitalism in practice.

More or less stable, formal and informal networks of power at local, state, territory and federal levels are also important elements within the Labor Party. These machines, which permeate the other components of the ALP, include not just union leaders, key figures in the parliamentary Labor parties and senior officials of the Party itself, but also extend to ordinary members.

In 1913, Lenin accurately identified the Australian Labor Party as a 'liberal [bourgeois] workers' party'.[28] In terms of its material constitution, the ALP is a capitalist workers' party. Labor is a capitalist workers' party, rather than a socialist workers' party, because of the class interests of the politicians and union officials who lead and control it, and because of the role it plays for the capitalist class. The actions of capitalist parties, whether social democratic like the ALP, or conservative like the Liberals, may improve workers' living standards in the short term or, inadvertently, enhance the working class's capacity to engage in class struggle. But their priority is to make capitalism work, and that means subordinating the interests of the working class to those of the capitalist class, which they identify as the national interest. A socialist workers' party, by contrast, regards the interests of capitalists and workers as fundamentally counterposed. In the words of the *Communist Manifesto*, a socialist workers' party would 'fight for the attainment of the immediate aims, for the enforcement of the momentary interests of the working class; but in the movement of the present . . . also represent and take care of the future of that movement',[29] which is the revolutionary struggle for socialism. There have been occasions when a socialist workers' party could have been built in Australia but the dominant forces in the ALP have never been interested in this project.

A grasp of the Labor Party's material constitution as a capitalist workers' party helps us understand how it has sometimes been more effective than the conservative parties in promoting capitalist interests. Two mechanisms have operated. First, because of its organic links with the working class, Labor, with the support of union officials, has at times been more successful than the conservative parties in getting workers to accept policies that hurt their interests. Unions were, for example, reluctant to lend their support to the wartime planning efforts of the Menzies government. After Labor took office in 1941, however, union officials accepted civilian conscription for the Civil Construction Corps, wage controls and bans on absenteeism.[30] Menzies was later to write 'The accession to office of the Labor Party had, therefore, some valuable results'.[31]

Communist Party leader Lance Sharkey explained a second way in which Labor governments can serve big business well. Although sections of the ALP have occasionally had strong, even corrupt, connections with business, the Party is not generally as directly dependent on particular capitalist interests as are the conservative parties. As a consequence, the ALP has often been in a better position to pursue the common interests of capital, despite the opposition of individual members of the bourgeoisie or even whole sections of the capitalist class. Hence, for example, the contrast between the Fraser government's weak record on tariff and banking reform, and the robust steps taken by the Hawke government in the 1980s.[32]

How much has changed recently?

Since the early 1970s, there has been a series of arguments about changes in the Labor Party. These debates were particularly strong when Labor was in office under Whitlam, Hawke and Keating. Some commentators have regarded transformations in the ALP as deplorable, others have applauded them. Others again, while acknowledging that the Party has adapted its policies and structures, have denied that it has fundamentally changed. What conclusions did these writers draw about changes, if any, in the material constitution of the Party – its relations with the trade unions, the capitalists and its electoral base? That is the focus of this book.

The heightened levels of class and social conflict during the late 1960s and early 1970s revived the radical left in Australia and, with it, critical assessment of the Labor Party. In 1972, historian Humphrey McQueen illuminated the various means by which 'the ALP operates as an agent for integrating the workforce within capitalism', stressing that

> [t]he decision to work within the system produces not a static arrange-
> ment but rather sets in motion a tangle of organisational linkages which
> initially impede and ultimately transform any party which has accepted their
> rationality.[33]

Other radical critics, such as Bruce McFarlane, Bob Catley and Kelvin Rowley, argued that the Party was undergoing a major change, from 'paleo-laborism' to 'technocratic laborism'. While they regarded Labor at both stages as a capitalist party, there were two elements in this transition. First, Labor under Whitlam had adopted policies advocated by the Organisation for Economic Co-operation and Development, designed to renovate Australian capitalism. Second, the character of the Party had changed with an influx of middle class professionals who had joined because its new technocratic policies provided a better way to advance their ideas and themselves than Labor's more closed minded conservative opponents.[34] While studies of technocratic laborism identified significant changes in the ALP's policies, leadership and membership in the 1960s and early 1970s, most critics did not attempt a systematic examination of the ALP's relationship with the union movement, internal structures or electoral base. Academic Melanie Beresford's assessment of the terminal phase of the Whitlam government foreshadowed our understanding of Labor as a capitalist workers' party, when she pointed out that

> The contradiction between [the interests of] the working class electoral and structural core of the Party and [the ALP's] objective function in office as the policy making body of the capitalist state is reflected in the crisis within the parliamentary Labor Party in 1975 . . . [35]

The discussion of technocratic laborism did not survive Whitlam's dismissal but some of its themes re-emerged later in debates about the Hawke and Keating governments.[36]

In the mid 1970s, David Kemp, a political scientist and later a Liberal member of parliament, maintained that Australian politics was changing for very different reasons: reflecting a decline in the salience of class identification, people were voting less along class lines.[37] The growing numbers of middle class supporters and members of the ALP, he speculated, could lead to conflict over the influence of union officials in the Party and consequently to fragmentation. But Kemp's preoccupation with data from opinion polls, his definition of class in terms of occupation rather than power at work and his neglect of political contexts meant that his study provided limited evidence about changes in the significance of class in Australian politics or even electoral behaviour.[38]

After half a decade of the Hawke Labor administration, political scientist Dean Jaensch used concepts drawn from conventional academic political science to argue that the ALP had undergone major changes since the 1960s. Labor had begun as a 'mass party', expressing the interests of the working class. Reforms introduced by Gough Whitlam since 1967 opened the way for Labor to become a 'catch-all party', concerned above all else with holding office and therefore becoming less ideological, more preoccupied with winning broad appeal and more responsive to changes in public opinion. 'The Hawke–Keating hijack', a change 'unparalleled' in the Party's history, was now propelling the ALP into 'a new, and more far-reaching stage . . . beyond "catch-all", then a stage that Jaensch labelled 'electoralism'. In admiring tones, he argued that Labor's new 'almost exclusive focus' on winning votes was essentially conservative. As the framework of Jaensch's analysis was competition among Australian parties, rather than the relationship between the ALP and major social forces, the logic of the hijack arose from electoral manoeuvring rather than class interests.[39]

Journalist Paul Kelly, in *The End of Certainty*, the best-selling book about the Hawke era, also celebrated Labor's break with tradition. The Party was liberating itself from the early 20th century 'Australian settlement', which had established a consensus around the White Australia policy, tariffs to build up local industry, management of industrial relations by government appointed arbitration judges or commissioners, exaggerated reliance on the state rather than the market or individuals' own efforts, and an alliance with an imperial power for military defence. Kelly delighted in Labor's transformation of itself and Australian society, noting that 'the more successful it was, the more it destroyed the basis of laborism'.[40] McQueen provided a devastating critique of this approach that complemented his class analysis of the Labor Party. 'The Australian Settlement' was the distorted product of 'free-trade apologists who structure the narrative of twentieth-century Australian history as a long march to the free market'.[41] It was a fable. During the supposed settlement, in sometimes intense class conflicts, workers still sought to raise their living standards against bosses' efforts to maintain and improve their profits. Long before Hawke took office, Labor had thrown its weight behind the capitalist side in these conflicts; in that sense, the 1980s did not represent a sharp break from the traditions of laborism at all.

A range of social democratic intellectuals and Party activists writing at this time agreed with Kelly that the Party had dramatically changed in the 1980s although, unlike him, they vehemently disapproved. Political theorist Graham Maddox looked back to a golden age when the ALP, under Curtin, Chifley and especially Whitlam, had been a moral party, committed to achieving greater equality by limiting the effects of the market. The Hawke government had departed from this tradition and now embraced policies similar to those of its opponents. This retreat was rooted in the Party's inappropriate, conservative reaction to the 1975 dismissal of the Whitlam government. Maddox did not explain why Labor's moral fibre had snapped after this particular crisis.[42] Another social democrat, Peter Beilharz, invoked Kelly's book, maintaining that the 'Labor Decade, 1983–93, involved the emptying out of Labor's century old identity or ideology'. Beilharz' analysis of Labor concentrated on its ideas rather than its material constitution and what it actually did.[43]

Peter Fairbrother, Stuart Svensen and Julian Teicher likewise believed that the Hawke and Keating governments had been 'captured' by neoliberal ideologues, and argued that 'The Labor governments were effectively hijacked by a cabal of Ministers, focussed around Keating, supported by senior officials in the Treasury and the increasingly independent Reserve Bank'.[44] This assessment played down the very long term consensus between the ALP and the conservative parties over changing economic strategies. These authors also failed to explain the underlying reasons why the neoliberal ideologues had become so influential in the Party. Nor could they explain why the lurch to economic rationalism was supported by the unions and much of the left of the Party.[45]

Another interpretation suggested that Labor and the Liberals had become 'cartel parties'. Contributors to a 2003 conference on this topic argued that public funding had allowed cartel parties to dispense with large, well organised memberships in favour of purchased professional services – especially market research and advertising. The policies of cartel parties converged and they resisted new competitors whose electoral success would reduce their share of public funds. The case that Labor had turned into, or was becoming, a cartel party rested not only on examinations of Labor policy but also on significant shifts in Labor's electoral support, membership and sources of funds. Former Keating government minister Gary Johns concluded that 'the Australian case is one where major parties have lost their party base'. Political scientist Ian Ward argued that 'the Labor and Liberal parties [are] now without firm foundations in civil society'. According to public policy researcher Ian Marsh,

> major party organisations have largely jettisoned interest aggregation. Established organisational linkages – the trade unions with Labor and business with the Liberals – have weakened.[46]

Labor and the conservative parties had, supposedly, undergone fundamental changes.

From a more radical perspective, Ashley Lavelle, in his comparative study, asserted that social democracy has died, not just in Australia but also in Europe. Social democratic parties had been committed to achieving socialism of some kind, usually amounting to reforms that benefited workers, through parliament. They had significant connections with the working class. According to Lavelle, the onset of a prolonged economic crisis in the 1970s meant reforms could no longer be achieved, so parties such as the ALP had abandoned 'any ambition to reform capitalism' and consequently their relationships with the working class 'no longer has any political content'.[47] The end of the long boom was, as Lavelle accurately pointed out, an important element in a convincing explanation of ALP's development since the early 1970s. But, as British Marxist Tony Cliff presciently remarked in 1957,

> Even when the economic roots of reformism wither away, reformism will not die by itself. Many an idea lingers on long after the disappearance of the material conditions which brought it forth.[48]

Workers may continue to vote for Labor's strategy of parliamentary reform even when the Party is unlikely to deliver. Furthermore, as Labor's reaction to the global financial crisis of 2008 demonstrated, with its stimulus packages and cash handouts, traditional reformist responses to economic crises are still, sometimes, possible.

The commentators who we have discussed so far diverge on many things but they do agree that Labor has undergone a qualitative transformation since the 1970s. Others reject this proposition. They include those on the right in the Party, such as former New South Wales Premier Neville Wran, for whom the policies of the Hawke and Keating governments were a consequence of its long standing commitment to national wellbeing.[49] On the left, Carol Johnson, a social democratic critic of the Party, identified the continuing distinctiveness of Labor's ideology of social harmony. In the economic and political circumstances of the 1980s, this led the ALP to sacrifice working class interests for the sake of the profitability of capital. Johnson's account was persuasive but neglected Labor's material constitution, in particular the role of union officials in the Party. Like Johnson, political scientist Haydon Manning highlighted elements of continuity, not only in Party policy but also in its relationship with the union movement.[50]

In a particularly useful 1991 study, Labor activist and researcher Andrew Scott documented long term changes in the Party's working class membership and the continuing importance of the union connection. He did not, however, identify the divergence of interests between union officials and the working class. In a follow up study published in 2000, Scott argued that Labor had begun to move away from its market orientation when Keating was prime minister. In the spirit of the ALP left, Scott hoped the Party could be won back to serve the interests of and revitalise its working class base.[51] Looking back almost a decade after the Hawke and Keating governments,

David Coates and Greg Patmore observed that 'in their propensity to use power to discipline the working class, they . . . very much still [operated] in an older [Labor] tradition'.[52]

We endorse the contention of those commentators who maintain that, despite a series of important changes, there is a fundamental continuity in the history of the ALP from the 1890s through to the first decade of the 21st century. We differ from these accounts by explaining this continuity not in terms of ideology, although social harmony, laborism and commitment to the national interest have been typical of Labor Party thinking, but rather in terms of the ALP's material constitution, its relationship with the capitalist class, which it serves, and the working class, which forms its base and whose trade unions are integrated into it. The role of parliamentarians and union officials within the Party has been crucial in sustaining this material constitution. There have been important changes in the influence of union officials, Party policy, the class backgrounds of members and leading figures alike, the ALP's machines, income sources, electoral fortunes and the characteristics of Labor voters. Nevertheless, the ALP remains a capitalist workers' party and a class analysis makes it easier to understand how and why these changes have occurred. The following chapters flesh out our case by examining these continuities and changes in the context of the Party's history, and focus on important episodes and events that highlight the characteristics of the ALP at different times, especially when the Party has held federal office.

Chapter 2

IN THE BEGINNING: LABOR'S FIRST QUARTER CENTURY

The ALP was born out of a period of prolonged economic boom followed by a devastating crash. The boom and subsequent bust and the social turmoil that went with it put a definite stamp on the character of the Party. In this chapter we describe the circumstances of the Party's formation, its initial electoral success, consolidation and early record in office, before turning to the tumultuous years of World War I when Labor experienced and survived its first convulsive split.

In the 30 years leading up to the Party's formation in 1891, the Australian colonies expanded at an unprecedented rate. Population increased by more than two and a half times while gross domestic product more than tripled. Medium and large businesses began to appear in the major cities and regional towns. These processes had a dramatic impact on the workforce and class divisions became more sharply defined. As the size of businesses grew, the scope for skilled workers and artisans to climb into the employer class declined and the proportion of self-employed people fell. In 1891 almost two-thirds of breadwinners in New South Wales were employees.[1]

With the sharpening of class distinctions, trade unions began to grow rapidly. Not only skilled workers – including those in urban trades and shearers – but also the semiskilled and unskilled – such as miners, most railway workers, urban and rural labourers – organised in large numbers in the Australian colonies. By 1891, there were almost 65 000 unionists in New South Wales, over one-fifth of the workforce and the highest proportion in the world.[2] The growth and consolidation of the union movement led to the emergence of a layer of full time union officials who could spend time and develop expertise in managing the affairs of their organisations.

As unions grew and divisions in the workforce between skilled and unskilled became less significant, trades and labour councils became more active, or were set up, in Melbourne, Sydney and Brisbane, to coordinate the activities of the whole union movement. As labour historian Raymond Markey argues, 'Organised labour at the end of the 1880s began to represent a class, rather than a craft elite, both quantitatively and in terms of outlook and policy'.[3] Employers looked on these developments with distaste and alarm. They resented paying higher wages and the unions' insistence on the closed shop, which prevented them from hiring non-union labour.

The expansion of the union movement reflected workers' growing consciousness of their class interests. But their ideas were uneven. The notion that they shared racial and national interests with their bosses was widespread, thanks to the efforts of politicians, the press and employers. Initially, trade unions tended to follow one or other wing of the capitalist class: in Victoria, the manufacturing unions tailed the protectionist employers who favoured high tariffs; in New South Wales, the shearers, coal miners and meat workers lined up behind their free trade employers.

Yet, as working class consciousness rose, workers became increasingly keen to develop their own political voice. From the late 1880s unions discussed the issue of political representation more systematically, including at Intercolonial Trade Union Congresses. The 1889 decisions by the New South Wales and Queensland governments to follow the Victorian parliament by introducing pay for parliamentarians lifted an important barrier to union involvement in parliamentary politics. The decisive impetus for the formation of the ALP came, however, from the immense class battles of the early 1890s.

In 1890, ships' officers decided to affiliate with the Melbourne Trades Hall Council. Facing a threat to their authority, the ship owners and port employers decided to respond. They were determined to beat back this latest assault on their prerogatives. The result was a mass strike that drew in ten of thousands of maritime, transport and mine workers, together with shearers, not just in Australia but also New Zealand.[4] Massive demonstrations and violent encounters with scabs, police and mounted troops broke out in all the major centres of resistance, from Townsville to Adelaide. Scabs were chased through the streets of Sydney. Miners' wives lay down in front of a locomotive carrying strike breakers near Wollongong to prevent it getting to the pits.

But bravery was not enough. The colonial governments and police backed the employers; magistrates and judges imposed harsh fines and jail sentences on hundreds of union activists and leaders. Strike breakers were plentiful given that there was high unemployment. By the end of 1890 the maritime workers and shearers had either been sacked or returned to work with inferior conditions and on lower pay. A similar pattern of mass action, state repression and bloody defeat marked the Queensland shearers' strike the following year.[5]

Labor's birth

The employer offensive, backed by the state, showed that pure and simple trade unionism was not enough. The capitalist class understood the necessity of buttressing its economic power with political power. The colonial leaderships of the union movement accelerated their efforts to remedy the situation. In 1891 the Trades and Labour Council in Sydney[6] established Labour Electoral Leagues in preparation for the colonial elections of that year. At its first outing the new party was stunningly successful. Thirty-five members of the new Legislative Assembly were associated with Labor. Twenty-one of them were unionists, most with experience on the executives of their unions.[7] The parliamentary allowance was £300 a year, more than three times average annual earnings in manufacturing.[8] This income could sustain Labor's representatives in a gentlemanly lifestyle. Their jobs also introduced them into exalted political and business circles. As Winspear and Childe pointed out, over years these experiences, very different from those of their working class constituents, influenced their perspectives.

After 1890, Labor parties became political forces not only in New South Wales but also in Queensland and South Australia. These new parties were predominantly, though not exclusively, working class in terms of their membership, their electoral base and the backgrounds of their political representatives. The local organisations of the Party were concentrated in the most working class suburbs of Australia's cities or were created by members of miners' or rural workers' unions in the country. Most of the planks in the Labor platform for the August 1891 elections in New South Wales were demands that reflected workers' interests, for improvements in conditions of employment, including the eight hour day, and greater political democracy. Other planks called for a national federation of the Australian colonies; the second last was a racist demand for the stamping of furniture made by Chinese in Australia (so it could be boycotted).

The foundation of the colonial Labor parties in the midst of massive class struggles created a powerful and enduring identification of large numbers of workers with the new organisations as expressions of their class interests.

The new parties had potential to evolve in more than one direction. Would they embrace the task of coordinating the industrial and political struggles of the working class in order to challenge the structures of capitalist state power? Would they act as a wing of liberalism that secured support from workers? Or would they observe a division of labour with the union movement and, while expanding their support and organisational autonomy from other political forces, subordinate the working class to the institutions and logic of capitalism? If the industrial confrontations of the early 1890s launched the colonial Labor parties, workers' defeat in these struggles had a decisive impact on the form they took.

The deepening Great Depression of the early 1890s soon came close to destroying the union movement. The price of rural products collapsed, throwing tens of thousands out of work. Between 1892 and 1896 the bosses demanded and won severe wage concessions and ended closed shops by defeating Broken Hill miners, seamen, New South Wales shearers and Hunter Valley coal miners in very hard fought disputes. Thousands of militants were sacked and blacklisted, and unions disappeared from most workplaces. For a period, the Labour Council in Sydney effectively ceased to exist and in Queensland the number of unionists slumped, with the Australian Workers Union (AWU) losing half of its membership.[9]

The defeats of the early 1890s undermined working class self-confidence and thus the credibility of a strategy based on class struggle. Initially, many unionists regarded parliamentary representation as a means to supplement their industrial muscle. As the industrial setbacks mounted and the Depression deepened many unionists and especially union officials began to look to parliamentary action, including legislation for industrial arbitration, as a substitute for working class struggle.

Labor's first parliamentary representatives in New South Wales were a motley crew. In order to prevent their conflicting free trade and protectionist sympathies from fracturing the Party, it imposed a pledge of solidarity on parliamentarians: henceforth, all Labor members of the Legislative Assembly (MLAs) had to vote according to the decisions they took when meeting together as a caucus. This collective discipline was too much for most sitting members, who quickly deserted the Party over the pledge. At the 1894 elections Labor's representation fell sharply, but those elected on a Labor ticket were now bound by the pledge, so the new Labor caucus was a far more coherent group.

Members of affiliated unions were also members of the Party. The AWU, even with its much diminished membership of 7700 in 1899, was by far the largest union in Australia in the late 1890s and became the decisive force within the New South Wales Party.[10] The AWU used its clout to put key people into parliament. Future premier William Holman, a political organiser with the AWU for a time, won a rural seat with AWU endorsement, as did future prime minister Chris Watson.

The relationship between politicians and the unions operated in both directions. The 1890s Depression did not hit the local organisations of the Labor Party as hard as it did the unions – in New South Wales in mid 1894 there were still 84 branches. When the union movement came close to collapsing, the Party helped to rebuild it. The unions of wharf labourers and carters in New South Wales disappeared during the Depression of the 1890s; New South Wales MLA Billy Hughes helped re-establish them and was a senior elected official in both. In 1902, as a member of the Commonwealth House of Representatives (MHR), Hughes played a prominent role in setting up the national Waterside Workers Federation and became its president. Another Labor politician, John Dacey, who owned a coach building factory in Sydney, helped organise the Wool and Basil Workers Union in 1901. With their backgrounds in the union movement and their parliamentary rail passes in their pockets, Queensland Labor politicians Harry Coyne, George Ryland and Ted Theodore travelled the state organising unions in the years before World War I.[11]

The outlook of most of the leaders of the AWU, with its bureaucratic, top down structure dominated by full time officials and a membership that included many small farmers, was populist. They contrasted the interests of a tiny layer of monopolists, imperialists and the money power with the national and racial interests of the (white) Australian people. This rhetoric sounded radical but did not criticise either capitalism or the core institutions of the capitalist state. In 1894, W. G. Spence, the secretary of the AWU, had even suggested an alliance between large land owners and the union against their common enemy, the banks.[12] Racist populism became the dominant perspective within the Labor Party.[13] In 1896 the New South Wales Party declared for 'Total exclusion of undesirable alien races'. Advocacy of white racial unity complemented efforts to bridge the class divide between workers and capitalists through arbitration of industrial disputes, which became a plank in Labor's platform in 1899.

In its early years, Labor's populism was challenged by a minority of socialists in its ranks. The most significant of these groups was the Australian Socialist League (ASL), which played an important role in the formation of the New South Wales and Queensland Labor Parties and had perhaps 900 members in New South Wales by 1893. The ASL was split between a moderate right wing led by Hughes and Holman, and a more left wing rank and file. To pragmatists such as Hughes and Holman socialism meant increased state ownership and welfare measures, rather than a systematic challenge to the capitalist order. They campaigned against the radicals and felt at home in the ALP as it moved to the right.[14] The left, however, was internally divided over the meaning of socialism and other issues. A majority of those sympathetic to working class struggle as a means of achieving change still generally thought that socialism could be legislated into existence. The ASL reached the height of its influence at the 1897 New South Wales conference when it succeeded in winning Labor to all out support for nationalisation. The Party machine nevertheless bureaucratically stifled any attempt to take the objective of nationalisation seriously. Individual ASL members began to resign in disgust. When the right wing dominated 1898 Party conference watered down any commitment to socialism even further, it was the final straw for the left wing rump of the ASL. Now numbering only 50 members, it abandoned Labor.

The 1898 conference marked the point at which the alliance between union officials, mainly from the AWU, and parliamentarians definitively consolidated their control over the New South Wales Party and established its distinctive material constitution. The Labor parties in the other Australian colonies and then states eventually adopted the pattern of Party organisation established in New South Wales.[15] In Victoria, Labor MLAs sponsored by unions from 1892, in effect, remained part of a liberal, protectionist political machine for a decade. Only in 1902 did the Victorian Party require candidates to pledge that they would act in accord with decisions of caucus. The Labor Party in South Australia was similarly a junior partner of the liberals for years and only adopted the caucus pledge in 1900.[16] In Western Australia and Tasmania, effective Party organisations only got going in 1900 and 1901.

Labor became the first modern political party in Australia with a formidable electoral organisation. The discipline of caucus solidarity among the parliamentarians was matched by the authority of the colonial (later state) conferences and executives in the extraparliamentary organisations. Powerful Party machines around ALP officials emerged. Local machines grew up in some working class areas. These were made up of activist individuals and families who exercised influence, through friendship networks, union connections and patronage that derived from holding office in the Party, municipal councils or parliaments. These local structures of power interacted with the state-level machines, at whose centre there were generally men on state executives and their allies among trade union officials and the leaderships of the parliamentary parties. At times there were rival factional machines that contended for influence or control in state Labor parties over policies and who would occupy ALP and public offices.

Unions affiliated with the Party provided its main funds.[17] The membership of the Party, through local branches and unions, helped get the vote out and rallied working class support. Street corner and other public meetings enabled Labor to build a loyal following and recruit many new members. So too did individual members talking to friends and fellow unionists, friends, workers, members of churches and other associations. During the 1890s, speaking with voters, door to door, became an important new method of campaigning that, in addition to public meetings and various forms of advertising, favoured parties with large memberships.[18]

Newspapers were the main mass medium through which workers learnt of political developments until the 1920s, when radio became increasingly important. The daily press in the cities was generally hostile to Labor, as were most of the weeklies in smaller towns, with the exception of the small number owned by Labor politicians or their friends. More reliable were the trade union papers, which were overwhelmingly pro-Labor. The most important union papers included the AWU's *Australian Worker* in

New South Wales and *Worker* in Queensland. The *Daily Standard*, owned by Brisbane unions, began to appear in 1912 and was only one of several metropolitan daily labour movement newspapers that circulated in Australia between the 1890s and the late 1930s.[19]

As it mustered its forces, the ALP began to make an impact in the field of legislative reform. Although it formed a government in its own right only once – for eight days in 1899 in Queensland – during the first 13 years of its existence, the new party began to influence government policy. In New South Wales, Labor supported the reforming liberal governments of free trade Premier George Reid between 1894 and 1899, and then the protectionist government of William Lyne in 1900. With Labor backing, Reid reduced the residency requirement for voters from six months to one, which enfranchised many itinerant workers, and introduced a land tax on large estates, which appealed particularly to small farmers, an important element of Labor's base. Working hours and conditions were also regulated by new legislation, although New South Wales lagged behind some other colonies where Labor was less influential. Lyne, pressed by the ALP, introduced old age pensions in New South Wales. The Party also supported the introduction of arbitration of industrial disputes, and then compulsory arbitration.[20] In Queensland, Labor participated in coalition governments with liberals between 1903 and 1907. Premier William Kidston's coalition government enfranchised women and enforced the principle of one person, one vote. It enacted laws to regulate working conditions and for old age pensions and workers' compensation. In Victoria, South Australia and Western Australia, Labor's support for liberal governments, or participation in coalitions with liberals, also had some limited influence on legislation.

The first conference of the national ALP, held after federation in 1901, adopted maintenance of White Australia and compulsory arbitration as the first two planks of its Fighting Platform. So the federal parliamentary Labor Party supported the racist 1901 Immigration Restriction Act, the first law of the new Commonwealth, and the Conciliation and Arbitration Act of 1904. Despite internal differences over the question, a large majority of Labor members supported the Lyne Tariff of 1907 on the basis of the New Protection legislation that made tariff protection dependent on an industry paying fair and reasonable wages. The High Court subsequently ruled the New Protection unconstitutional, but from 1908 the formula was included in the ALP platform. In 1919 the Labor Party formally embraced tariff protection for its own sake.[21] From the Lyne Tariff until the 1970s, there was consensus between Labor and the conservative parties in support of tariffs, quotas and bounties as a means to boost local manufacturing.

Labor's early record in office

Labor tasted power federally for the first time in 1904, albeit not for long. Chris Watson's minority government, elected in April, fell after less than four months in a no confidence motion. Yet, four years later, Labor began to enjoy a string of electoral successes at federal and state levels. Between 1908 and 1915, Watson's successor, Andrew Fisher, held office on three occasions, with only brief interludes of conservative rule. Nineteen hundred and ten was a particularly auspicious year: the first majority Labor governments took office federally, in South Australia and in New South Wales. The following year, Western Australia was secured by Labor and in 1915 the Party won a majority of seats in Queensland.[22] In mid 1915, Labor ruled at the federal level and in all states except Victoria. From just 19 per cent of the vote in 1901, Labor polled 50 per cent in House of Representatives seats in 1910; it reached its all time high of 51 per cent of the popular vote in 1914. What had started with hesitant steps by the infant Party in 1891 had become a victory march. No other working class party in the world could boast of such electoral success at such a young age.

Underpinning Labor's success was the recovery of the broader working class movement. Although unionism had been virtually smashed by the mid 1890s, it slowly began to recover towards the end of the decade and surged forward in the new century. Between 1901 and 1909 union membership tripled and the number of unions doubled.[23] Sections of the working class regained self-confidence and the level of class struggle increased. Labor benefited electorally from this trend. In addition, the Party began to be infected by the more radical mood in sections of the working class. At the 1905 New South Wales conference, the Broken Hill miners' union proposed as the Party's goal 'a Cooperative Commonwealth founded upon the socialization of the production and distribution of wealth'. In the same year the Queensland and Victorian Labor Parties adopted a 'socialist objective', while in New South Wales and federally the Party decided to demand the nationalisation of monopolies.[24] Labor now had the opportunity, provided it could overcome opposition from hostile upper houses, to dramatically change Australian society, a prospect that was met with trepidation by businesspeople.

The capitalists need not have feared. In government, it was apparent from early on that Labor was content to pursue a strategy of modest reform. The socialist objective did not shape the way the state and federal parties campaigned in elections, still less their actions when they eventually took office. The Party's practical agenda, whatever its formal objectives or platform, was not guided primarily by the needs of its working class supporters, let alone the goal of achieving socialism. Rather, Labor positioned itself as *the* party of the Australian nation and people. The conservatives were too tangled up, the ALP argued, with the squabbling factions of urban and rural capital – the banks, the manufacturers, the squatters and the shipowners – and owed their primary allegiance to narrow vested interests, Mother England or both, rather than Australia. It was only Labor that could be trusted to promote the interests of the nation.

Labor's nationalism, while purporting to stand above the unsavoury business of class, was oriented towards the requirements of capital accumulation. And so, while Labor's new programs of social security, most notably the age pension, benefited the working class, they also met the needs of Australian capitalism and matched the policies in the federal parliament of the liberals, led by Alfred Deakin. The emerging nation state needed healthy and educated workers for the factories and the battlefields. At the same time, welfare measures were concessions to, and a means to defuse, working class militancy, as they could be used to encourage workers to accept the established capitalist order.

Both the ALP and its political opponents on the right drew on a broad policy tradition that predated the formation of the Labor Party. During the 19th century, (non-Labor) colonial governments in Australia had played a crucial role in economic development. They established armed forces and police to maintain order at home and fend off challenges to business interests from abroad. They expanded the labour force by promoting migration and regulating access to land. Much more so than in Britain or the United States, they also built infrastructure – roads, ports, railroads and, eventually, telecommunications – to promote the growth of the private sector.[25]

Labor maintained and extended this tradition. In particular, from 1910 until the mid 1920s, ALP governments in several states expanded the scope of public enterprise. Labor in Queensland led the way in this respect. T. J. Ryan's and Ted Theodore's governments set up butcher shops, sawmills, coal mines, a fishery, a cannery, a hotel and a number of cattle stations to compete with the private sector and to develop the state. Similar experiments were conducted by Labor governments in New South Wales and Western Australia. But Labor governments were by no means unique in this respect. Non-Labor governments had, for example, established banks in all the colonies. Later, in 1916, the Peacock Liberal government in Victoria set up a state insurance office. In Western Australia, before the Scaddan Labor government of 1910–16 began to escalate the establishment of public enterprises, non-Labor governments already ran ore batteries, hotels and a sawmill. So, if the ALP was particularly keen on state run enterprises, this was a difference in degree rather than in kind from the conservatives.[26]

Labor governments' overarching commitment to capitalism meant that, despite their (state) socialist rhetoric, they were as prepared to subsidise strategic private initiatives as were their conservative counterparts. In New South Wales in 1912, despite the ALP's policy of establishing a state owned iron and steel industry, Jim McGowen's government agreed to provide land and dredge a shipping channel for Broken Hill Proprietary (BHP) Company Limited's new works in Newcastle.[27]

Labor diversified the Commonwealth's sources of revenue away from tariffs and excise duties that were mainly levied on basic goods consumed by workers. Money was needed not just to prevent deficits but also to pay for escalating military expenditure. A land tax on big properties was a key plank in Labor's platform.[28] Land taxation was not a specifically Labor concern. Radical single taxers, followers of Henry George, had advocated such a tax since the 1880s. In New South Wales a free trade government had legislated for a land tax in 1895. Popular pressure from smallholders and would-be small landowners who wanted large estates broken up also played a role in the introduction of the tax. It was thus an element in an economic strategy that, while appealing to Labor's working class base, could also be used to encourage more intensive agriculture. Labor made land taxation an important issue in the 1910 federal election, at which it won almost two-thirds of seats in country areas. The incoming Fisher government promptly imposed a federal land tax in 1910, and reinstated it in 1914 after the conservative government of Joseph Cook reversed the legislation.

With the onset of war in August 1914, the need to expand Commonwealth income became much more pressing. In 1914 Labor introduced death duties. In 1915, the Fisher government brought in federal income tax, which was structured in such a way as to exempt most workers.[29] While these measures were met with opposition from the wealthy backers of the conservative parties, subsequent conservative governments did not reverse them, thereby demonstrating the essential policy consensus that developed in the area of government finance.

Labor governments also increased the role of the national state in monetary policy. Legislation in 1910 increased public control over the financial system by giving Treasury responsibility for issuing Australia's currency, a right previously exercised by trading banks and the government of Queensland. Such a move had been envisaged by the conservatives and liberals who had designed the Commonwealth Constitution. In 1911 the Fisher government also set up the Commonwealth Bank, which was unique in that it had a government guarantee for its trading as well as its savings bank functions. But, to the disappointment of its radical proponents, the new bank was to operate like its private sector competitors.[30] It was no threat to capitalism, a fact recognised by Hughes when, in 1920 as Nationalist prime minister, his government began the process of transforming it into Australia's central bank with responsibilities for managing the financial system.[31]

As a party seeking to position itself as the most committed to the Australian nation, Labor was also strongly committed to military expansion and to the British empire. There were republicans on the left of the colonial Labor parties who favoured severing all ties with Britain and sections of the Party that were critical of particular policies of the British government, notably, during the Boer War. But the ALP as a whole was just as committed to the British empire as were the conservative parties. Both sides of mainstream politics recognised that Australia's bargaining power over imperial policy would grow if the country made a contribution to the armed forces of the empire. Racism and the defence of White Australia justified the imperial link and the construction of military forces that assisted in the maintenance of Britain's status as a great power. Australia's own nascent imperialist interests could prosper in the bosom of the empire rather than in opposition to it. In a theme that was to be repeated through the 20th and into the 21st century, Labor under Andrew Fisher returned again and again to the need for national defence and the expansion of local military capacity.

In 1910, building on the legislation of its conservative predecessor, the Fisher government established the Royal Australian Navy – as a unit of the British Royal Navy. It imposed compulsory military service on males aged 12 to 26, 'boy conscription', which resulted in the jailing of 7000 who refused to participate over the life of the scheme.[32]

Labor's determination to take responsibility for the successful functioning of the Australian state meant that the Party systematically opposed working class militancy, which was a threat to profits and national security. So, even though Labor benefited from the surge of industrial struggle in the decade leading up to World War I, the Party often came into conflict with the actions of militant workers. Early in 1909, police in Port Pirie were sent in on the orders of South Australian Labor Premier Tom Price's coalition government to protect scabs as they broke a picket line set up by metal mining unions who had been locked out for five months. Fellow locked out unionists in Broken Hill were brushed off by New South Wales Labor opposition leader Jim McGowen who told them to take their case to arbitration. BHP simply ignored a ruling of the Commonwealth Arbitration Court on the lockout and delayed the resumption of mining until metal prices rose two years later.[33] The following year, the ALP under McGowen took power in New South Wales and promptly took a stick to the unions, threatening to recruit scabs to break strikes by wharfies in 1911 and by gas workers in 1913.[34] Outside the Party, small revolutionary socialist organisations that advocated militant class struggle grew and won support among militant workers, notably Broken Hill and Hunter Valley miners. The most influential group, set up in 1911, was the anti-political Industrial Workers of the World (IWW, or Wobblies). The IWW was too small to have any decisive effect on the course of events in the short term. It was, however, to achieve much greater prominence in coming years.

War, crisis and split

War is an extreme test for a political party, a world war still more so. It poses the questions of class and nationalism in the starkest terms. Sections of the Labor Party had opposed the Boer War, and Holman, then a member of the Anti-War League, had risked losing votes in 1901 by advocating self-government for the Boers. Even so, when war broke out in August 1914, the leaders of the ALP, Holman among them, marched in step with the empire. During the election campaign that returned Labor to office shortly before the hostilities began, Fisher pledged that Australia would support Britain to the 'last man and last shilling'. He was as good as his word. The new government soon established the Australian Imperial Force on a volunteer only basis to fight for the empire. In New South Wales, the Labor government entered into a truce with the opposition and allowed its own legislation for the eight hour day, fair rents, mine inspection and shearers' accommodation to gather dust in the Legislative Assembly.

During the first period of the war, the Australian economy was in recession and the level of class struggle was low. The war itself was broadly popular. Yet, by the middle of 1915, war fever was cooling. Wages had been frozen since January but prices were continuing to rise rapidly. Many unionists were not only increasingly dissatisfied with the Labor government's economic policies but also with its commitment to Britain and the war effort. Fisher resigned in October and was replaced by Hughes.

Responding to the pressure from the working class and within the Party for relief from the inflationary squeeze on living standards, the Hughes government promised a referendum to give the Commonwealth the capacity to control prices. Most Labor supporters were delighted, but state Labor governments, jealous of their prerogatives, and business, fearful lest its profits be curbed, campaigned fiercely against the proposal. Hughes, previously a strong advocate of the referendum, backed down and scrapped it, which led to widespread criticism from unionists and Party members.

As the government would not protect their living standards, workers took action themselves, with or without the backing of their union leaders. Members of Hughes' Waterside Workers Federation, who were particularly militant in Sydney and the north Queensland ports, staged wildcat strikes. As the economy began to revive in 1916, the scale of industrial action rapidly increased. With metal prices high because of the war, miners in Broken Hill imposed the 44 hour week by refusing to work on Saturday afternoons, defying their union officials. When some miners were dismissed, the rest struck. Neither the New South Wales nor the federal Labor governments were sympathetic. The Holman Labor government in New South Wales was collaborating with BHP in the company's steel making operation in Newcastle. For his part, Hughes said the Broken Hill strikers were following 'the advice of German sympathisers who are insidiously active in fomenting disturbances'.[35] Despite attempts by Hughes and Holman to label them as enemy agents, the metal miners won; their campaign emboldened coal miners to strike, with some success, for shorter hours. In Queensland and western New South Wales, shearers went out over wages. All in all, 1916 saw a record number of strike days. Militancy was achieving better results than arbitration.

Meanwhile, antiwar sentiment was growing. The IWW was the most outspoken organisation in denouncing the war, suggesting that 'those who own Australia do the fighting'. The Wobblies also advocated direct action over wages and conditions and it was this that initially won them a wider audience. Their syndicalism, the idea that industrial action is the key to social change, also influenced socialists who won control of the Broken Hill miners' union and a group of radical union officials that emerged in Sydney. Increasingly, industrial and political issues overlapped. Conscription became the key battleground. In September 1915, the Melbourne Trades Hall Council voted to oppose conscription. The Labour Council in Sydney condemned state direction of labour, 'industrial conscription', while businesses were free to invest their capital wherever they saw fit. State control of the deployment of labour had obvious implications for workers' capacity to defend their wages and conditions. Then, in a highly significant move, the AWU, the bulwark of the trade union right inside the Labor Party, unanimously opposed conscription at its national conference in January 1916.

The left was buoyed by the willingness of rank and file workers to fight in their own interests. Trade union officials, even those in the AWU, responded to the pressure from below. During the first half of 1916 the Queensland, Victorian and New South Wales Labor Party conferences followed the AWU in rejecting conscription. In Sydney, the Party organised a rally of between 60 000 and 100 000 anti-conscriptionists. In August Hughes announced that a referendum on conscription for overseas military service would be held in October. Hughes' decision split the Party and opened up the biggest schism in Australian social and political life since federation.

Under pressure from the Party's members, and acting in its own interests, Labor's extraparliamentary machine, dominated by union officials, stepped in to bring the parliamentarians to heel. In circumstances of sharp political polarisation and enormous hostility to conscription in the ranks of the ALP, the union leaders could not allow the Hughes government to defy the Party.

Had Hughes won there was the very real prospect of thousands of working class members quitting the ALP in search of a more radical alternative. The unions campaigned hard, with widespread strikes and demonstrations against conscription in the lead up to the referendum.

The conscription referendum was narrowly defeated. Hughes and 24 others walked out of the federal caucus. Forty remained. Conscriptionist parliamentarians were expelled from the ALP and ultimately went over to the conservatives, along with many of their more middle class and well to do supporters. The immediate result of the split was an electoral disaster. The ALP lost office federally, in New South Wales and South Australia. While there were six Labor governments in Australia in mid 1915, less than two years later there was only one, in Queensland, where the AWU's massive influence meant that the Ryan government opposed conscription. Despite the loss of government, the price of the split was worth paying: by their actions, the union leaders had reasserted control over the ALP and prevented the desertion of large numbers of working class members and supporters from the Party.

There were, however, distinct limits to the leftward shift in the Labor Party at this time. While opposed to conscription, Labor was still in favour of Australian participation in the war. Another indication that the Party had not become a threat to the established order was its leadership's reaction to the biggest industrial dispute in Australian history: the 1917 New South Wales general strike. The confrontation began with an attempt by management to speed up work in the tramway workshops in Randwick in Sydney. There was widespread working class dissatisfaction with conditions of work and falling wages at this time, and sympathy for the unionists in the workshops was widespread. Ordinary workers in the main, rather than union officials, decided to spread the strike to include other engineering works, the trams, railways, maritime, road transport and mining industries and also into other states, particularly Victoria, and even New Zealand. Around 97 000 workers participated in the strike, the core for about five weeks. Up to 150 000 people participated in weekly processions organised by the strike defence committee.[36]

The dispute was significantly larger than any of the strikes of the early 1890s and was a greater potential threat to Australian capitalism. It also disrupted the war effort. Employers and the conservative governments were clear about this and were determined to crush the strike. The Nationalist

New South Wales and Commonwealth governments, led by Labor rats Holman and Hughes, organised scabs to operate trams, trains, shipping and coal mines.

ALP parliamentarians, committed as they were to prosecuting the war effort, for the most part simply sat on their hands. New South Wales Labor leader John Storey said, 'If it be possible for one to take no attitude, I will plead guilty to the offence'. He wanted a quick resolution of the 'industrial difficulties without humiliating either side'.[37] The strike ended in a serious defeat. Workers suffered a major setback in Queensland as well when the Ryan government broke a strike by militant railway employees in the north of the state by threatening to sack them all.[38]

Politicians, union officials and the nature of the ALP

The ALP had come a long way since its foundation in the midst of the class confrontations of the early 1890s. By the turn of the century, the core features of its material constitution were pretty much settled. Its base of support was in the working class, while the power brokers in the Party were senior union officials and politicians, both groups committed to Australian capitalism. In office, far from challenging capitalism, the ALP pursued policies of reform aimed at stabilising and expanding the Australian economy. When the short term interests of bosses and workers coincided, the working class might benefit from reforms. When they did not, Labor governments were prepared to repress militant working class activity. These features of Labor's material constitution were refined and reinforced during the course of several conflicts within the Party in the first quarter century of its existence.

The challenges faced by the Party took several forms that were to recur throughout its history. First, the politicians wanted greater autonomy from the extra parliamentary organisation so that they could more easily make deals to form, enter or influence governments and secure their own re-election. They were resisted by the new Party machine and the union leaders who insisted that the parliamentarians operate in a disciplined manner through caucus. The all out fight over conscription during World War I demonstrated that when battle was joined, the union officials and the ALP machine had the power to eject any politicians, no matter how prominent, who would raise themselves above the Party. The machine and union officials also fiercely resisted pressure from the left to convert the Party into a socialist workers' party. If Labor was to appeal to the capitalist class by proving itself fit to govern, it had to demonstrate its capacity to keep the left in check. Hence the determined fight by Hughes, Holman and others to repel efforts by the left wing of the Australian Socialist League to push the ALP in a more radical direction, culminating in the right's triumph at the 1898 New South Wales conference. The right was helped by the fact that most of the left inside the Party believed in parliamentary reform and thus were committed to working through, rather than challenging, the parliamentary set up that is an essential bulwark of capitalist power. Furthermore, the presence of a left within the Party gave the ALP a radical veneer that was in following decades to prove very useful in attracting new generations of radical young members, rebuilding the Labor vote after crushing electoral defeats and squeezing the space for the creation of a socialist, rather than a capitalist, workers' party.

Chapter 3

BETWEEN THE WARS

Having seen off threats from the right and left, the ALP recovered quite quickly from the split of 1917. Although Labor did not hold federal office between 1916 and 1929, the Party won every election in Queensland from 1915 until 1929, and formed governments in several other states.

Labor's recovery in New South Wales was particularly important. The defeat of the general strike was a setback for the unions but its effects were only temporary; the process of radicalisation that began in 1915 continued apace. Although repression, initiated by ALP governments, had destroyed the IWW,[1] the syndicalist idea that the key to effective working class organisation was one big union attracted widespread support among rank and file unionists and left wing union officials. Industrial militancy soared after the war: workers in Australia struck for a total of 8 million days in 1919–20, one-quarter more than in the previous peak of 1916–17.

Working class radicalisation and industrial militancy pushed the ALP further to the left. In 1919, militant unions, led by the Miners Federation, set up the Industrial Socialist Labour Party and succeeded in getting Percy Brookfield elected as the MLA for Broken Hill. Under pressure from below, the federal Labor Party adopted 'the socialisation of industry, production, distribution and exchange' as an objective in 1921. The ALP was now formally committed to socialism, albeit only as a distant goal – it was not included in the Fighting Platform on which Labor contested elections. The 1921 conference also affirmed that any instrument of production 'utilised by its owner in a socially useful manner and without exploitation' could remain securely in private hands.[2] This formulation, the Blackburn Declaration, was designed to reassure big and small business alike. Although state Labor (and non-Labor) governments maintained or set up some new public enterprises in the interests of competition or economic development in the 1920s, no systematic nationalisations followed the 1921 conference.[3] Indeed, until the Depression, no significant current in the Party tried to do anything about the socialisation objective. When socialists in the ALP, such as Vere Gordon Childe, called for workers' control over public enterprises they received little support at state ALP conferences.

The Ryan, and then the Theodore, Labor governments in Queensland demonstrate the extent of Labor's reform programs in this period, the obstacles that they had to deal with and their limitations. Facing obstruction from the conservative and unelected Legislative Council, which mangled and blocked their legislation, successive ALP governments swamped it with Labor appointees, and then abolished it. In 1919, the Ryan government pushed amendments to the Land Act that allowed large increases in rents on pastoral leases, through the Council. Its main motive was not to soak the rich but to provide funds for road, rail, irrigation and other infrastructure as well as loans for small farmers.

Labor's reforms outraged local pastoralists who were backed by London finance houses that had large investments in the Queensland rural sector. These financial institutions boycotted loans to the Queensland government, which, in the circumstances of a deep recession in the early 1920s, was forced to cut public spending. In 1924, Theodore capitulated to the London financiers and put a cap on pastoral rents. Thus the ALP learnt to avoid tangling with big capital.[4]

Labor's retreat from the radical but nevertheless pro-capitalist development programs of the Ryan and Theodore governments was accompanied by measures to attack workers. In response to the budgetary problems caused by the London financiers' boycott of Queensland, in 1922 Theodore cut the basic wage for public sector workers.

The premiership of Bill McCormack from 1925 to 1929 marked a definite end to Labor's reform era in Queensland. His government shut down the state's most expensive public business ventures in pastoral production and the Chillagoe mining and metal refining operation. When McCormack targeted militant railway workers, he had a crucial ally in the AWU, which was threatened by the rise of the combative and socialist led Australian

Railways Union (ARU). McCormack cynically used the anti-communist pledge required of all Labor branches and affiliates to exclude ARU representatives from the central executive of the Party in November 1925, and then, in the following year, from the Party conference. As a result, the ARU and several other unions disaffiliated from the ALP.

Having defeated the ARU within the Party, McCormack and the AWU proceeded to isolate and humiliate the railway workers industrially when they took action in solidarity with AWU members on strike at the South Johnstone sugar mill in north Queensland. McCormack sacked all the railway employees and required them to sign a pledge to follow the Railway Commissioner's orders before they would be re-employed. The AWU leadership ordered its South Johnstone members to return to work on the mill management's terms. After being locked out for eight days and now completely isolated, the ARU instructed its members to accept the pledge and return to work. Membership of the ARU dropped by more than one-quarter in the aftermath. Disillusionment with the Labor government's treatment of its own employees in particular and its industrial relations policies in general was a factor in the ALP's devastating defeat in the 1929 Queensland election.[5]

Where the alliance between the AWU and the leaders of the parliamentary Labor Party continued to dominate the ALP in Queensland through to the 1950s, the union's influence in New South Wales began to decline in the 1920s. This reflected a much higher rate of industrialisation and consequently the declining weight of rural workers – the bulk of the AWU's membership – in the New South Wales working class. The eclipse of the AWU was apparent in the outcome of the intense factional brawling during the early 1920s. Jack Lang, whose base was a coalition of moderate and militant unions opposed to the AWU, won the leadership of the state Party in 1923.

Lang was the most controversial Labor figure between the world wars. As treasurer in the ALP government of the early 1920s, he had pursued conventional economic policies to deal with budget deficits: increasing indirect taxes, raising government charges and restraining the expenditure of his ministerial colleagues. After Labor returned to office in 1925, Premier Lang gained a reputation as a radical. He reinstituted the 44 hour week granted by the Arbitration Court in 1921 but withdrawn by his conservative predecessor, and restored the seniority of public employees who had participated in the 1917 General Strike. His government also extended the workers' compensation system and set up the Government Insurance Office to compete with private firms. In 1926, Lang introduced the widows pensions and, in 1927, child endowment.

Under Lang, the balance of power in the Party initially swung towards union officials. Through a complicated structure of union groups, the new 'red rules' introduced by the Lang machine gave unions 60 per cent of the 150 state conference delegates and direct representation (33 of 46 positions) on the state executive.[6] The powers of the parliamentary Party were reduced: caucus no longer elected the leader or the front bench. Instead, conference, dominated by Lang's union allies, appointed him to lead the Party and empowered him to decide the makeup of his ministry. The union officials who backed Lang also helped provide the numbers in preselections to purge his opponents from the parliamentary Labor caucus.

Labor responses to the Depression

The Great Depression was the definitive event of the interwar period. It made and broke governments across the continent. The crisis in Australia began before the Wall Street crash of October 1929. Business conditions slumped and unemployment climbed to 12 per cent in 1928. Employers sought to impose the burden of restoring profitability onto the working class. The bosses' offensive started in September 1928 when they smashed a national strike by wharfies against wage cuts and casualisation. Timber workers struck from February 1929 for eight and a half months before they too were forced back to work under inferior conditions. Both unions were shattered. In March 1929, owners of Hunter Valley coal mines locked out 10 000 employees for 16 months until they accepted a 20 per cent wage cut. In each case conservative governments and the police intervened to break picket lines and intimidate unionists. After the defeats on the industrial front, politics became the crucial arena in the struggle to defend wages and conditions.

The October 1929 federal election saw a huge swing to Labor. After 13 years in the wilderness, the federal Party under Jim Scullin won a resounding victory, although the conservatives hung on to their majority in the Senate. Success followed in Victoria (December 1929), South Australia (April 1930) and New South Wales (November 1930). In each case, the number of Labor seats swelled to record numbers.

The new Labor governments faced a severe challenge. If they wanted to keep the support of their core voters they had to maintain workers' wages and government services. But there was pressure from business, expressed in the language of sound public finance, to cut public spending and wages. Four major currents emerged within the ALP in response to these contradictory pressures, ranging from a conservative right to a socialist left. Joe Lyons, a senior member of the federal parliament and Cabinet, totally capitulated to the demands of big business; Scullin reluctantly pursued 'responsible' economic policies; Lang adopted a radical, populist rhetoric and made concessions to capital and labour; and the most serious left wing in the Party's history, the Socialisation Units in New South Wales, agitated for 'socialism in our time'.

It was apparent from the outset that the response to the Depression by Scullin and his treasurer, Ted Theodore, who had moved from Queensland into federal politics, had nothing to do with socialism. Labor had campaigned in 1929 on a promise to support the locked out New South Wales coal miners, but the new government quickly reneged.

The government's economic policies were no more effective. In response to the economic collapse, Scullin dramatically increased tariffs, but this did not prevent bosses from continuing to sack large numbers of workers. The Bank of England, concerned about the security of Australian debts to financial institutions in Britain, sent Sir Otto Niemeyer to advise the Australian authorities. Under his influence federal and state governments, Labor and Nationalist alike, signed the Melbourne Agreement in August 1930, which committed them to balance their budgets. Scullin's treasurer put together an alternative strategy, the Theodore Plan. This provided for mild inflation, government expansion of credit and the devaluation of the Australian pound.

Parliamentarians on the right wing of federal Labor, grouped around Joe Lyons, regarded the Theodore Plan as irresponsible. Lyons had been the premier of Tasmania and held a Tasmanian seat in the House of Representatives. The state had a small working class and relatively weak union movement. Used to dealing with business people and with limited pressure on him from the working class, Lyons ratted on the ALP and, together with his supporters, joined forces with the former Nationalists in setting up the new, conservative United Australia Party (UAP) under his leadership in May 1931.

Before the October 1930 election in New South Wales, Jack Lang had campaigned against Thomas Bavin's Nationalist government, which had reduced public spending, cut wages and reinstituted the 48 hour week.[7] In contrast to Tasmania, the working class in New South Wales was large and well organised. It had, however, been seriously weakened by mass unemployment and industrial defeats; the union officials who had supported Lang in the 1920s put pressure on him to defend workers' interests. Lang promised to restore the 44 hour week, withdraw public service pay cuts and fight to dissolve the Loans Council so that New South Wales could borrow additional funds for 'revenue producing works'.[8] At the election, Lang thrashed Bavin; Labor won 55 per cent of the vote and 55 of the 70 seats in the Legislative Assembly.

Lang quickly lived up to one of his main promises, legislating in January 1931 for the 44 hour week. At a time when the federal Arbitration Court reduced award wages across the board by 10 per cent, under the Lang government wages set by the state Industrial Commission were not cut, and pay cuts for public employees in New South Wales were more moderate than in other states.[9] Lang hoped that wage stability would put a floor under household spending and promote economic growth.[10]

Despite Lang's efforts, the Depression deepened and unemployment rose to one-third of the workforce. The worsening economic situation precipitated a crisis in the ALP that was played out in the Battle of the Plans. The premiers' conference in February 1931 saw a contest between the Theodore Plan, presented by the federal government, and the Lang Plan of the New South Wales government. The Lang Plan called for the suspension of interest payments on governments' overseas debt, lower interest rates and an end to the gold standard (the valuation of the Australian pound in terms of a specific quantity of gold). Wrapped in radical rhetoric, the Lang Plan became a rallying point for many in the ALP, including a number of federal parliamentarians. To large numbers of workers in New South Wales and beyond, Lang seemed to be the only Labor leader prepared to resist retrenchment, wage cuts and austerity. The Party in New South Wales split over the plans. Scullin, with the help of his defence minister, Ben Chifley, established an official, federally recognised Party in New South Wales in direct competition with the Langite Party. All significant affiliated unions, apart from the AWU, and a very large majority of the membership remained loyal to Lang.

In April 1931, the dispute escalated when New South Wales failed to pay interest to British bondholders. The Labor federal government paid instead and began legal action to recover the money from New South Wales. Scullin's willingness to take on the Lang government in the name of financial creditworthiness did not help him much. The Commonwealth Bank and the Senate blocked the Theodore Plan and insisted on drastic retrenchment. Scullin and Theodore gave in, agreeing to abide by the June 1931 Premiers' Plan, which included a 20 per cent cut in government spending, and consequently slashing public works, welfare benefits and public service salaries. The ALP federal executive formally opposed the Premiers' Plan but gave Labor parliamentarians a free vote on the issue in order to achieve the highest goal: keeping the Party in office.[11]

South Australian premier, Lionel Hill, and his ministers signed the Plan and were promptly expelled by the state Party in August 1931, under pressure from rank and file members, union officials and a rising Lang organisation in that state. Hill remained in office, propped up by the Nationalists. In Victoria, Premier Edmond Hogan also signed the Plan, but his own ministers repudiated him, which brought down the Labor government in April 1932. The state executive expelled Hogan and other right wing politicians three months later.

In New South Wales, the Lang government played a two-sided game. On the one hand, Lang, like his fellow Labor premiers, signed the Premiers' Plan and cut public employees' pay. On the other, under pressure from the unions and the working class, his government protected tenants from eviction if they were unable to pay rents, did not compel the unemployed to work for the dole and made attempts – blocked by the Legislative Council – to increase taxes on the rich and to force insurance companies to make loans to the government. The Lang administration did cut its employees' wages, but with proportionately larger reductions for those on higher pay.

In November 1931 crossbench Langite Labor MHRs joined with the UAP in a vote of no confidence in the Scullin government, bringing it down in a round of mutual acrimony. At the following election, in December 1931, the UAP romped home. In a stunning reversal of fortunes, the combined primary vote of the official and New South Wales Labor Parties fell by more than 11 per cent.

The political situation in New South Wales was by now deeply polarised. The economic crisis was going from bad to worse. Unemployment continued to rise. The state's public finances were in disastrous shape. As the state's budget deficit deepened, the new UAP federal government attempted to seize control of the Lang government's funds. The far right was also on the move. Armed organisations, the New Guard, a fascist movement with a base in the middle class, and the more substantial Old Guard with supporters in the New South Wales political, judicial and military establishment, began to rally their forces. Workers' meetings were attacked by the fascists. Meanwhile, on the left, Lang attracted huge crowds to meetings and hundreds were flocking to join the ALP in the hope that it would institute a new socialist order.

The political crisis in New South Wales climaxed in May 1932. State governor Sir Philip Game sacked the government after the Legislative Council, swamped by Labor appointees, passed a 10 per cent tax on mortgage creditors. For hundreds of thousands of Labor supporters, Lang's dismissal exposed parliamentary democracy as a hollow sham. They looked to Lang for a lead. The circulation of the *Labor Daily* reached over 160 000.[12] The high point of Labor's 1932 election campaign was a huge rally of, according to various estimates, between 200 000 and 750 000 people. Lang continued to play by the parliamentary and legal rules that were stacked against him and, more profoundly, against the working class. Over the previous year and a half, his policies had failed to overcome the Depression, and it was apparent that more drastic measures were needed but the ALP would not countenance them. The very large but far from militant mobilisations around Lang's modest program in times that demanded radical action could not persuade the lower ranks of the middle class and the less class conscious sections of the working class to support Labor in the face of the unremitting campaign conducted against the ALP by the right. Lang's failure to raise the stakes led to Labor's rout at the election.

Langism was not the only manifestation of the deep seated anger among large numbers of working class people towards the wage cuts, mass sackings, evictions and even starvation that resulted from the Depression. Revulsion against capitalism led to a sharp shift leftwards within the ALP, beyond Lang's radical populism. This shift took the form of the Socialisation Units.

Labor had adopted the socialisation objective at its 1921 federal conference but its leaders had done nothing to promote let alone implement it.

Now, in the midst of capitalism's worst ever crisis, many in the Party concluded it was time for socialism. In 1930, the New South Wales state conference authorised the establishment of committees by local branches, Socialisation Units, to promote the objective and the goal of 'socialism in our time'.[13] This movement was the most systematic and best supported attempt in the Party's history to translate the ALP's purely formal objective into practical action. Before long many Units were larger than the local branches that created them. There were 97 Units in early 1931 and almost 180 by late 1932, with strongholds in Sydney and Newcastle. To promote the idea of socialism inside and outside the Party, the Units published a monthly newspaper, *Socialisation Call*, which was sold around working class suburbs, and organised lectures and classes. The ALP quickly recruited hundreds of new members through the Units, many of them ardent socialists. As a result, Party members committed to socialism controlled many local branches and state electorate councils and so were strongly represented at state conferences.

The Units straddled a contradiction at the heart of the Labor Party, between its need to appeal to its working class base and its reformist, pro-capitalist leadership. The more the Units pursued a thoroughgoing fight for socialism, in line with the strong desires of many Party members and supporters, the more they came into conflict with the politicians and union officials who dominated the ALP. This was evident at the 1931 New South Wales Party conference where the Units succeeded in getting up a motion calling for 'socialism within three years'. Their triumph was short lived. Members of the Inner Group – influential union officials and confidants of Lang – were livid, concerned about the defection of moderate Party members and voters. They sprang into action and the conference rescinded the decision the next day.

A different fight over the achievement of socialism flared up inside the Party after the release of the *Payne Report* in August 1931. Tom Payne was a militant socialist and former communist who had been commissioned by the Socialisation Units to draw up recommendations on strategies for socialism, which became the *Payne Report*, a blueprint for socialist revolution. It argued that the Units' current strategy of relying on propaganda alone was not enough to deliver socialism and that the Labor Party should lead working class struggles. The *Report*'s clear call for action rallied the more radical members of the Socialisation Units. Most of the leaders of the

Units were, however, reformists who believed that the ALP, once sufficiently determined, could use parliament to rapidly legislate a new social order into existence. Close Lang allies and reformist socialists, who had a majority in the leadership of the socialisation movement, rejected the *Payne Report*. But Lang was increasingly concerned about the rising influence of the Units.

In October 1931, to boost his own credentials and blur the distinction between reform and revolution, Lang said that 'the revolution has come . . . by Act of Parliament', meaning the Lang Plan.[14] Yet the behaviour of the private banks, the Commonwealth Bank and the federal Labor government demonstrated very clearly that a revolution had not occurred – the workers of New South Wales were a long way from holding political power. And, regardless of his rhetoric, Lang remained committed to managing Australian capitalism within the existing legal framework. By inclination and Catholic faith on the right wing of the ALP, Lang was never a socialist.

The 1932 New South Wales conference unanimously resolved that Labor's election campaigns should emphasise the Socialisation Objective. Lang paid no attention to this decision during the campaign for the May 1932 election that followed his dismissal by the governor. The informal leadership of the Units, now without Payne who had led a handful of revolutionaries into the Communist Party of Australia (CPA) earlier in the year, decided to challenge the Inner Group for control of the ALP.

Lang and his supporters had tolerated the Units as a means to channel the surge of working class radicalism into safe activities within the structures of the Party. In particular, the Units seemed to provide an alternative to the CPA, which Lang loathed with a passion. Now the Units were a threat to the Inner Group's control over the New South Wales ALP and had to be crushed. Lang's offensive against the Units disoriented many of their supporters, who had believed that pressure within the Party could nudge its leaders to fight for socialism. They did not understand that those in control of the ALP were committed to capitalism. The Inner Group secured a majority at the Party's annual conference in 1933, which voted to dissolve the Socialisation Units. After the ALP cut them loose, the Units withered and died. Most of those who had joined the Party in order to fight for socialism quit in disgust and demoralisation, and disappeared from political life.

Unlike the ALP, the CPA, Lang's *bête noire*, was committed to the revolutionary overthrow of capitalism. Though small, it grew rapidly, from around 300 members in 1930 to about 2400 by 1934. Its ability to grow further and build a mass base in the working class was, however, limited by its strident denunciation, in accord with the line from Moscow, of the Labor Party's leaders as social fascists and, even more damaging, the leaders of the Socialisation Units as left social fascists. This attitude isolated the CPA from many workers who still retained some loyalty to the ALP, and especially its left. Communists were incapable of offering members of the Socialisation Units, let alone straightforward Lang supporters looking to defeat the bosses' offensive, a credible alternative to electoral politics. The CPA let the immense opportunities of the Socialisation Units and Lang's dismissal almost completely pass it by, picking up only handfuls of new members from the ALP.

The differences among the policies of the state and federal Labor governments during the Depression can be explained in terms of the ALP's material constitution. The working class and union movement was largest and strongest in New South Wales. Lang's policies complied less with the demands of business and the advice of senior public servants and were less hostile to working class interests than those of other Labor governments. For their part, federal politicians were more insulated by distance and the structures of the ALP than their state counterparts from Labor's working class supporters, and were able to rely on a conservative base of support from the smaller states at the federal ALP conference.

The Socialisation Units wanted the Lang government to challenge capitalism and advance workers' interests by parliamentary means. They failed to take over the New South Wales Party because the parliamentarians and union leaders, whose domination of the ALP was fundamental to its material constitution, were solidly opposed to them. It was impossible to alter Labor's nature as a capitalist workers' party without blowing it apart.

Recovery

Labor's electoral record in the aftermath of its devastating defeats during the Great Depression was mixed. In South Australia the Party did not return to government until 1965. In New South Wales and federally, the ALP only won office again in 1941. Where it had been out of office during the Depression it fared best, winning government in Queensland and Western Australia in 1932 and in Tasmania in 1934. Labor governments went on to rule Queensland until 1957. From the mid 1930s, the Labor Party rebuilt its electoral support in New South Wales and union officials reasserted their power in the New South Wales organisation as employment and membership began to recover; eventually, Lang was deposed.

During the late 1930s, the Party's economic outlook was quietly changing. As the economy pulled out from the Depression, the emerging new orthodoxy among academic and professional economists, developed by John Maynard Keynes, began to win favour within the ALP. Labor politicians and union officials recognised the usefulness of a respectable academic theory with which they could justify the moderate economic policies they had long supported. Keynes' emphasis on public spending, for example, provided an additional justification – stimulating growth – for public works that both Labor and non-Labor politicians had funded as relief for the unemployed since the 19th century.[15] The testimony of W. Brian Reddaway, a 'star pupil' of Keynes, in favour of a pay rise during the Arbitration Court's basic wage hearings in 1937, seemed to confirm the value of Keynesian economics to the labour movement. Union leaders and parliamentarians abandoned the underconsumptionist theories, most systematically expressed by the English economist John Hobson, that had for decades distinguished them from their conservative opponents.[16] The new ideas, which many conservatives also adopted, proved invaluable during World War II, when Labor again took responsibility for managing Australian capitalism at a federal level.

Chapter 4

HOT WAR, COLD WAR, SPLIT

Today, ALP supporters and even many critics regard the Curtin and Chifley governments between 1941 and 1949 as a period of achievement, exemplifying the best in the Party's traditions. There is no doubt that the Labor governments of the 1940s did a great deal. It is, however, worth asking whose interests they served. This chapter briefly considers their actions and ALP policies in several key areas. While these governments were responsible for the rapid expansion of the Australian welfare state and attempted to nationalise the banks, they also devoted a great deal of effort to containing and even defeating working class struggles, and to promoting capitalists' profits. Contradictory pressures from workers and bosses in the late 1940s help to explain the eventual fall of the Chifley government in 1949. They also contributed to the great split of the mid 1950s that had devastating consequences for the Party in Victoria, Queensland and federally.

Still smarting from its internal turmoil in the 1930s, Labor lost the 1940 federal elections with a primary vote of only 40 per cent. But the UAP–Country Party coalition was not in a commanding position because it was incapable of mobilising the working class for war. Workers simply did not trust Prime Minister 'Pig Iron Bob' Menzies, who had been an admirer of Hitler, had prosecuted wharfies for banning the export of scrap metal to Japan in 1938, and had supported Chamberlain's Munich Agreement. Menzies' parliamentary majority depended on two conservative independents and his government was riddled with competing factions. Labor leader John Curtin understood that it was a weak government and astutely rejected offers to join an all party government (as the Labour Party had done in Britain).

Although it would not join the government, the ALP did join the Advisory War Council to help prosecute the war. From the outset of the conflict in Europe in September 1939, the leaders of the Party were as enthusiastic about Australian involvement in this second round of global conflict as their forerunners had been about the first in 1914. Both the ALP and the conservative parties understood that Australian national interests could only be secured through alliances with more powerful countries. Labor did not hesitate to back Britain in 1939 and supported the dispatch of Australian troops to Europe and North Africa. Compared to the conservative parties, however, Labor had certain advantages in winning working class support for the war. Curtin had been an anti-war activist during World War I and had been on the left of the ALP. He was not tainted by any pro-fascist sympathies and Labor's connections with the unions meant that workers were far more likely to trust him than Menzies. Even before the war broke out, Curtin had persuaded the ACTU to end its boycott of the government's National Register of the labour force, a measure crucial to planning the redeployment of human resources in case war broke out.

In October 1941 the Menzies government collapsed and the ALP took office for the first time in a decade. No dramatic shift in policy followed. Two months later, when Japan attacked Pearl Harbor, Curtin put the country onto a full war footing. Japanese successes against the Western imperial powers in Asia, in particular its seizure of Singapore, made it clear that Britain could no longer secure Australian interests. Curtin recalled Australian forces in the Middle East and reoriented foreign policy towards the United States as a new military ally, though he did not forsake Britain. There was no disagreement between government and opposition about the overall conduct of the war, just as there had been a consensus over foreign policy fundamentals throughout the interwar period.

The Japanese bombing of Darwin in February 1942 and submarine raid on Sydney Harbour in May reinforced the perception that the country faced imminent invasion, an idea that the government vigorously encouraged. Yet senior politicians were well aware that there was no such prospect. Japanese codes had been cracked so, by May 1942, the government knew very well that Japan did not intend to invade, even before its navy was defeated in the Battles of the Coral Sea and Midway in May and June. The Curtin government nevertheless repeated the lie that the Australian mainland was under threat of invasion because it served the useful purposes of boosting recruitment for the army and encouraging the intensification of work at home.[1]

Racism towards the Japanese was a central feature of the invasion scare. Labor portrayed the 'Japs' as subhuman beasts who had to be destroyed. The hysteria about invasion by Asians, something that tapped into the deep seated racist paranoia associated with Australia's status as a white colonial settler state in Asia, gave Labor the opportunity to introduce conscription for military service outside Australia, something that the conservatives had not been game to attempt. Although Curtin had to fight hard to overturn Labor's long standing opposition to overseas conscription, a decision that was very unpopular in sections of the ALP and the wider labour movement, the Party did not split as it had in 1916, not least because the leadership faced no organised opposition to the decision on its left.[2]

As the war drew to its close, the Labor government sought to extend Australia's otherwise limited influence by helping to construct a series of international institutions that were to be used by the victorious allies once the armed conflict was over. These included the United Nations, the International Monetary Fund and, later, the General Agreement on Trade and Tariffs. Australia's ability to leverage these was limited by the Cold War polarisation of the world into two imperialist blocs, led by the United States and the Soviet Union, the veto powers of the permanent members of the UN Security Council and the subordination of the IMF and World Bank to their main creditor, the United States. Alliances with Britain and the United States therefore remained Australia's main means to influence world events.

Australia under Labor was firmly on the side of the United States. It backed British and American intervention in the Greek civil war, dubbed 'the first round in the Cold War'.[3] Rather than assist decolonisation in Asia, Foreign Minister Bert Evatt initially supported the return of the old colonial masters to Malaya, the Dutch East Indies and East Timor immediately after the war. Under pressure from a campaign of solidarity action by Australian unions, however, and fearing that obstructing independence would only further radicalise the Indonesian nationalists, Evatt changed tack. Acting as a mediator between the nationalists and the Dutch, he oversaw a transition to Indonesian independence from 1947. Evatt backed colonial ventures elsewhere, including the formation of the state of Israel in 1948.[4]

The ALP's dedication to the stability of Australian capitalism and its enthusiastic support for the USA led the Chifley government to expand the local security apparatus. Labor established the Australian Security Intelligence Organisation in 1949 to root out foreign agents and spy on subversives, and it relentlessly played up the red threat in Asia, which leveraged the twin right-wing bogeys of communist dictatorship and the yellow peril.

While the ALP and the conservative parties agreed on a primary foreign policy orientation to the United States, they differed on the specifics of the relationship and secondary issues. The United Nations was more prominent in Labor rhetoric but, far from encouraging peace initiatives, the Party was often bellicose. The ALP favoured, for example, a more punitive peace agreement with Japan than the one that the USA promoted and the Menzies government signed. Following its defeat at the 1949 election, the ALP endorsed the 1951 Australia, New Zealand and United States (ANZUS) agreement. Labor criticised the terms of the 1954 pact that created the South East Asia Treaty Organisation (SEATO), which included the USA, Britain, Australia and their allies in the region, on the grounds that the treaty lacked teeth.

Labor against labour

Just as foreign policy under Curtin and Chifley sought to secure Australia's strategic position, Labor's management of industrial relations and the economy was designed to protect the interests of Australian capitalism, although the ALP's material constitution enabled it to use tactics that the conservatives could not.

Following Japan's entry into the war, the Curtin government dramatically increased the role of the state in the economy in order to concentrate resources for the war. It established enterprises to produce munitions and other equipment necessary for the conflict, closely regulated the use of raw materials and rationed many consumer goods. The February 1942 National Economic Plan provided for limits on profits, restrictions on property transfers and investments, supervision of interest rates, tighter control over prices and labour (including civilian conscription for the Civil Construction Corps) and wage pegging. But Labor was not interested in threatening capitalism. Within 6 months the government's promise to regulate profits was dropped.[5] Indeed, it guaranteed profits, through the cost plus system of pricing for the vastly increased quantity of war related goods purchased by the state and by subsidising increased costs of production for other goods. The system ensured a healthy rate of return on their investments to private capitalists.

The government made no effort to use its enhanced, emergency legislative powers to nationalise privately owned industries. In fact, the Curtin government's position on nationalisation, let alone genuine socialism, was unequivocal: during the campaigns for the 1943 federal election and the 1944 referendum on increasing the powers of the Commonwealth, Curtin explicitly ruled out any socialist measures. Attorney-General and External Affairs Minister Evatt promised that 'There will be more room for private enterprise and business initiative after this war than ever before in Australia's history'.[6]

The Curtin government embraced Keynesianism and introduced legislation to control the banks along the lines recommended by the UAP appointed royal commission into the Australian financial system, which had reported in 1937. It did not implement the ALP platform's bank nationalisation plank.

The government and its economic advisers were worried about inflation but it was workers who were to bear the brunt of bringing it down. Wage pegging meant cuts in living standards as inflation raced ahead of earnings. Workers responded by going on strike for higher wages. The strike rate, which had slumped in the 12 months after Pearl Harbor, soared in 1943. Workers struck without much support from their own union leaders who, for the most part, went along with the state direction of labour and wage controls.[7] Compared with activities during World War I, when the Wobblies criticised the Fisher and Hughes governments from the left, opposed the slaughter and encouraged workers to strike in defence of their wages and conditions, there was no significant current to the left of the ALP during World War II. The CPA, which had initially criticised the war as an inter-imperialist conflict, changed tack after the German invasion of the Soviet Union in June 1941. The war was now a fight against fascism. The CPA demonstrated at least as much enthusiasm about work intensification and industrial discipline as did Labor Party supporters and conservatives, to the point of encouraging scabs to cross picket lines.

At war's end, workers saw no reason for continued restraint. Uncertainty about how long the economy would hold up before a new depression set in made their struggles all the more urgent. The level of strike action increased even further. Key demands were for higher wages, still pegged under wartime regulations, and for the 40 hour week. While reluctant to undermine the government, Labor-oriented union officials were now under substantial pressure from their members to lead effective struggles.[8] The ALP also faced competition on its left from the Communist Party, many of whose members held senior positions in the unions. Even before the CPA, prompted by Moscow, lurched to the left in 1947–8, the discontent of union members had an effect on the willingness of Communist union officials to lead militant struggles.

In early December 1945, 30 000 workers, including coal miners, wharfies, seamen and Newcastle steel workers, went on strike against the victimisation of a union delegate and over the New South Wales Industrial Commission's deregistration of the Communist-led Federated Ironworkers' Association. Despite the hostility of the New South Wales and federal Labor governments, the New South Wales Labor Council and the ACTU, the workers won a partial victory.[9] During the following year, Queensland pastoral workers, Victorian tramway and railway workers, and coal miners all struck for and won shorter hours, pay increases or longer holidays. The high point of the postwar working class offensive was the 6 month strike by Victorian metal workers in 1946–47, roundly condemned by the state and federal Labor governments, which achieved a substantial wage increase that flowed on to other sectors.

A head of steam was now building up around the demand for a 40 hour week. Sydney daily newspaper workers had already struck for and won the 40 hour week in 1944. Subsequent strikes by pastoral, metal and transport workers in New South Wales and Queensland forced state Labor govern-ments to promise shorter hours under state awards. In September 1947 the ACTU Congress threatened a 24 hour stoppage on 20 October. Faced with the prospect of widespread strike action, the Arbitration Court capitulated and granted the 40 hour week, to be effective from the beginning of 1948. The Chifley government's policies for controlling wages and conditions were now in tatters.

ALP governments went further than simply taking the employers' side in industrial disputes. In New South Wales, the Party leadership also set up industrial groups within the unions to combat the influence of the CPA. The Victorian, South Australian and Queensland state branches of the Party soon followed. Although the groups were ALP bodies, the proposal to set them up and their overall strategic direction came from the Catholic Social Studies Movement, a secretive right wing organisation sponsored by the Catholic church.[10]

Labor and capitalist development during the 1940s

Following war's end, Labor's industry policy was geared to developing the economy around the needs of business. It initiated the Snowy Mountains Scheme Agreement, established the Overseas Telecommunications Commission and the Bureau of Mineral Resources to provide important infrastructure or support for private capitalist development, offered big subsidies to stimulate the domestic car and aluminium industries, and created Trans Australia Airlines to compete with Ansett Airlines and prevent a private monopoly in domestic air transport.[11]

Labor encouraged the introduction of incentive payments in private industry and set an example by pushing up productivity through Taylorist techniques of detailed control over workers' time, activity and movements in the Commonwealth public service.[12] Another measure designed to raise private sector profits and investment across the board was an accelerated tax depreciation rate of 20 per cent per annum for plant and machinery.[13]

The coal industry provides one of the clearest examples of the government's commitment to private capitalist development rather than to socialism. Here was a technologically backward sector, crucial for the entire Australian economy, whose employees worked in appalling, unsafe conditions and whose nationalisation was identified by two professional economists as the most effective means of overcoming the coal shortage and rationalising the industry.[14] Not only the Communist Party but also the ACTU and, until 1946, the New South Wales ALP campaigned for nationalisation of the industry and improved conditions for miners. The Curtin and Chifley governments were having none of it and remained strongly opposed to nationalisation. Instead a new Joint Coal Board supervised technological modernisation and the improvement of working conditions in the private mining industry.[15]

Labour was the most important component of productive infrastructure provided by the government, which set up the Commonwealth Employment Service to encourage labour mobility and better matching of skilled workers to jobs. It introduced a program of mass, assisted migration. Between 1947 and 1951, an average of 117 000 migrants entered Australia each year, a figure, in proportion to the population, never matched before or since. Migrants generally went into lower paid work and '[p]rovided an easily directed, mobile reserve army to overcome the bottleneck areas of building and construction, heavy industry and public utilities'.[16] To mollify the opposition of the trade unions towards such a large inflow of migrants, the Labor government played on racism, invoking the need to increase Australia's population in the face of the yellow peril.[17]

The Curtin and Chifley governments are celebrated by the ALP for their contribution to improving the social security and health systems. They were not, however, the first to be convinced of the need for these programs. By the late 1930s there was already a consensus between the two sides of politics on the need for a healthier and more reliable workforce, which, protected by social services, might be more accepting of capitalism. The major issues in dispute were who should pay, the capitalist class or workers, and who should control health services, government or private doctors.

The UAP had legislated in the late 1930s to expand the welfare state through a national insurance scheme to which workers would contribute, but it was never implemented. At that time, Labor favoured a system funded from consolidated revenue and higher taxes on the wealthy. But the Curtin government chose to extend income taxation to most wage earners in order to pay for the war and new social security measures. In 1943 it introduced funeral benefits, higher maternity payments and allowances for dependents of pensioners, at the same time as income tax was brought in for all but the lowest paid. Unemployment and sickness benefits, already foreshadowed, followed in 1944, pharmaceutical benefits in 1945. Free hospital care became available in public wards. The costs of the expanded social security and public health systems were more than offset by the additional revenue from income tax on workers. Maurice Blackburn, an independent labour MHR, observed that the government stole a sheep and gave 'the trotters away in charity'.[18]

Labor's approach made workers pay for the war and involved some income redistribution within the working class rather between social classes.

The welfare schemes served to bolster public commitment to the war effort and offset the unpopularity of the Curtin government's introduction of conscription for overseas service. The new health services and social security helped the ALP win an impressive primary vote of just below 50 per cent at the August 1943 federal elections.

Chifley's fall and the Split

By the end of the 1940s, the Chifley government was having increasing difficulties balancing demands from the capitalist class with those from its working class base. Employers increasingly felt that Labor was caving in to workers, at the expense of their profits. The banks and a powerful section of the middle class – doctors – campaigned against what they deemed to be socialist policies that affected their sectional interests. They were the spearhead of a wider mobilisation by the capitalist class against the ALP. The medical profession used legal action, and then a boycott, to sabotage a vital element of the Chifley government's national health scheme – the provision of free medicine, despite Labor's successes in September 1946, when the Party was returned to office with a high primary vote and won a referendum to expand the Commonwealth's powers in the areas of social security and health.

The banks mounted a ferocious campaign against an attempt by the Chifley government to nationalise them in 1947. The High Court had struck down a section of Labor's 1945 Banking Act, which required all government instrumentalities, Commonwealth, state and local, to hold accounts only with the Commonwealth Bank. The section was not critical to the general thrust of the legislation, but Chifley anticipated, incorrectly as it turned out, legal challenges to more vital provisions and sought to pre-empt these by nationalising the banks. Bank nationalisation was a defensive manoeuvre designed to bolster earlier legislation.[19] Far from being socialist, its intent was to ensure that the central bank and government had the capacity to keep the capitalist economy on a stable course and was inspired by Maynard Keynes rather than Karl Marx.[20] The banks rallied other sections of Australian business behind their cause, sponsored intense advertising campaigns and mobilised their own staff against Labor. The media warned darkly of creeping socialism. The legislation was passed but was soon struck down by that conservative bastion, the High Court.

The final major act of the Chifley government – its battle with the coal miners – was a clear demonstration of Labor's preparedness to crush working class militancy in order to safeguard the interests of Australian capitalism. It was preceded by a two month railway strike in Queensland in 1948, successfully coordinated by Communist union officials, that saw the Hanlon Labor government introduce emergency powers legislation and police violently attack strikers. Undeterred, the railway workers eventually won large wage gains. The national miners' strike in 1949 led to an even deeper and wider confrontation between Labor and labour. More than 20 000 coal miners struck to win the 35 hour week that Broken Hill miners had achieved 30 years before, a 30 shilling wage rise and long service leave. With coal supplies already short, the 7 week strike brought more and more sectors of the economy to a halt. The Chifley government, which placed a higher priority on the profitability of the coal industry than on improving miners' conditions, identified not only a threat to the national economy but also an attempt by the CPA to discredit the ALP.

Labor leaders introduced tough measures to break the strike and the influence of the CPA. The government outlawed financial support for striking miners or their families, took control of the Miners' Federations' funds and jailed seven strike leaders. Promising to fight 'boots and all', Chifley was already preparing to use troops to mine coal early in the strike, arguing that 'The Reds must be taught a lesson'.[21] On 1 August, the soldiers went in, the first time that the armed forces had been used to break a strike in peacetime. The miners' industrial action collapsed two weeks later. Many militants, on and well beyond the coal fields, were bitter about the actions of the Labor government.

Labor's agenda of austerity, union busting and Cold War mongering in 1948 and 1949 did not save the Chifley government. On the contrary, its witch hunts against communism steered national politics sharply to the right and its persecution of militant unionists demoralised sections of its own most active support base. As the prospect of a new postwar depression and the threat of working class combativity receded, the capitalist class and sections of the middle class chafed at the government's efforts to control their activities. The Liberal Party, formed by Menzies in 1944, surged to victory at the December 1949 elections.

In these early days of the Cold War, ALP leaders lined up with the West against the Soviet Union and used coercion against the CPA and militant workers regardless of their party loyalties. The ALP Industrial Groups came increasingly to the fore, fighting the Communists in Labor-affiliated and unaffiliated unions and, with financial help from employers, scoring some spectacular successes in court supervised elections.

As the Groupers prospered, the Movement expanded its influence within the ALP, which started to sound alarm bells. ALP union officials were happy to help the Groupers get rid of their Communist opponents but were not so pleased when the Groups began to move against Labor union leaders and politicians labelled corrupt or insufficiently anti-communist. The right wing state president of the powerful Queensland AWU, Joe Bukowski, and Victorian Trades Hall Council Secretary Vic Stout, for example, had collaborated with the Movement to set up and expand the Groups during the 1940s. Now they turned against it. Among the anti-Grouper parliamentarians were Party leader Evatt, who had taken over when Chifley died in 1951, and his eventual successor, Arthur Calwell.

The internal tensions between the Groupers, and behind them the Movement, and the anti-Group forces came to a head at the federal Party conference in 1955. The conference expelled the whole Victorian executive and ended the connection between the Groups and the ALP. In the resulting bloody and debilitating split, the ALP lost office in Victoria. Menzies called a snap election to capitalise on his opponents' disarray. At the 1954 election Labor had won over half of the primary vote, only the second time in its history that it had done so. A year and a half later, its primary vote slid to 45 per cent. The Split enveloped Queensland in 1957, ending Labor's long rule in that state, when the central executive expelled Premier Vince Gair over his refusal to legislate for 3 weeks annual leave. Party membership, which had been massively boosted by widespread branch stacking, plummeted nationally from 75 000 in 1953 to under 45 000 in 1958, and in Victoria by more than half to a mere 10 000.[22]

The ALP into the 1960s

The Split purged the Party of its most right wing and pro-capitalist elements who were seeking to fundamentally change its nature, but the purge came at a cost. The expelled Groupers formed the Democratic Labor Party, whose allocation of preferences to the Liberals helped keep the ALP out of federal office until 1972. In the 1958 federal election Labor's primary vote fell further to just 43 per cent, its lowest since 1940. Evatt was pushed out and in 1960 Calwell was elected leader.

The prosperity of the long postwar boom consolidated Menzies' hold on office. The Coalition government, and Australian capitalism more generally, seemed to be delivering the goods. The scope of the welfare state expanded modestly. Although poverty did not disappear and the middle and capitalist classes gained disproportionately from the boom, workers' incomes rose, so that home and car ownership and holidays away were within the reach of millions more. In conditions of low unemployment, short strikes were often sufficient to extract pay rises from the bosses. Union coverage reached record levels during the 1950s.

While the 1955 Split had serious ramifications for the Party federally, and in Victoria and Queensland, its consequences were not so damaging in other states. In New South Wales, where most of the Groupers stayed in the ALP, Premier Joe Cahill's government did not fall and the right soon regained control of the branch. No official groups were ever set up in Tasmania or Western Australia, and in South Australia they existed for only a few years. The ALP's dominance of Tasmanian politics continued. Nor was Albert Hawke's Labor government in Western Australia dislodged by the Split.

In 1961, Labor came within a whisker of defeating the Coalition parties at the federal election. The government had slammed on the economic brakes and brought growth to a halt. Unemployment soared to what was then the unacceptably high rate of 2.6 per cent. The ALP gained a majority of the two party preferred vote and was one seat and a handful of preferences shy of victory. After this sudden leap in the Party's federal fortunes, the Menzies government recovered in the following two elections.

Despite their fierce rivalry, the ALP and the Liberal–Country Party coalition both understood economic growth in the same Keynesian terms. According to Gough Whitlam, 'During the years of the post-war economic boom, questions of economic management were scarcely deemed to require original answers'.[23] According to another account, politics in New South Wales, where Labor remained in office until 1965, was 'little more than a battle of tactics with only vestigial ideological overtones. Pragmatism was dominant'.[24] The Menzies government retained, and in some respects expanded, the welfare state in the basic form established under Curtin and Chifley, although it reversed Labor's few steps towards a comprehensive, free health system.

If there was little to separate Labor from the conservatives in economic policy during these years, a serious difference between the Menzies government and Labor opened up on the question of Australian involvement in Vietnam. Menzies' decision in November 1964 to introduce conscription and in June 1965 to send troops to Vietnam was a watershed in Australian politics. Labor leader Calwell took a strong stand against both decisions. He had been one of the few Labor figures to oppose conscription for overseas service during World War II. He was not, however, an anti-imperialist or an advocate of Vietnamese self-determination. According to Calwell,

> On three great issues, there is agreement between the two parties. These issues are: the American alliance, opposition to Communism, and the common determination to keep Australia safe and inviolable.[25]

The problem with the war in Vietnam, according to Calwell, was that the Americans could not win. And the conservatives in Australia were too supine in their attitude to the United States to argue this point to the US administration. Rather than pursue a futile war that would only damage the reputation of the United States and its allies, the ALP leader argued that Australia should steer well clear. Labor went into the November 1966 election campaign supported by hundreds of ardent anti-war activists who threw themselves into getting out the vote for the Party. The Liberal–Country Party government under leader Harold Holt, who had succeeded Menzies earlier in the year, banged the anti-communist drum, arguing that a Labor victory would open the country to the threat of invasion. Labor was trounced, its vote dropping below 40 per cent for the first time since the fall of the Scullin government.

Class, power and the ALP from the 1940s to the 1960s

The Curtin and Chifley governments mark an important milestone in the history of the ALP. They proved that Labor could govern in the interests of capitalism during a period of intense military and economic stress and working class struggle without tearing itself apart, in the way it had in 1916 and 1931. Indeed, the Party's working class base and links with the unions placed it in a better position during World War II to sell wage pegging, conscription for military service overseas and the imposition of federal income tax on all but the poorest sections of the working class without a matching improvement in the welfare state. After the war, Labor continued to hold down workers' living standards and discipline union militants.

The ALP's relative independence from individual capitalists and specific sectors of the capitalist class, thanks to its working class base, enabled it to regulate the financial system and expand the welfare state in the long term interests of the capital in general, even if these policies came at the expense of particular capitalists or sections of the middle class. But when Labor went beyond what the capitalist class as a whole was prepared to accept, those sectional interests found wider support. Self-employed doctors, encouraged by conservative politicians, mobilised to defend their privilege; when Chifley sought to take over the banks they portrayed nationalisation as a threat to civilisation and were able to rally other sections of the capitalist class in an anti-Labor mobilisation.

Labor's leaders were incapable of inspiring workers in a countermobilisation that could successfully defend its program of bank nationalisation, a national health service and more extensive welfare because of its own commitment to prosecuting the Cold War in foreign and domestic policy. The ALP's identification of strikes with communism, its hostility to industrial campaigns and sponsorship of the most right wing elements in the union movement disillusioned many of the activists who would have been the mainstay of any effective response to the capitalist class's anti-Labor campaigns.

On the other hand most of the parliamentary and trade union powerbrokers in the ALP turned against those in the Party who wanted to drive it hard to the right. They defended themselves by forcing the most extreme adherents of Cold War policies and naked capitalist interests out of the Party. But unlike the splits of 1916 and 1931, the Split of 1955 was not driven by any upturn in working class activity or radicalisation. It was essentially engineered from the top and removed the influence of the Movement while preserving the Labor Party's material constitution and the decisive role of union officials and politicians within it.

Chapter 5

LABOR AFTER 70 YEARS

During its first 70 years, the ALP became one of Australia's two main parliamentary forces, went through three major and other minor splits, and held office federally for six periods. For long stretches, Queensland, Tasmania and New South Wales almost seemed to be one party Labor states. In comparison with labour or social democratic parties in other countries, the ALP was remarkably successful. Had its years in office changed it significantly? To answer this question and to provide a point of comparison when we come to consider the Party in the 21st century in Chapter 10, this chapter assesses important features of the ALP around the time of its 70th birthday. We focus on the three most powerful elements within the organisation: the union officials, the parliamentarians and the Party machines; we also consider the rank and file members, branches and Labor voters.

Union officials

Trade unions established the Labor Party in the 1890s; 70 years later the relationship between unions and the Party was still very close. Before considering this relationship, it is worth making two points about the nature of the union movement in the early 1960s. First, workers affiliated with the Labor Party through the unions were at this time still overwhelmingly members of blue collar unions. The exceptions, in states where they remained affiliated after the 1955 Split, were mainly members of the private sector clerks' and shop assistants' unions. Most white collar and professional workers' organisations were affiliated to neither the ALP nor the ACTU, although many of their officials were Labor Party members.[1] Second, a large majority of full time union officials still had backgrounds as ordinary members of their unions. With some exceptions, until the 1970s trade union officials came from the trade or calling that they represented and had worked in for several years as rank and file union members or job delegates before being appointed as organisers or elected to leading positions.

Trade union officials exercised power within the ALP in several ways. Before the 1970s, affiliated unions controlled up to 85 per cent of state conference delegates.[2] State conferences determined branch rules and policies, with which parliamentarians were required, at least on paper, to comply. State conferences also elected state executives and delegates to the federal conference.

Union leaders had a large say in the Party, not only through the votes of their delegations at Party conferences, but also through union officials who were representatives of local branches. The fact that affiliated unions provided a large proportion of the Party's funds and substantial additional in kind resources during election campaigns also underpinned the power of these senior union officials.[3]

The exact relationship between the unions and the Party varied across states and over time. Between 1927 and 1940 trade unions in New South Wales had direct representation on the New South Wales state executive. Even after this provision was eliminated, the formal power of union officials was not noticeably reduced: in 1964, 27 of the 40 members of the New South Wales state executive elected by the state conference were secretaries of trade unions.[4] In Western Australia, the ALP state executive served as the peak body of the state's trade union movement until an independent labour council was established in 1963.[5] In Queensland, unions enjoyed direct representation on the state central executive. Until 1980 rank and file unionists could also vote in Queensland Labor preselections,[6] a practice that had ceased in New South Wales in 1954. In Victoria, as the central Party organisation assumed greater control after the 1955 Split, the influence of rank and file unionists in preselections was rather more attenuated.

The very extensive interpenetration of unions and Party also operated through less formal mechanisms. Many former union officials became parliamentarians. Current union leaders also held powerful positions in the Party. They included Charlie Oliver of the AWU in New South Wales, Jack Egerton of the Boilermakers' Society and Trades and Labour Council in Queensland, Vic Stout of the Victorian Trades Hall Council and successive New South Wales Labor Council secretaries who had billets as part-time legislative councillors.

Regular lobbying of Labor politicians was another means by which union leaders exercised influence within the ALP. Party events and personal relationships provided ample opportunities for informal discussions. Unions also sent formal delegations to Labor ministers over specific issues. In New South Wales, Reg Downing, ALP fixer, minister, member of the Legislative Council and former union leader, presided for years over weekly meetings between members of the Party and Labor Council executives to sort out common positions on issues of mutual interest.[7]

In general, however, the influence union officials had on politicians through the Party was rather more limited than the resources at their disposal suggest. Labor came under pressure, of course, not just from unions but also from business. Other things being equal, pressure on Labor politicians from business and the public service was more intense when the ALP was in government than when it was in opposition.[8] Union influence on Party policy tended to be greatest when there was little prospect of policy actually being implemented, particularly in states where Labor had been out of office for long periods.

As we saw in chapters 2 to 4, the main difference between Labor and non-Labor governments between the 1890s and the early 1960s was a somewhat different style of managing public affairs in the interests of the capitalist class. Under ALP and conservative governments workers sometimes made gains and sometimes experienced setbacks in their living conditions. The key variables influencing government actions were the levels of class struggle and the state of the economy. Generally speaking, the more militant the working class and the more buoyant the economy, the more likely were Labor governments to carry out measures that directly benefited the working class. Yet the union officials did not always capitalise on these situations to extract the maximum advantage for their members. Their class position generally led them to stress their own role in mediating between capital and labour. They tended to emphasise their political influence within the ALP, rather than class struggle, as the means to bring about change. Union leaders stressed the need to maintain good relations with those who headed the parliamentary parties and avoid actions that jeopardised Labor's electoral chances to dampen militancy among rank and file unionists. Yet in doing so they weakened the very force that could put the most effective pressure on the politicians.

The structures of the Party and the inclinations of union leaders meant that it was the parliamentary Labor caucuses, particularly the front benchers and ministers, and, at the local level, municipal caucuses, that formulated and implemented the Party's day to day policies. Tensions between parliamentarians and union officials reflected the distinct roles of the two groups. The parliamentary leaders, in government, took direct responsibility for managing Australian capitalism and were more preoccupied with winning the electoral middle ground. The union officials had to perform their own industrial balancing act between bosses and workers. Their relations were further complicated by factional allegiances. Only rarely were union officials and Party machines prepared to discipline and, if necessary, drive out leading politicians. This occurred in spectacular fashion on three occasions: during the conscription fight in 1916, in some states during the Depression and in the battle with the Groupers in 1955. Thereafter, the union leaders pulled back from head on confrontations for fear of the electoral consequences.

Parliamentarians

If the union officials mainly exercised their power within the ALP in smoke filled rooms, the politicians were the public face of the Party. What were their characteristics? Most of Labor's federal leaders from Watson to Chifley had held working class jobs prior to becoming a union official or parliamentarian. They generally came from working class families.[9] Chris Watson had been a manual worker, Andrew Fisher and Matthew Charlton had both been coal miners. Curtin's father ran a pub, but the family was not well off and he left school at 13. None of Labor's leaders until Evatt completed secondary school. Evatt's family was more prosperous and he had a dazzling academic and legal career; by 1930 he was earning a very high income of £8000 to £10 000 a year as a barrister. He then became a judge on the High Court before entering the federal parliament in 1940. Although the background of his successor, Calwell, a former Victorian public service clerk, was more plebeian, Evatt's election to the leadership was the first sign of an important shift that became more pronounced in the following decades.

With the notable exception of Evatt, most Labor leaders had extensive experience as union activists, followed in most cases by full time union posts before entering parliament. Some had been sacked, blacklisted and, in Curtin's case, gaoled for their political or union activism prior to entering parliament during the stormy industrial and political conflicts of the first 40 years of the 20th century.

Labor's leaders reflected the Party's strong base among Catholics and those with an Irish heritage. Scullin, Curtin, Chifley and Calwell had Roman Catholic backgrounds, although Curtin broke with the church at a young age and Chifley was non-observant. Six of the eight Labor premiers of New South Wales between 1920 and 1965 had also been brought up Catholic, as had five of the eight Queensland Labor premiers between 1915 and 1957. Most of these leaders also had Irish antecedents.

As did their leaders, most of Labor's federal parliamentarians had working class backgrounds. According to Party historian L. F. Crisp, two-thirds of federal ALP politicians had either blue collar or white collar backgrounds in 1962. Forty-four per cent of Labor parliamentarians had been union officials, down sharply from 79 per cent in 1901 but still very significant. Roman Catholics were also significantly over-represented among Labor politicians. In the early 1960s, Catholics made up 45 per cent of ALP federal parliamentarians, as against only one-quarter of the Australian population.[10]

In terms of lifestyle, Labor MPs were still very privileged compared with their constituents, as they had been in the 1890s. Between 1921 and about 1950, the basic pay of junior federal MPs was around five times average earnings, and subsequently remained around three times average pay.[11]

Labor politics was male dominated. There were no female ALP members in any Australian parliament, state or federal, until 1925.[12] The situation improved from that point on, but at a snail's pace. Over the next 20 years, six ALP women held state seats and another dozen women were elected between 1945 and 1970. The only Labor woman in federal politics during this period was Western Australian Senator Dorothy Tangney, elected in 1943. Women were also severely underrepresented in elected positions in the extra parliamentary Party.

Machines

The ALP had early evolved its own formal and informal apparatuses – state branch and factional machines – that exercised power within the Party. These embraced union officials, parliamentarians and rank and file members. The machines were networks and there were no clear boundaries between them and the other elements that made up the Party. The machines did enhance the power within the ALP of their senior members, including some who were neither union officials nor parliamentary leaders.

Labor's formal structures, established under its constitutions and rules, included state and federal officer positions, executives and conferences, local branches and electorate organisations with their own officers, and arrangements in the parliamentary and municipal caucuses. These bodies and individuals controlled the Party's funds,[13] decided policy and tactics, and conducted state and federal election campaigns. They operated through votes in committees, local branches, preselections, caucuses and at conferences or through the prerogatives of ALP officers and leadership bodies to interpret and enforce the rules, set agendas and spend money. The number of full time Party officers was tiny, but those who held honorary posts or otherwise played a leading role in machines often had union jobs or parliamentary seats, which allowed them time to wheel and deal within the Party.

In the early 1960s, power was still very concentrated in the state branches of the Labor Party, each with its own constitution and rules for the conduct of its affairs. The state parliamentary parties and municipal caucuses, as we have seen, had considerable autonomy.

The Party's rules and hence its official structures were important aspects of its operations but an account confined to them cannot explain how the ALP worked in practice. The rules cannot capture the relations of ideological agreement, loyalty, friendship, family and patronage that bound groups of parliamentarians, union officials and rank and file members into political machines. The machines mobilised resources and organised the numbers in important votes, preselections and internal Party elections, in line with their policies and the judgements of their leaders. Given their control over human and financial resources, union leaders were powerful figures within the informal machines, just as they were in the formal Party structures defined by the rules.

In some circumstances, these informal relationships and the official Party apparatus were closely aligned in a machine that dominated a state branch.[14] The main forces in South Australia, including left and right wing unions, collaborated in a single Party machine. As a consequence of the departure of most of the right during the Split in Victoria, the dominant left exercised tight control of and could operate through the official structures of the ALP. The Egerton machine, with its very firm grip on the Queensland Branch in the mid 1960s, was also identified with the left, as was the machine that dominated the Western Australian apparatus of the Party.

In New South Wales, where the Split had not been as severe, the machine of the dominant right wing mainly organised through the ALP's official apparatus. The New South Wales left, whose members occupied a few Party posts only by grace of the right, had its own factional machine, known as the Combined Unions' and Branches' Steering Committee, that stretched from branches and affiliated left unions to the state conference and into parliament. The Steering Committee had its own formal constitution and rules.

The resources controlled by the federal extra parliamentary machine remained minute in the early 1960s. The position of federal Party secretary only became full time in 1963. The authority of the Labor Party's federal conference and executive in relation to the state branches had, however, increased in the decades before the 1960s. The federal executive had inter-vened in the faction fights in the New South Wales ALP during the 1920s and 1930s. Both the federal executive and federal conference were important arenas for the contending forces in the lead up to the 1950s Split, which involved federal interventions in Victoria and New South Wales.

Each of the six states sent six delegates to federal conference and the federal executive was made up of two representatives from each state. While leaders of the local parliamentary parties had *ex officio* membership of state Party executives, this was not true of the federal executive.

Federal politicians owed their positions and continued preselection to the state branches of the Party, just as state Labor politicians did. Most members of Caucus were more or less aligned with a state head office or factional machine, which meant that the influence of the state-based machines extended into the federal parliament. Machine allegiances were a major factor in, for example, the election of Calwell in 1960 and Whitlam in 1967 to the leadership of the federal Labor Party.

Largely thanks to the Party's own federal structure, federal parliamentarians were more insulated from Labor's working class base than were their state and municipal counterparts. The federal executive ruled in the 1920s and 1930s that state branches could not direct federal politicians and only once itself pushed the parliamentarians to act in contradiction with a Caucus decision.[15] The inaccessibility of MHRs and senators, at least during sitting weeks, due to the physical distance between Canberra and Australia's population centres, was another factor that enhanced the autonomy of the federal politicians.

If the reach of the machines spread out from ALP state executives into the state parliaments and up into the Labor's federal institutions it also spread down, not only into unions, but also into the local branches. In electorates and branches, local parliamentarians, councillors and candidates for these positions were often pivotal figures in friendship groups, family circles and cliques that might shade into more highly organised machines. These local formations were often connected with head office or factional machines. Particularly during the mobilisation and countermobilisation, stacking and counterstacking leading up to the Split in Victoria and New South Wales, there were contending personal or factional machines in some branches and, more frequently, in electorate-wide councils or committees.

Members, branches and voters

The ALP's local branches were vital for the Party's contact with voters. In some states, their members determined preselections and in all they provided a wider pool of potential parliamentary candidates than the limited pond of those already employed in the apparatuses of the ALP or trade unions. Branches also had representation at Party conferences, which, as the experience of the New South Wales Socialisation Units demonstrated, could be used to force the Party's leadership to pay attention to, if not act upon, their demands.

Although far smaller than European social democratic parties in absolute terms and in relation to its voting base, the Australian Labor Party was still a mass party with tens of thousands of members in the early 1960s. The exodus of members during and after the Split came to a halt by 1958 and the membership stabilised at about 44 000 for a decade. But the Party's social weight had significantly declined by the early 1960s. In 1929, the 24 361 members of the New South Wales branch were roughly 1 per cent of the state's population and 4 per cent of the ALP vote.[16] By 1963 the national membership represented only 0.4 per cent of the population and 2 per cent of the ALP vote. Two years later, Federal Secretary Cyril Wyndham lamented, in a report on Party organisation that

> [t]he individual Party membership is appalling... Some electorates have a pitiful handful of devoted stalwarts to keep the Party alive. As electorate vote grows, so our membership lessens.[17]

The membership remained strongly working class in the early postwar decades. Approximately 80 per cent of ALP members in the Victorian and New South Wales branches in the early 1960s were in working class occupations, compared to 69 per cent of the adult population.[18] The Party was a workers' party in that it had a mass membership of individual workers who complemented its connection to the working class through the affiliated trade unions. Its working class character was reinforced by Catholic and Irish associations, giving it a certain outsider ethos, counterposed to the Protestant and Anglophile ruling class associations of the Liberal Party. With religious sectarianism still a powerful force in Australian society in the early 1960s,[19] this distinction mattered in shaping the way members and non-members related to the Party. So, although the Party had proved itself capable of overseeing the affairs of Australian capitalism quite effectively during the 1940s, it was not quite respectable among the middle and upper classes, which were firmly wedded to the UAP, and then the Liberals. The Split may have drawn some Catholics away from the ALP, but it reinforced the feeling among Party members that they were part of an organisation that represented the underdog in Australian society, targeted by reactionary conspiracies. Voting Labor was often virtually hereditary; a vote for the UAP or Liberals was simply inconceivable for most class conscious working class families, tantamount to scabbing on a strike.

As a working class party, in composition and in political identity, Labor's internal affairs were a matter of great interest to many workers. The early 1930s split in the New South Wales ALP between supporters of Lang and Scullin excited great passions. One was either a Lang man or a Scullin man. About 20 years later, the Split in the ALP caused estrangements in Labor supporting families, with DLPers and Labor supporters at loggerheads for decades.

As an electoral machine focused on getting its candidates into parliaments and onto municipal councils, Labor needed activists in branches, people able to stay in touch with local issues and to mobilise support. But the importance of this base was declining. In the 1890s, house to house canvassing became an important campaign technique that favoured parties with numerous members. Even as late as the 1950s, the campaign books of the local ALP branch in Melbourne's working class suburb of Richmond still recorded door to door canvassers' assessments of the political inclinations of all voters in the suburb, house by house, street by street.[20] Committed members, rather than large amounts of money, were the key ingredient for such organising. For a period, newspapers owned by the Party, unions, ALP candidates or their close mates played an important role. But labour dailies in Hobart and Adelaide had closed in 1924, and the Brisbane *Daily Standard* went under in 1936. The last of these metropolitan publications, Sydney's *Labor Daily*, closed at the end of the 1930s, which signalled the decline of this medium. Apart from the *Barrier Daily Truth* in Broken Hill and the *National Advocate* in Bathurst, the most frequent labour-oriented publications remaining in Australia were subsequently weeklies.[21] The New South Wales Labour Council, the Victorian Trades Hall Council and the Queensland ALP all owned Labor-oriented radio stations,[22] but the Party was overwhelmingly reliant on the conservative mass media for coverage of its policies and activities.

With changes in the mass media in the postwar decades, the growth of less densely populated working class suburbs away from the inner cities and the falling ratio of ALP members to voters, the importance of local branch activism began to decline and an increasing role was played by paid publicity in the mass media and public relations strategies to secure favourable news coverage.[23] Services – especially advertising and professional advice – purchased with central office funds were more and more displacing the efforts of local ALP branch members in getting the Party's message out to potential

Labor voters. Furthermore, while the costs of political campaigning were rising rapidly, the contributions of local branches and their members to Labor's coffers were small. Most funds raised by the local branches went straight back into financing their own activities.[24]

Although by the 1960s local branch members were no longer as decisive a force for success in elections as they had been, Labor candidates, especially in marginal electorates, could not afford to alienate or entirely ignore them. This was especially true in New South Wales, where rank and file preselections were the norm. But in every state, the efforts of knockers on doors, persuaders of friends and acquaintances, and distributors of flyers, posters and placards were still useful in hoisting a candidate into office. In return, politicians and factional organisers might reinforce the ideological commitment and solidarity of rank and file ALP members by offering support in contests for internal Party posts, providing references or finding jobs with the local council for close supporters. In her history of the Melbourne suburb of Richmond, Janet McCalman records that

> The out-door staff [of the Richmond Council] saw their role as political agitators rather than as servants of the ratepayers: disrupting DLP meetings, painting graffiti, harassing the enemies of the machine were all so much more fun than cleaning streets.[25]

Studies by political scientist Michael Hogan and former New South Wales education minister Rodney Cavalier of Labor Party branches in four very different Sydney suburbs give us a good feel for branch life during the late 1950s or early 1960s and provide a baseline for comparisons with the situation in the 21st century.[26]

The inner suburb of Glebe was an old and densely populated working class neighbourhood of many terrace houses and was a long time Labor stronghold, with three branches. Guildford had been a residential suburb for decades, but a major public housing development begun after World War II altered its character. On the rural margin of Sydney, most of Panania's inhabitants lived in homes very recently built by the Housing Commission. Unlike these three working class suburbs, the residents of Hunters Hill were mainly middle and ruling class and staunch Liberal supporters. The membership of the Party in all of these branches was overwhelmingly working class, even in Hunters Hill, where the vast majority were unionists and housewives. Nearly one-quarter of Party members in Glebe whose industrial affiliation was known belonged to the Municipal Employees Union demonstrating the close connection between ALP membership and jobs with the local council.

Where figures are available, average attendance at monthly branch meetings ranged from one-quarter to one-half of the branch membership (which averaged 40–50, except for one branch in Glebe that had 210 members). The turn up to meetings when there were elections for branch officers and representatives could be very much higher. At some points, particularly during the conflicts of the mid 1950s, branch stacking by cliques and organised factions was endemic, continuing a tradition that stretched back to the early years of the Party. Membership turnover was high; in the Guildford branch at any time from the 1940s to the 1980s, two-thirds of the membership had been in the Party for less than six years.

The main concerns of branch meetings and activists were fund raising (which achieved very modest success), improving local public amenities, influencing the policies of state and national governments, and factional manoeuvring. During local council, state and national election campaigns, the more active branch members were also involved in securing votes for Labor by door knocking, leafleting and, along with many otherwise inactive members, handing out how to vote leaflets on election day.

The core of Labor's membership and electoral support in the early 1960s was still densely populated inner urban areas, along with newer working class suburbs further out from the centres of Australia's capital and industrial cities, and mining districts. Inner city gentrification was yet to have much impact. The federal and, especially, the state seats Labor held through thick and thin were precisely such predominantly working class electorates as West Sydney, Melbourne Ports and those on the northern coal fields of New South Wales.

The parts and the whole

We started this chapter by asking whether Labor's character had fundamentally changed over the course of its first 70 years. Together with earlier chapters, this brief review of the Party in the early 1960s indicates that it had not.

The officials of affiliated unions were still very prominent in the decision making bodies of the extra parliamentary Party; many still followed the trajectory from a senior union post into a state or federal parliament. If they acted in concert, union officials had the numbers to get their way at state conferences and their unions' contributions were still the mainstay of the ALP's finances.

The social backgrounds of Labor leaders and parliamentarians were changing, but it remained the case in 1962 that at least two-thirds of federal Labor politicians had been workers. In office they did not challenge the logic of capitalist accumulation or the national interest, defined in terms of the interests of locally based capital. Like the conservatives, Labor was capable of making concessions to workers in the face of pressure from below and when they could be afforded. When they could not, Labor proved willing to attack working class living standards.

The Party's state-based machines, whether organised around its official structures or in the form of factions, bound together leading figures in the unions and parliaments, less prominent union officials and parliamentarians, and rank and file unionists and members of local branches through formal and informal connections. While linking the main elements of the Party, the machines cushioned pressure from the ranks of ALP and union members on the politicians. This was particularly true of the embryonic federal organisation. Although it possessed no full time staff of its own until 1963 and there were major geographical obstacles to it meeting frequently, the federal executive protected federal parliamentarians from direction by state branches of the Party while exerting only modest control itself.

The Party's membership shrank dramatically in the 1950s. Compared to mass media campaigning, controlled and funded centrally by the Party's official machines, the role of the membership in Labor's approach to winning elections was declining too. Nevertheless, the ALP remained a small mass Party whose members were overwhelmingly working class.

Although there was a gradual shift of workers away from densely packed, inner city areas towards the less prestigious suburbs further out, all the way to the urban fringe, Labor seats were still precisely those inhabited by the highest proportion of workers. The Party had been able to sustain a working class base over generations. For many working class families, support for or membership of the ALP was an important aspect of their identity.

By the 1950s and 1960s, the working class had become more white collar, more educated and, with fewer jobs in the pastoral and railway industries, more urban than it had been in the late 19th century. Workers were still exploited and they organised in trade unions to defend themselves. Despite some shifts, the ALP's relationships with the working class in the early 1960s – through trade unions, local branches and the ballot box – were still much as they had been for decades. And the Party still served to bind workers to a program for the management of Australian capitalism. It remained a capitalist workers' party.

Chapter 6

THE WHITLAM ERA

If many Labor supporters regard the Curtin and Chifley governments as a period of great achievements and greater ambitions frustrated by conservative forces, their illusions in the Whitlam government are even more heroic. After nearly a quarter of a century of stagnant conservative rule during which Australia seemed to be a backward looking outpost of the British empire run by monarchists and reactionaries, Gough Whitlam, the Mighty Gough, broke through and during his first 12 months in office remade Australia forever. Then, as in a Victorian melodrama, the forces of evil began to organise and eventually brought down the Whitlam government through a dastardly anti-constitutional conspiracy that involved the Liberals, the High Court, the governor-general and the Melbourne Club, all backed by, if not working at the behest of, the CIA. After just three years of Labor in power, Australia was once again thrown back into the dark days of Liberal government, now led by Malcolm Fraser, grazier from the Western Districts and prime exemplar of the born to rule set.

There is of course a germ of truth in this heroic myth. The December 1972 election was a watershed in Australian electoral history, and the Whitlam government did represent a break from the past in important respects. No matter the demonisation of the Whitlam government by the conservatives and many ALP leaders since its defeat, it left behind a legacy of reforms that its more conservative successors have never tried to eliminate completely. And the Whitlam government *was* brought down by a constitutional coup that trashed some basic principles of parliamentary democracy.

The heroic myth is, however, an incomplete if not positively misleading story. While the Whitlam government was a break, there were also some important continuities with its immediate predecessors. The components of the Whitlam reform program were no challenge to capitalism and indeed were welcomed by important representatives of the Australian business sector. And Labor's progressive reforms were not the result of any particular predisposition to radicalism on Whitlam's part but reflected the much broader radicalisation in Australian society during the late 1960s and early 1970s.

Whitlam and the rising tide of struggle

To understand the Whitlam government it is first necessary to identify three crucial developments in the late 1960s that made a Labor victory in 1972 possible and shaped the government's actions during its first 12 to 18 months in office. These were an upsurge in working class militancy, the revival of the antiwar movement and a wave of student radicalism.

While the postwar boom helped win votes for the conservatives and underpinned their 23 years in office, it also had a contradictory effect. From the early 1960s, a new generation of workers emerged who had not known the mass unemployment, the wartime austerity and the industrial defeats of the 1930s and 1940s. They took full employment as a given. In the new economic circumstances, workers began to flex their muscles.

A wave of strikes in the metal industry erupted in the first half of 1968 and the powerful metal trades unions broke the chokehold of arbitration and forced employers to concede significant wage rises. Then, just 12 months later, tramways union leader Clarrie O'Shea, who had been jailed in May 1969 for refusing to pay harsh fines imposed on his union by the Industrial Court using its penal powers, was sprung from prison by a massive general strike in Victoria and solidarity action around the country.

The impact was immediate. The number of strikes began to escalate. Workers had not only won the right to strike, they had also gained the confidence to use that right. Wages soared and working hours were cut. Migrant workers increasingly took a stand for their rights. A short 'riot' at the Ford Broadmeadows car factory in Melbourne in 1973 turned a national spotlight on their conditions of work. Employees in one or two sectors, most notably construction and the power stations, began to take up issues of workers' control. The building industry was probably the most radical union arena at this time, especially in Sydney, where the Builders' Labourers' Federation (BLF) was particularly notable for militant on the job organising and lively participation by members in union affairs.[1] It also took a stand to protect the natural environment and cheap inner city working class housing with its famous Green Bans campaign.[2]

The strike wave was not restricted to blue collar workers. In the late 1960s and early 1970s a range of white collar workers, including teachers, bank workers, insurance clerks, pharmacists, nurses and ancillary staff in hospitals, took industrial action.[3] Women began to play an increasingly important role in the trade unions. The influence of the right wing Groupers, who still held power in several unions, declined.

The new union confidence was reflected in and reinforced by the movement against the Vietnam War which, by early 1969, was gathering pace. Public opinion was steadily shifting against the war. The movement grew more daring: draft resistance became more widespread. Unions took a leading role in the campaign against the war, particularly in Victoria. In December 1969, a meeting of 300 Melbourne representatives from 32 unions called for Australian troops in Vietnam to mutiny.[4] Workers marched, stopped work and raised funds in support of draft resisters. Three huge Vietnam Moratorium marches in 1970 and 1971 gave vivid public expression to the growing opposition to the war.

The third factor was a wave of radicalisation on the university campuses.[5] The stirrings began in the early and mid 1960s when students and academics campaigned against White Australia, anti-Aboriginal racism, the death penalty and censorship. The breakthrough came in 1967–8 in the aftermath of the Coalition's victory in the 1966 election. Labor's failure, and Whitlam's subsequent dilution of Labor's opposition to Australian involvement in the Vietnam War, encouraged young radicals to look beyond the ALP for a means to change the world. They took direct action – demonstrated, sat in, occupied and marched. Their goal was to stop the war. Starting at the University of Queensland, Monash University and Sydney University, student radicalism soon spread to other campuses. The revolutionary left quickly gained recruits among the militant students. In the heyday of the movement, from 1968 to 1971, radical students mounted a frontal assault on the authority of university administrations. Arrests and disciplinary cases only stimulated further protests.

The convergence of the three great mass movements of the time – the rising tide of industrial action, the anti-war movement and the student movement – demonstrated the power of the working class to challenge capital and the state and the limitations of the conventional political process. Together they created the space for a series of other radical campaigns. These included movements for Aboriginal land rights, women's rights, gay and lesbian rights, and against apartheid in South Africa.

The upsurge of class and social struggles had a big impact on the ALP. The membership began to grow – from 43 000 to 46 000 between 1968 and 1973.[6] This was not much but it was the first rise since the stack recruitment associated with the internal fights of the 1950s. Unlike the traditional blue-collar membership, new recruits were much more likely to be university graduates and upper echelon professionals in government jobs and the private sector, a trend that had been under way since the early 1960s but now became more pronounced. It was particularly evident among Labor MPs. In 1971, only five Labor MPs had held jobs as an artisan or tradesperson and a further five as clerks. By contrast 24 had been journalists, lecturers, solicitors, barristers, doctors or teachers.

The Party reacted in different ways to the rising struggles. In New South Wales the Labor right did its best to prevent unions from supporting the anti-war moratorium movement.[7] In Victoria, the Party played a more positive role: Victorian Labor MHR Jim Cairns emerged as a central figure and local branches were active in building the campaign. Even though the ALP and Gough Whitlam benefited greatly from the radicalisation of Australian society in the late 1960s and early 1970s, he was no radical. Whitlam, a QC whose father had been Crown solicitor, was a creature of the Establishment. He may not have followed the right wing career path that was clearly open to a man with his credentials, but he advocated gradualism and moderation rather than the radicalism that was manifest on the streets, the university campuses and in the trade unions at this time. One of his first acts as leader in 1967 was to scrap Labor's commitment to immediately pull conscripts out of Vietnam. Whitlam supported state aid to private schools, opposed union action on political issues and strongly backed the US alliance. He joined the Coalition government and media in denouncing the 1969 motion passed by Victorian trade unionists calling on Australian soldiers in

Vietnam to mutiny. His effort to distance the Party from its working class traditions was part of a conscious strategy, designed to attract support from the middle and capitalist classes.

In order to enhance Labor's appeal to business, Whitlam had to squeeze the left in its Victorian heartland. Although its bark was worse than its bite, the Victorian central executive of the Australian Labor Party was regarded by many in the business community as a hotbed of radicalism. With the support of the left's Clyde Cameron from South Australia, the national executive imposed on the Victorian Branch a new state executive and proportional representation in elections for Party posts, crimping the power of the left. A parallel intervention into the New South Wales branch gave the left more senior positions in the Party, but the right remained overwhelmingly dominant there.[8]

Whitlam referred frequently to 'the Australian people' but rarely to trade unionism or strikes. Within the union movement he was, in fact, widely distrusted, a feeling he returned in full measure. Indeed, as deputy leader between 1960 and 1967, Whitlam had made a name for himself by trying to rein in union power within the Party.[9] In 1967, federal and state parliamentary leaders became *ex officio* members of the national executive for the first time, diluting the power of delegates elected directly by state conferences, dominated by union delegates. The 1970 federal interventions by Whitlam and Cameron fixed union representation at state Party conferences in Victoria and New South Wales at 60 per cent of delegates, down from 75 per cent in New South Wales.[10] The impact of these changes should not be exaggerated though: with the upsurge in strikes, the union leaders were an important force in society and could not just be pushed aside.[11]

Labor's attitude to strikes while in opposition was indicative of the political environment at this time – the Party's leaders sought to ride the tiger, the better to rein it in. In opposition, Cameron defended the right to strike against the penal powers.[12] But this was not the same as encouraging strikes. Far from it. ALP leaders portrayed the Party's links with the trade unions as the means by which it could more effectively restrain working class militancy than the Coalition.[13]

Labor's material constitution had advantages in other areas as well. The Party could defuse the radical wing of the anti-war movement by offering a parliamentary response to the issues of conscription and the Vietnam War, an option that seemed increasingly realistic following a swing of

7 per cent to the ALP at the 1969 election. Labor could appeal to young people and radicalising women who were thoroughly alienated from the political establishment after 23 years of conservative rule. Less hidebound by Cold War rhetoric, Labor offered business a strategy for the renovation of Australian capitalism and a new approach to the increasingly important Asian region without jeopardising the US alliance.

Labor's reform agenda

The ALP's 1972 election slogan, 'It's Time', captured the public mood well.[14] Labor's extensive reforms during its first term in office were the high water mark of Australian postwar social democracy. The new government granted federal public servants large pace-setting wage rises, a $36\frac{1}{4}$ hour week, four weeks annual leave and paid maternity leave. It passed laws providing for equal pay for women. It introduced the sole parent pension, Medibank and free tertiary education. Divorce laws were liberalised. Labor was responsible for the country's first legislation against racial discrimination and introduced national land rights laws. Federal health expenditure rose by 20 per cent, education outlays doubled and spending on housing quadrupled.[15]

Before examining Labor's reform agenda in a little more detail it is important to put it in perspective. The ALP's victory was welcomed by sections of big business, including the Murdoch press and mining magnate Lang Hancock.[16] Whitlam was eager to reassure his business backers, telling them that

> The program of social reform embarked upon by the present Government cannot be achieved without a strong and growing private sector. Nothing could be further from the truth than that we are anti-business or hostile to business.[17]

After years of drift under a succession of lacklustre Liberals, business leaders looked to Whitlam as a figure who could give a new direction to the Australian economy. This was particularly true when it came to foreign trade. The long-standing protectionist consensus had begun to crack in the 1960s. Economists, supported by the newly appointed chairman of the Tariff Board, Alf Rattigan, together with businessmen in export oriented industries increasingly recognised that high tariffs were hurting not just the export sectors but also the very manufacturing sector it was intended to protect.[18] But the Coalition government was paralysed; its parties and politicians were too closely tied to tariff protected industries.

Not for the first time, and not for the last, the ALP led the way in overhauling industry policy. In July 1973, the Whitlam government cut tariffs by 25 per cent. This action and the replacement of the Tariff Board by the Industries Assistance Commission were the most significant industry policy initiatives in Australia for several decades, and paved the way for the still more extensive changes introduced by the Hawke government in the 1980s. Revaluations of the Australian dollar in 1973 had similar structural and anti-inflationary logics.[19]

The Whitlam government took other initiatives to improve the profitability of Australian capitalism. It expanded the scope of the state owned Australian Industry Development Corporation, established in 1970 by John Gorton's Coalition government to fund private sector expansion of important industries in Australia.[20] Minister for Minerals and Energy Rex Connor attempted to maximise returns to Australian capital from the country's resource exports by expanding state regulation and ownership of the mining sector.[21] These steps were not radical; they were consistent with the recommendations of the rich countries' think tank, the Organisation of Economic Cooperation and Development (OECD), which Australia had joined in 1971.

The OECD also regarded an incomes policy as an important means to achieve stable economic growth. OECD reports conceded that securing the agreement of workers to wage restraint might require concessions in the form of expanded social services and higher minimum wages.[22] This analysis was particularly appropriate for the situation faced by the Whitlam government. With a self-confident working class winning substantial improvements in real wages through industrial action, sufficient sweeteners had to be granted if the government was to implement a successful incomes policy capable of holding down wages.

The Whitlam government's most important welfare reforms can be understood in this light. They were definitely advances for the working class, but they were compatible with and did not threaten capital accumulation. Medibank, for example, was a system of universal health insurance that significantly improved the access of poorer people to health care, but it did not diminish the power of private doctors and the Australian Medical Association. The abolition of the means test on age pensions for those older than 70 was a progressive reform, but universal access was also calculated to serve as a substitute for the redistribution of income to workers through higher wages or a greater tax burden on corporations and the rich. The government's approach was to redistribute income within the working class, rather than from capital to labour.[23]

Medibank, along with increased funding for schools and higher education, had other advantages. By improving the health and skills of the workforce they helped raise labour productivity. The abolition of university fees in 1973 did open higher education up to working class students a little more, but it did not go far enough, because it was not accompanied by sufficient complementary policies to raise the achievements of working class students at school. It was still disproportionately the children of the well off who attended university.

Expanding equal pay for women and access to childcare were likewise concessions to workers that also served capitalist interests; they assisted efforts to expand the labour force without recourse to migration, a more expensive policy. It was on these grounds that the measures were commended by the OECD and the *Australian Financial Review*.[24] The requirement that big business submit proposals for price increases to a Prices Justification Tribunal was designed to promote competitive efficiency, as was the Trade Practices Act, which sought to prevent monopolistic or collusive behaviour. Some changes introduced by Whitlam enshrined in legislation advances that had already been won in some sectors through industrial action, for example, longer paid holidays and equal pay for women.

The Whitlam government is commonly remembered as an early pioneer in the area of land rights – sympathetic academic Will Sanders argues that after years of neglect by the Liberals 'the Whitlam government unleashed a whirlwind of reform in Indigenous affairs'.[25] But the impetus for the reforms came from strikes in the Northern Territory and the land rights campaigns on the streets of the southern capitals.

Whitlam's achievements in the field of land rights were, in any case, rather more limited than his rhetoric. His proposed legislation applied only to the Northern Territory, would have granted Aborigines secure title over land already set aside as reserves and only made it possible for Aborigines to gain ownership of unalienated Crown land, that is, land that no one else had wanted.[26] But it also specified that any Aboriginal veto over mineral exploration and development of their land could be overridden 'in the national interest'. The Whitlam government was dismissed before its land rights legislation was passed. But its main provisions were implemented by the Fraser government.

Throughout Whitlam's terms in office relations with black activists were testy. The 41-strong National Aboriginal Consultative Committee, which was elected by Aboriginal voters in December 1973, never had more than advisory powers, and the newly created Department of Aboriginal Affairs was run by white bureaucrats. Communist Party newspaper *Tribune* noted in February 1974 that 'Despite greater financial allocations, the plight of Black Australian communities as objects of discrimination in job, land and other basic rights has so far been only marginally improved, if at all'.[27]

Another change often associated with the Whitlam legacy is the abolition of White Australia and the first steps towards multiculturalism. Whitlam was an early advocate of overturning the ALP's racist migration policy. After a series of defeats, the reformers were finally successful in having White Australia removed from the Party platform in 1965 and its last vestiges were removed from ALP policy in 1971.[28]

These changes were in line with a bipartisan trend that had been under way for decades. The White Australia policy had already started to become a problem for Australian capitalism in the 1950s. Trade was increasingly shifting away from Britain and the white dominions towards Asia. More-over, the days of white colonial domination in Asia were over. Independent Indonesia, Malaya and Singapore now had to be treated as equals and anti-communist allies. Foreign sensitivities about Australia's racist migration policy could no longer be ignored. The Australian state, through a variety of mechanisms, including the Colombo Plan, increasingly saw itself as playing a leadership role in Asia, rather than shunning it in favour of ties with the motherland.

Nor did White Australia match the needs of employers any longer. During the 1950s and 1960s, labour shortages limited the expansion of industry, and the days when factory, mining and construction labour could be sourced almost exclusively from Britain and Ireland were long past. Under Coalition migration ministers, the definition of 'white' became increasingly elastic. Well before the White Australia policy was formally dropped, Turks and, later, Lebanese were recruited to the Australian migration program. This shift to a non-discriminatory migration policy required a change in key tenets of Australian nationalism. Public attitudes to the White Australia policy shifted. By 1966 more than three-quarters of Australians supported 'limited Asian migration'.

For decades White Australia had served an important purpose for the capitalist class by providing a means to blur class distinctions, so important in winning working class compliance with demands for equal sacrifice in times of economic crisis or war. Rich or poor, 'we' were all white. As the composition of the workforce changed, the use of whiteness as a unifying force binding the Australian nation became increasingly outmoded as a means to smooth over class contradictions. According to sociologist Robert Tierney, 'governments faced the spectre of a series of migrant communities who felt they had little stake in Australian capitalism'.[29]

By the early 1970s, conservative politicians were playing down the need to assimilate non-English speaking migrants and granting migrant groups public funds to carry out welfare work and some cultural activities. During the 1972 election campaign Liberal Minister for Customs Don Chipp said, 'I would like to see a stage in the 1980s where Australia is becoming the only truly multi-racial country in the world'.[30] His statement recognised that the political atmosphere, and particularly attitudes to race, were changing and that a new approach to promoting national unity was necessary.

The 1973 riot by predominantly Southern European workers at the Ford Broadmeadows plant in Melbourne threw the alienation of migrant workers and their rejection of assimilation into sharp relief. Employers knew that there were, potentially, dozens of other Broadmeadows – in the steel plants, food processing, plastics and glass factories, on construction sites and so forth. This gave added urgency to the steps already under way to embed what became known as multiculturalism as the centrepiece of a remodelled Australian nationalism. More appealing and racially inclusive, the new variant could replace but perform the same important role as the old nationalism in generating a sense of cross-class unity. Nor did this remodelled nationalism challenge the 'great achievements' of British colonialism.[31]

The relatively generous disbursement of government grants to various ethnic community bodies served the ALP well in elections – Southern European migrants, in particular, tended to support the ALP.[32] In some areas, local Labor Party branches became segmented along ethnic lines, as leaders of the various community bodies mobilised their supporters behind various parliamentarians or candidates for preselection. The traditional sectarian division between 'Micks' (Roman Catholics) and 'Masons' (Freemasons) was now supplanted in Australian society by a more complex array of ethnic and national identifications. The decision of the Whitlam government to respond to escalating unemployment in 1975 by slashing the migrant intake,[33] on the spurious basis that migrants took jobs from locals, demonstrated that multiculturalism did not necessarily rule out racist policies.

In the field of foreign policy, Labor's position on the Vietnam War underwent several modifications. Following Labor's severe defeat at the 1966 election, when Calwell campaigned strongly against Australian involvement and called for an immediate end to conscription, Whitlam took over and promptly pulled Labor's policy on Vietnam to the right. He was an even more enthusiastic supporter of the US alliance than his predecessor. Whitlam's critique of the war in Vietnam was no more connected to any condemnation of US imperialism than Calwell's had been. As he later wrote: 'All of us were entangled in Labor's central dilemma: how to oppose American intervention without opposing America; how to denounce the war without denouncing the US'.[34] At Whitlam's urging the 1967 federal ALP conference watered down the Party's position. The resolution expressed general opposition to the continuation of the war and Australian involvement in it. But there was no call for the immediate withdrawal of Australian conscripts.

Labor's policy began to shift back to the left again in 1969 under the impact of two factors: the shifting balance of opinion at home and broader geostrategic considerations. In August the majority of Australians for the first time indicated opposition to Australia's continued involvement in the war. Years of campaigning by anti-war activists in the context of a radicalising society had had its effect. Second, the US was caught in a quagmire in Vietnam and wanted a way out before it sustained more damage to its imperial reputation. China, furthermore, was open to a rapprochement with the United States as a means to isolate the USSR. The opening of the Paris Peace Talks in 1968, Nixon's trip to Beijing in February 1972 and the gradual shift to détente between the US and the USSR made it clear that, in domestic political terms, the Coalition's former reliance on the Cold War domino theory had to give way to a rather different approach to international relations. Under Liberal Prime Ministers Gorton and Billy McMahon Australian troops were gradually withdrawn from Vietnam, in line with President Nixon's attempt to cut US losses by 'Vietnamising' the conflict. By 1972 very few Australian soldiers were left in the country.

In stark contrast to 1966, the 1972 election was marked by consensus over Vietnam. International relations academic Jim Richardson was to write soon afterwards that 'The political aims and sympathies of ALP leader Whitlam, so far as South-East Asia was concerned, were indistinguishable from those of the government, although this was not true of the Party's left wing'.[35] Thus, Whitlam's withdrawal of the last soldiers and liberation of imprisoned draft resisters was politically symbolic and very popular, but it was only the conclusion of an established process. The evolution of Labor's policy on the Vietnam War illustrated not the triumph of principles but a profound pragmatism.

Other examples of pragmatism in foreign policy included the government's relations with Australia's immediate neighbours. The Whitlam government granted independence to Papua New Guinea (PNG) in 1975, but Australian business and finance continued to dominate the new state's economy and the PNG government was dependent on Australian aid. Whitlam's response to the independence movement in East Timor, which grew rapidly as Portugal, the former colonial power, withdrew during 1974 and 1975, indicates that *realpolitik* always trumped support for self-determination. Fearing instability to Australia's north, in other words the possible emergence of a new independent state led by a radical left wing government, and the weakening of the grip of General Suharto's military dictatorship over the Indonesian archipelago, the Australian government made clear to Indonesia that it would not oppose the annexation of East Timor, giving Jakarta the green light to invade.

The onset of economic crisis and the Kerr coup

The Whitlam government assumed that the buoyancy of the domestic and international economies would continue to generate the tax revenues to pay for its social reform program. This expectation was initially met in full – despite a large increase in spending, the government actually ran a budget surplus in 1973, thanks to a surge in tax receipts. Unemployment fell to 1 per cent. Business was reasonably satisfied too, as the rate of profit, which had fallen in the last years of the Coalition government, stabilised in 1973.[36] All of this changed in 1973–4 when Australia was hit hard by two shocks. The first was a worldwide burst of inflation. The Labor government tried to hold back inflation by organising a referendum in December 1973 to give it wage and price fixing powers. It was stymied by the unions, who successfully campaigned against wage controls. In the following year the unions launched a massive strike wave that won hefty wage increases. The government's response was vigorous. Early in 1974, Clyde Cameron slammed militant unionism in the first of what was to be a series of increasingly bitter attacks:

> The general public – including that section of the public that consists of trade
> unionists themselves – are sick and tired of the near anarchy that pervades the
> industrial scene. It is this bloody-mindedness on the part of a small section
> of the trade union movement that is slowly, but surely, pricing thousands of
> Australian workers out of employment.[37]

In an attempt to rein in inflation Treasurer Frank Crean announced plans to raise interest rates and cut government spending in a July 1974 mini budget.

The second shock was the sharp downturn in the world economy that began in 1974. Business around the world shut factories and laid off millions of workers. Unemployment in Australia began to rise. The coincidence of high inflation and unemployment was a puzzle that Keynesian economics could not cope with. Keen to continue with its ambitious plans and to avert unemployment, the government rejected Treasury's line of 'fighting inflation first'. It eased credit conditions and budgeted for a deficit to stimulate economic activity. Jim Cairns, who advocated this approach, took over as treasurer from Crean. Spending cuts announced in the July 1974 mini budget were dropped once it became clear that the economy was rapidly contracting and unemployment was rising. Unemployment reached a postwar high of 3.2 per cent in October 1974.

The economic slowdown changed the entire political environment within which the Whitlam government operated. The capitalist class had been mildly supportive of Whitlam on his election in 1972. Over the following 18 months, however, business became increasingly dissatisfied over a range of issues. With the onset of recession, capitalist hostility mounted. The rate of profit took a steep dive from 13 per cent in 1973 to only 9 per cent in 1975.[38] Business responded with a right wing ideological offensive and a virulent anti-Labor press campaign, which blamed the crisis on the demands of trade unions and government incompetence. Monetarist arguments were prominent. The core of monetarism (like its successor, neoliberalism) boiled down to restoring profitability by capping, if not cutting, workers' wages and undermining the welfare state.

As the economic crisis intensified, Labor shifted to the right. Government attacks on militant unionism increased.[39] On the other side of the ledger, the government cut business taxes and granted subsidies to companies that were threatening to sack workers. The Prices Justification Tribunal authorised a 14 per cent price rise by BHP, while blaming unions for rising unemployment and inflation. In February 1975 the ALP federal conference at Terrigal, which Labor economist Barry Hughes would later call 'a pro-business orgy', witnessed the final interment of the reform agenda. Whitlam told delegates that profitability had to be lifted. The private sector had to be boosted and the case for greater public spending got short shrift. Labor's left wrung its hands but went along with it all. The government now began to cut public sector positions in earnest, eliminating 1500 civilian jobs in the Department of Defence and freezing recruitment to the public service. In May 1975 the Arbitration Commission, with the support of the government, introduced wage indexation to peg pay increases to the level of inflation. The leadership of the union movement, demoralised by rising unemployment, accepted wage restraint. The result was a sharp reduction in the rate of wage increases and, just as importantly for business and the government, a decline in workplace militancy and a reassertion of power by the union leaders over rank and file militants.

As a sop to business, Cairns was replaced as treasurer by Bill Hayden in July 1975. In his first budget the new treasurer slashed public spending, including outlays on welfare, and tightened credit, while granting tax concessions to business.[40] Whitlam's problem was that, try as he might, he could not move fast enough to keep big business happy. The working class offensive was too recent and the pressure by the unions inside the ALP was too great to allow Whitlam to quickly wind back the social and economic gains that workers had made over the previous two decades. In the view of business, Whitlam had to make way for a government that could do just this. The right wing mobilisation against his government gathered steam.

From early in 1975 the Opposition, with the help of Treasury Secretary Sir Fred Wheeler, began to make great play of the so-called loans scandal. This scandal comprised an attempt by Rex Connor to borrow funds from oil rich Middle Eastern states to develop the mineral resources of the North West Shelf. In the end no funds were borrowed and no financial impropriety was uncovered but the Liberals and the media confected outrage over this issue that associated the Whitlam government with corruption and incompetence.

In February, the Liberal–Country Party government in New South Wales appointed a conservative independent to fill a vacancy in the Senate caused by the appointment of Labor Senator Lionel Murphy to the High Court, breaching the convention that the replacement should come from the party that the previous incumbent had belonged to. In March, ineffectual Liberal leader Billy Snedden was dumped in favour of Malcolm Fraser, who promised a more strident attack on the government. In April, US right wing economist Milton Friedman, fresh from advising Chilean dictator Augusto Pinochet, addressed meetings around Australia on measures to restore business confidence. There was a strike by capital. Many big businesses stopped investing and the inflow of foreign capital dried up. In September, the conservative government of Premier Joh Bjelke-Petersen in Queensland appointed another conservative to the Senate to replace Labor's Senator Bert Milliner who had died in office. The Coalition now had a majority in the Upper House and its leaders, the Liberal Fraser and the Country Party's Doug Anthony, barnstormed the country demanding that Whitlam call an early election. On 15 October, the Senate, citing the loans affair as a pretext, blocked supply (budget funding) in an attempt to bring down the government.

The situation was now deeply polarised. Although workers' attitudes to the Whitlam government had cooled, they understood the significance of the right wing offensive against it – a conservative victory would usher in a Liberal government that might destroy all the gains that they had won over the previous period. They responded vigorously. In the nine days following the blocking of supply, 50 000 workers attended rallies and a further 100 000 struck in defence of the Whitlam government.[41] Workplaces in every corner of the country took action, from meatworkers in Townsville and office workers in Adelaide to brewery workers in Perth.[42] Every state labour council passed strong resolutions condemning the Opposition for withholding supply.[43]

Working class resistance to the Coalition's attempt to financially throttle the government produced a sharp lift in Labor's popularity, particularly among blue collar workers. According to a Gallup poll, Labor's support rose by 6 per cent in late October. The union mobilisation threatened to derail the Liberal attack. The Melbourne *Age* and Brisbane *Courier Mail* took fright at Fraser's high stakes tactics and urged the Senate to pass supply. There were rumblings inside the Liberal Party and a real possibility that one Liberal senator would cross the floor to ensure that supply was passed. With the situation on a knife edge, Governor-General Sir John Kerr dismissed Whitlam on 11 November and appointed Fraser in his place as interim prime minister. Fraser rapidly called an election.

Led by the militants, workers poured out of their workplaces to strike and join mass demonstrations against what quickly became known as the Kerr Coup. The overwhelming demand on the streets and from the leaders of all the key left wing unions was for a general strike, a proposal that was backed by resolutions from labour councils and worksite meetings. ACTU (and ALP) President Bob Hawke and the parliamentary leadership were, however, determined that the campaign would be contained within the traditional boundaries of an electoral contest. Warning of 'violence in the streets' and 'anarchy' if a strike went ahead, Hawke directed the resistance off the streets and into a conventional electoral contest.[44] Defeat was preferable to a serious fight that would break the bounds of parliamentary politics.

Other elements in the union movement were initially prepared to put up more of a fight. On the morning of Wednesday, 12 November, the leaders of 30 left wing Victorian unions called a half day general strike and mass rally in the city centre for Friday. But, having made the announcement, they almost immediately began to retreat. This became clear on the day, when more than 400 000 workers struck and 50 000 attended the rally in Melbourne's City Square. Union militants were boiling with anger against the coup and were only waiting on their leaders' call for a general strike. It never came. Hawke told them to 'cool it', to direct their energy (and a day's pay) to Labor's election campaign, and to go home. He misjudged the mood; workers wanted action and refused to leave. Amalgamated Metal Workers Union (AMWU) Victorian secretary and leading Communist Party figure John Halfpenny made a fiery speech and led the crowd on a march to state parliament where he then urged them to leave. Even then there was a substantial number of workers who still wanted to vent their rage; the far left led them on a march to protest outside the Stock Exchange. But if the far left could lead a march, it could not lead a movement. It was far too small to challenge the authority of the left wing union leaders who had put themselves at the head of the demand for action only in order to head it off. The CPA at this crucial juncture refused to mobilise its networks of worker militants for a general strike, preferring instead to tail the ALP.

As the momentum for a general strike had been lost, the campaign switched to election mode. The ALP organised mass rallies to pull support behind the government, and workers stopped work in large numbers to attend them. Labor's campaign opening at the Sydney Domain attracted 40 000 supporters and a rally in Brisbane's King George Square drew more than 15 000. Eight thousand attended an election rally at Festival Hall in Melbourne, and in Perth meatworkers, seamen and wharfies walked off the job to join a crowd of 7000 to hear Whitlam speak.

As the movement on the streets was diverted into a campaign dominated by orthodox electioneering, the political focus shifted. At first, Labor emphasised its defence of democracy and the Constitution. Under attack from the Liberals on questions of economic policy, Labor's leaders switched over to selling their fiscal conservatism. Whitlam's most right wing ministers, Bill Hayden and Jim McClelland, promoted a platform of sound economic management, commitment to wage restraint and their ability to control the unions. The ALP only legitimised the main thrust of the Liberals' campaign, and Labor's early poll lead ebbed away.

Moreover, having been sacked quite illegitimately by the governor-general, Whitlam insisted that Labor had to play by the rules of the game, just as Lang had in 1932. The ALP still had control of the House of Representatives after the dismissal and Whitlam could have blocked supply for Fraser's caretaker government had he chosen. Instead, Labor passed Fraser's bills. Whitlam declared in retrospect:

> What humbugs we would have been if, after condemning the Liberals for refusing to vote on the Budget, we ourselves had delayed a vote on the Budget. We had fought a great fight by the rules. We stuck by the rules to the bitter end.[45]

Labor was swept out of office on 12 December. The new government won 91 seats out of 127 in the House of Representatives and took control of the Senate with a six seat majority.

The essential contradiction embedded in Labor's reform project was exposed: in order to stay in power, the Whitlam government had to placate business, a process that so alienated the Party's base that it lost office at the elections. This process had become clear at the by-election in the Tasmanian seat of Bass in July when even right wing loyalists, such as the New South Wales secretary of the AWU, Barry Egan, complained that 'The traditional Labor voter has deserted them [the ALP] in herds because they have lost touch with realities and with their own supporters'.[46]

The Whitlam government's defeat, like that of Jack Lang in the 1930s, provides a good case study of the limits of the parliamentary road to reform, let alone socialism. In both cases, when business and the Establishment felt that its interests were not being met by the government of the day, they mobilised to bring it down. The Westminster system of parliamentary democracy was revealed as flimsy and dispensable when confronted by the raw power of the capitalist class on the offensive.

From nadir to recovery

Two conclusions were possible from the Kerr coup. One was that any attempt to bring about fundamental social reforms through parliament was utopian, and that a strategy based on a more direct challenge to the conservative vested interests of big business, the High Court and the public service bureaucracy was necessary. The other was that Whitlam had gone too far, too fast, and that, in conditions of economic crisis, Labor had to be more amenable to business. Given the Party's makeup and entire previous history, only one of these conclusions was ever likely to be drawn. Labor was established as a party that operated within the parameters of the capitalist state in order to introduce reforms for its working class supporters. If the capitalist state and big business would not allow this, then Labor's ambitions would have to be scaled back.

So the ALP leadership, after an initial period of disorientation in early 1976, quickly forged a new consensus that further social and political reform had to be suspended until business profitability was restored. Wages would have to be strictly controlled under a future Labor government. The rightward drift in the Party was accentuated by the sharp decline in the strike rate in 1976–7 and the decline or greater moderation of most social movements, which reduced pressure on the Party from the left. Neville Wran's new Labor government in New South Wales, elected in a landslide at the 1976 state election after nearly 10 years of corrupt conservative administration, became the template for the Party federally and in other states. An economically conservative platform, promising budget restraint and responsible government, along with wage moderation and a few minor welfare reforms, was the centrepiece of Labor's platform at the 1977 federal elections. This turn to moderation did nothing to help the Party: its primary vote sank to its lowest level since 1931. Whitlam stood down and was replaced by Hayden who consolidated the Party's shift to the right. Hayden told ALP supporters: 'Much and all as we may regret it, now is not the time for the visionary reform programs of earlier years'.[47] Senior Labor figures were now outspoken in their condemnation of strikes.[48] Labor also had a hard time condemning the Fraser government's use of indexation to cut wages; the Whitlam government had established the machinery that made this possible.[49]

Given that there was little to distinguish Labor policy from that of the Coalition, the ALP was largely irrelevant as a source of opposition to the Fraser government between 1976 and 1980. The unions now came to the fore.[50] The Kerr coup had been a serious setback for the Australian working class, but it was only the first skirmish in a series of battles between employers and workers during Fraser's terms in office. After several defeats in 1976–7, trade unions began to recover and move onto the offensive. With rapid growth and plentiful jobs, the strike rate soared. Worker militancy broke wage indexation and the government's industrial watchdog, the Industrial Relations Bureau. One of the bases of the Fraser government's appeal to big business – its ability to contain the unions – was destroyed. The recovery in strike activity and the resultant working class self-confidence boosted support for Labor, even though the Party had done nothing to support the workers. At the 1980 election Labor's primary vote for the House of Representatives shot up by 600 000, a swing of 5.5 per cent.

The other basis of the Fraser government's appeal to business was its ability to manage the economy and promote international competitiveness. Here too it failed. Pressure from industry lobbies prevented it from cutting tariffs in the most sheltered sectors of the economy – cars, clothing, textiles and footwear – and it shied away from deregulating the financial sector on the lines recommended in the 1981 *Campbell Report*, which it had commissioned. The last nail in the Fraser government's coffin was the deep recession that took hold in 1982. The rate of profit in industry, which had crawled back up from 9 per cent in 1975 to 11 per cent by 1980, slumped to 6 per cent in 1982, a new postwar low. Employers slashed jobs, and unemployment soared from less than 6 to more than 10 per cent, the highest level since the 1930s. The government's economic credibility was shattered. While Fraser offered no strategic perspective for the future of the Australian economy Labor had developed a plan, its Prices and Incomes Accord with the unions.

For a number of years in the mid to late 1970s Hawke had made several pleas to the Fraser government to include the ACTU in some form of consensus economic management, involving state and territory governments, the federal government, unions and employer organisations. Fraser rebuffed every one of Hawke's advances and the proposals were stillborn. Hawke then promoted the idea of a tripartite business–union–government arrangement to take effect when the ALP regained office; discussions to this end began to feature regularly at Labor Party conferences. In 1981 the ACTU Congress carried a motion for an incomes policy under a Labor government: it proposed that unions would accept wage indexation and a pledge not to strike for further wage rises in return for increased spending on health, education and social security.

The ACTU's acceptance of wage restraint was backed not only by the leaders of the more conservative unions but also, crucially, by the leaders of the left wing unions, including the AMWU and Building Workers Industrial Union (BWIU) whose members had the greatest capacity to wreck any wage restraint mechanism. Indeed, it was these left leaders who, with the help of an ideological framework supplied by the CPA, did most to win support for the Accord among worker militants. They were assisted by changes within the union movement in the latter half of the 1970s. The wages breakout of 1979–81 showed that the unions still had industrial muscle, but unlike the industrial struggle of the early 1970s, this wave of strikes was not accompanied by any broader leftward shift in Australian society. Furthermore, numerous union strongholds were hit hard by redundancies in the early 1980s. Many former shopfloor militants were demoralised and became more open to the conservative argument that a continued wages push would simply exacerbate unemployment. Caution was now the watchword.

In August 1982, with the left unions locked in behind the pact, the ACTU and ALP announced their prices and incomes policy, followed in December by the final version of the Accord document that was endorsed at a special unions conference on 22 February 1983. Labor promised to support a return to wage indexation, an expansionary budget policy to reduce unemployment, repeal of Fraser's anti-union laws, the reintroduction of universal health care, expansion of the welfare state and the establishment of a series of joint committees to oversee industry restructuring. In exchange, the ACTU gave a commitment not to make claims on employers for wage increases beyond those resulting from indexation, in other words, a no strike pledge.

Labor's agenda at the 1983 election was based on a simple appeal. Fraser had divided Australian society and his economic policies had led to a wage breakout followed by recession. Labor promised social consensus, arguing that unemployment could be reduced if unions moderated wage demands, and that only the ALP could convince unions to do so on a sustained basis. Furthermore, the Wran government had been in power in New South Wales since 1976 and had proven to be a safe pair of hands for business. Moderate Labor governments had also been elected in Victoria and South Australia in 1982 with no worrying consequences. At the 1982 national conference, leading left figure Bob Hogg led the charge to eliminate any elements of Labor's platform that might alienate the business community. Opposition to uranium mining was replaced by a three mines policy that allowed existing operations to continue. A motion to ban visits by US nuclear warships, already imposed by the recently elected New Zealand Labour government, was defeated. Abortion law reform was sidelined. A motion to introduce a capital gains tax was voted down.

Finally, in a last minute switch, the more popular Hawke, who had proven his credentials as a man with whom business could do business, and who had more credibility in the eyes of union officials and workers, pushed Hayden aside and became the Labor leader, a change that was followed within a few hours by Fraser's announcement of the date of the forthcoming election. Some sections of the capitalist class were won over by Labor's pitch. Others were neutralised. For the first time in its long history the conservative Melbourne *Herald* endorsed the ALP.

Widespread working class disaffection with the Fraser government and the decline in business support for it led to a sweeping Labor victory at the 5 March 1983 election. The ALP achieved a primary vote just shy of 50 per cent. The ALP and the ACTU now had the opportunity to put their Accord into effect.

Chapter 7

ECONOMIC RATIONALISM UNDER HAWKE AND KEATING

*The Hawke Government has proved itself to be, not only a great reform govern-
ment, but a government in the highest traditions of Labor reform. It is a Labor
Government not only in the true tradition; it is a government restoring and
renewing, strengthening and entrenching the best traditions of Labor reform.*
Neville Wran, 1986 John Curtin Memorial Lecture[1]

If the Whitlam government is upheld by many ALP supporters as the shining
example of postwar social democracy, the Hawke and Keating governments
evoke a much more ambiguous response. There are their defenders, such as
former New South Wales Premier Neville Wran, and there are those, such as
long time ALP member and academic Graham Maddox, who lamented in
his 1989 book *The Hawke Government and the Labor Tradition* that Hawke

> gladly presided over an economy in which, as the fortunes of our richest
> people rose and fell by hundreds of millions of dollars and entrepreneurs made
> millions in overnight deals, real wages continued to decline, poverty traps
> closed sharply over the unemployed and the employed poor and propertyless
> pensioners despaired over an inadequate subsidy.[2]

Then there is the fact that, between them, Hawke and Keating won five
successive elections, a Labor record. Set against that achievement is the
stunningly low Labor vote in 1996, when the Party lost office with its lowest
primary vote in 65 years. While assessments of these governments by ALP

supporters have been contradictory, BHP–Billiton Chairman Don Argus still insisted, in 2010, that 'the courage and the foresight' of their economic policies benefited Australian business.[3] As the Accord with the unions was central to Labor's economic and industrial relations achievements under Hawke and Keating, it is with this that we start our account of their record in office.

The Accord

After years of being marginalised by the hated Fraser government, Australian union leaders initially had high hopes for the Accord. At last they were consulted over government policy and could help implement important reforms. The jewel in the crown was a promise to reintroduce a national health scheme in a single public insurance fund (Medicare), and the removal of means testing for access to public hospitals and community health services. Left wing union leaders and supportive academics also highlighted the Accord's references to 'planning' mechanisms and discerned in them a vehicle for introducing socialism along Swedish lines.[4]

Their hopes about such a transition to socialism were profoundly misplaced. If the Accord had actually been a means for unions to guide government policy along socialist lines, or anything remotely like it, it would hardly have received business backing. Hawke had already made clear the nature of the government's consensus relationship with capital and labour. At the February 1983 ACTU conference that ratified the Accord, he had told the unions that

> We as a Government will certainly not be your handmaiden, and this historic document makes it clear that you do not expect that . . . There will be just as much opportunity for consultation with employers as with you.[5]

So it was at the May Economic Summit, which was convened five weeks after Labor took office. The Summit brought together the prime minister and his senior Cabinet colleagues, the state premiers, the ACTU executive, big employers and leaders of business associations, and a smattering of representatives from community groups and welfare agencies.[6] It became clear that the proposed redistribution of income discussed in the Accord was, if anything, to favour business and the wealthy, and that the Accord's collective restraint was to weigh disproportionately on workers. The joint communiqué published at the conclusion of the Summit reiterated that the Accord's promise to maintain real wages would be an objective 'over time'. Unions would agree to 'an offset in wage increases on account of the health insurance scheme'. While employers respected 'the legitimate expectation that incomes of the employed shall be increased in real terms through time in line with productivity', the crux of the Summit communiqué was acceptance by the unions that 'the preservation of the private sector as a profitable operating sector' was essential.[7] Hawke's decision to retain Fraser's right wing Treasury Secretary John Stone only reinforced the impression that the government was committed to a conservative economic policy.

The suppression of strikes and militant unionism was probably the single most important contribution made by the Accord to the fortunes of Australian capitalism. When members of the Food Preservers Union, mainly women, went on strike at the Heinz factory near Melbourne in 1983, the government sought to exclude it from national wage increases. In 1985 a joint operation of the New South Wales, Victorian and federal governments, the ACTU and other building industry unions deregistered and dismembered the Builders' Labourers' Federation (BLF), which had secured substantial wage increases for its members. In 1986, the Plumbers and Gasfitters Union was threatened with similar treatment over its pursuit of a $70 wage rise outside the Accord. In 1989–90 the government used the Royal Australian Air Force to defeat domestic airline pilots striking for higher pay.[8] John Stone, by 1989 a National Party senator and leading light in the anti-union H. R. Nicholls Society, could only stand back and admire the government's handiwork during the pilots' dispute: 'Mr Hawke's zeal in all these matters thus went even further than our own'.[9]

During the first four years of the Accord, a period of economic recovery and falling unemployment, Australian Labor cut real wages, something that the conservative government of Margaret Thatcher in Britain failed to achieve. The leadership of the union movement played a crucial role in this respect. In 1989, ACTU Secretary Bill Kelty bluntly argued that the economy was in good shape because, 'Fundamental number one: the profit share has shifted back'.[10]

After several years of centralised wage fixing by the Arbitration Commission, the Accord system, from 1987, took the form of trading off working conditions to win pay rises. CPA and ALP union officials alike enforced this policy. The *Financial Review* recorded in 1987 that 'In one instance recently, the central office of the AMWU sent back a deal to an AMWU steward because it involved a trade-off of wages in return for the lifting of industrial bans'.[11] The union office could not countenance wage rises without productivity increases.

In 1991, localised trade-offs were replaced by enterprise bargaining, initially advocated in 1987 by the peak body of the large corporations, the Business Council of Australia (BCA), but roundly condemned by the unions at that time. Now, the union leaders were converts to the cause. Productivity improvements negotiated at the enterprise level replaced industry-wide awards as the way most workers maintained, let alone improved, their real wages. The outcome of enterprise bargaining in the 1990s was longer working hours, increased use of shift work, reduced penalty rates for work during unsocial hours and more casual and part time employment.[12]

Contrary to the Accord's initial promise, real wages were not maintained over time. Measured in terms of full time award wages of the non-managerial workforce, workers' pay fell by 12.8 per cent in real terms between 1983 and 1990 and by a further 3.2 per cent before Labor lost power in 1996. Those covered by enterprise agreements saw their wages increase in the 1990s, but only at the cost of work intensification. Sacrifice was not shared equally: average weekly earnings, unadjusted for inflation, rose by 70 per cent between 1985 and 1995 while managerial salaries increased by 125 per cent.[13] During the terms of the Hawke and Keating governments, the profit share of national income rose from 17.5 to 22.8 per cent, while the wages share fell from 60.8 to 55.7 per cent.[14] All of this took place without an industrial rebellion in the ranks of the unions. Strikes fell to very low levels in the 1980s and remained subdued in the 1990s, thanks to the discipline exerted by the ACTU. Under Labor's Accord, Australian business enjoyed 13 years of industrial peace.

Not only was business happy to see labour costs and union strength wound back, but Labor also successfully promoted an extensive program of economic rationalism in the private and public sectors.[15] Where Fraser had been strong on free trade rhetoric but weak on action, ALP governments from 1983 to 1996 delivered dramatic cuts in tariffs and import quotas.[16]

Labor's approach was not simply to combine wage cuts with market liberalisation that might have jeopardised investment. The government also

provided big subsidies for investment and the retraining of redundant workers, as well as industry specific measures, to improve the international competitiveness of key Australian sectors. In particular, the textile, clothing and
footwear, iron and steel, and car industries were restructured under the
aegis of tripartite industry plans involving union, company and government representatives.[17] The result was substantial increases in exports and
labour productivity and large scale redundancies.[18]

Union leaders' involvement in various industry restructuring committees
accelerated a shift already under way within the ranks of leading Australian
union officials – their adoption of an explicitly pro-business agenda, sys-
tematised in the ACTU's 1987 report, *Australia Reconstructed*. But it was
not just the full time union leaders. Job delegates who were prepared to
follow instructions from their union's headquarters now became the front
line of employer efforts to convince workers that redundancies and major
changes to work practices were inevitable and, indeed, desirable.[19] The
transformation in the politics of the union movement was most obvious
in the case of union officials associated with the CPA. During the 1960s
and into the 1970s the CPA had led militant strikes, and in the early
1970s the Party announced its intention to challenge the 'sacred rights
of the capitalists' to control industry. During the Accord years, however,
CPA-aligned union leaders became industrial disciplinarians and advocated
wage restraint. Now content merely to tail the ALP, the Communist Party
lost its political reason for existence and finally dissolved in 1991, some
years after it had ceased in any sense to be a coherent force on the Australian
left.[20]

Labor used its distance from individual business sectors to shake up
the banking industry, long term supporters of the conservative parties.
ALP leaders had historically regarded international bankers and the foreign
exchange markets with suspicion. Under Hawke and Treasurer Keating,
however, the power of big business to move its capital offshore was radically
increased. In December 1983, the Australian dollar was floated, government
control over banks modified and foreign banks allowed to set up operations
along the lines of the recommendations of the *Campbell Report* to the Fraser
government. Labor also relaxed rules for the ownership of print and electronic media (which enabled Rupert Murdoch to expand his empire) and
permitted the entry of new competitors into the domestic airline industry.
In 1989, Jeffrey Babb, an advocate of New Right politics, told the *Financial*

Review that 'It is quite clear that the Hawke Government has done far more to implement the neoconservative agenda than the Fraser government did'.[21]

Under Hawke and Keating, Labor politicians became keen exponents of privatisation. Telecom (subsequently renamed Telstra) was corporatised in 1988; the state monopoly on telecommunications ended in 1991. After Keating ousted Hawke as prime minister in December 1991, the government went further: it privatised the Commonwealth Bank and corporatised large federal government agencies. In 1993, with the adoption of a National Competition Policy, contracting out and compulsory competitive tendering in the public sector became government policy. In cooperation with state governments, Keating significantly cut the national rail transport network and in 1994 began moves to privatise the Australian National Line shipping concern. Privatisations and corporatisations were often followed by mass redundancies.[22]

The hopes harboured by Australian capitalists in 1983 that Labor would be able to succeed in restructuring the economy where Fraser had failed proved justified. Australian business became increasingly integrated into international circuits of trade and finance. Exports and imports leapt and Labor presided over a big increase in exports of advanced manufactures. Australian businesses became major foreign investors outside Australia's traditional southwest Pacific base for the first time. Australia's profile as a mid range power in the Asia–Pacific region began to grow.

The taxation system was similarly reshaped to satisfy the demands of business. Tax cuts for the rich and more extensive user charges for public services shifted the cost of government functions onto low and average income earners. Personal income taxation was made less progressive, the rate of company tax was pruned and the significance of indirect taxation increased. In each case, capital benefited at the expense of the working class. Compulsory superannuation was introduced in order to reduce future public outlays on means tested pensions and to increase the pool of savings available for investment.

Years later, ALP President Senator Stephen Loosley spelt out the political significance of the Hawke and Keating governments. The legacy of the Whitlam government had been a perception that Labor could not effectively manage the economy, whereas Hawke and Keating demonstrated that the capitalist class could trust Labor once again. Under their governments,

All those areas neglected by the Fraser governments were taken up with a measure of zeal during those years. Floating the dollar, permitting the entry of foreign banks, dismantling the tariff wall that had been the centrepiece of the Chifley Government's post-war planning, liberalising the labour market and injecting competition into many stagnant areas of the economy were the hallmarks of reforming Labor governments. Legitimacy was earned.[23]

One result of this restoration of legitimacy was a healthy flow of business donations to the ALP and friendly relationships with leading businessmen and women, including Kerry Packer, Alan Bond, Sir Peter Abeles, Sir Rupert Murdoch and Janet Holmes à Court.

Social policy

The Hawke and Keating governments made much of their commitment to fairness.[24] In 1988 Hawke claimed that, 'Side by side with its economic strategy of making Australia a wealthier society, the government has been developing a social justice strategy aimed at fairly distributing that wealth throughout the community' through increased spending on health, education and social security.[25] At the launch of Labor's campaign for the 1987 election Hawke famously announced his ambition that by 1990 'no Australian child will be living in poverty'. There was some substance to these claims. The introduction of Medicare in 1983 was undoubtedly an important reform, and the real level of welfare benefits did increase under the Hawke and Keating governments.

These reforms were, nevertheless, very limited. Medicare was a form of socialised health insurance, not health provision. It fell well short of the British National Health Service, a much bolder attempt to tackle structural inequalities in health. Even in the form of insurance, it had drawbacks. In particular, only 85 per cent of scheduled medical fees were covered by Medicare benefits, and the official schedule did not consistently reflect what medical practitioners actually charged.

The increased level of welfare payments has to be set against other changes under Labor: tighter grounds for eligibility, increased pressure on recipients to participate in or return to the paid workforce, more vigorous harassment of claimants by an increased number of Department of Social Security fraud inspectors and the elimination of the unemployment benefit for people under 18. The scope for an all round improvement in the welfare state was limited by the government's commitment to budget discipline – public spending as a percentage of GDP declined from 30 per cent in 1984 to 27 per cent 10 years later. The number of students in tertiary education rose by 44 per cent between 1987 and 1995, but this was paid for not through increased taxes on business, the ultimate end users of this new 'resource', but by reintroducing university fees in the form of the Higher Education Contribution Scheme, a tax on university graduates. Despite the government's social justice rhetoric, inequality rose sharply during the Hawke and Keating governments, reversing years of decline, and child poverty was still a blight on Australian society when Labor lost office in 1996.[26] There was some income redistribution within the working class to the poorest, but the main flow was from workers as a group to the rich.

Labor's ambiguous social policies and the steady decline in real wages in the 1980s, alongside the further enrichment of the wealthy, began to weigh on the ALP's electoral popularity, as Neville Wran acknowledged in his 1986 Curtin Memorial Lecture with which we began this chapter:

> I realise very well that gaining acceptance for change, much less active support for it, is no easy task. I certainly don't underestimate the difficulty for a Labor government in asking the nation's workforce to take a cut in real wages, when there have never been so many overnight millionaires... when the Stock Exchange soars to record levels; when company after company chalks up record profits.[27]

Wran's insight was to prove correct in two devastating elections that were to follow. Before turning to these, it is worth assessing Labor's performance in three other respects – Aboriginal rights, asylum seekers and foreign policy, which tells us a great deal about its priorities.

Aboriginal dispossession continues

Labor went to the 1983 election with a commitment to establish national land rights legislation that would override state governments that, other than South Australia, had stymied reform for years. Initially, it looked as if Labor would deliver. But when, early in 1984, the federal government released its plan to legislate nationally for land rights, it immediately faced a barrage of opposition from big business, mining companies in particular. Business paid for television advertisements aimed at scaring people into the belief that, if Labor's legislation went ahead, their backyards were under threat from Aboriginal land claims. The public relations campaign had its desired effect. Brian Burke, Western Australia's Labor premier, threatened to resign if the legislation was not withdrawn. Hawke buckled, dropping the proposed Aboriginal veto over mining. Aborigines and their allies were furious at Labor's backdown and held protest rallies in Canberra in May 1985, to no avail. In March 1986, Aboriginal Affairs Minister Clyde Holding abandoned federal land rights legislation altogether, a decision described by the *Canberra Times* as a 'shameful backdown'.[28]

Lavish celebrations to mark the bicentennial in 1988, organised by federal and state Labor governments, only rubbed salt into the wound. Forty thousand Aborigines and their supporters protested in Sydney on 26 January against the whitewashing of Australia's history. In order to deflect criticism of his government's abandonment of land rights, Hawke and new Aboriginal Affairs Minister Gerry Hand began to speak of a treaty or compact with Aboriginal peoples, yet nothing had come of this by the time Labor lost office in 1996.

The dissolution of the Department of Aboriginal Affairs and its replacement by the Aboriginal and Torres Strait Islander Commission (ATSIC) in 1990 was small comfort. Even though its budget was modest, ATSIC did provide for elected regional Indigenous councils and a national board of commissioners. But ATSIC did not emerge from Aboriginal aspirations; rather, it was imposed by the Hawke government, eager to give the impression of progress. Charles Perkins, who served from 1981 until 1988 as the first Indigenous secretary of the Department of Aboriginal Affairs, railed against the decision, arguing that ATSIC meant 'there was to be more, not less, ministerial power . . . less, not more, Aboriginal self-determination'.[29] Aborigines were also fed the small crumbs of a reconciliation process, something so innocuous that it was backed by the Coalition when tabled in parliament in August 1991. Other than intervening in 1991 to stop a proposed gold mine at Coronation Hill in Kakadu National Park, Hawke did nothing to advance the cause of land rights.

The Keating government was no better. Paul Keating is often remembered in the field of Aboriginal rights for his speech in Redfern on 10 December

1992, in which he referred to some of the genocidal crimes that were a fundamental feature of white settlement:

> It begins, I think, with the act of recognition. Recognition that it was we who did the dispossessing. We took the traditional lands and smashed the traditional way of life. We brought the disasters. The alcohol. We committed the murders. We took the children from their mothers. We practised discrimination and exclusion.[30]

Although the speech was couched in a liberal vein and did not pin the responsibility for the genocide on the major beneficiaries of dispossession – the pastoralists and later the mining industry – it was nonetheless a remarkable speech for an Australian politician, a mainstream recognition that the white settlement of Australia was based on genocide. But, when it came to practice, the Keating government continued the theft of the land. The test came with the High Court's Mabo decision in June 1992 which found that Australia was not *terra nullius* at the time of the British invasion, and that the Indigenous peoples had a common law title to their land, except where it had been overridden by an Act of a settler government. There were significant limits to this decision.[31] For the two-thirds of Aboriginal people who lived in urban areas, Mabo was a moral victory at best. Nonetheless, business reacted sharply. Profits and investments were now at risk. Business fears escalated when the Wik people of north Queensland and the Wiradjuri of New South Wales filed large land claims on the basis of the Mabo decision. Mining companies, the Coalition parties, the media and right wing think tanks mounted a scare campaign, claiming that Australia was now threatened by 'reverse apartheid' and 'cultural McCarthyism'. Business demanded validation of existing land title, that is, unqualified legal recognition of their control of the land. If this were not granted, the mining companies threatened an investment strike.

In his Redfern speech, Keating had said that the Mabo decision was the 'basis of a new relationship between Indigenous and non-Indigenous Australians'.[32] Yet the Keating government did all that it could to undermine even the highly restricted benefits of the Mabo decision.[33] Leading Aboriginal activists denounced the government's draft legislation in their August 1993 Eva Valley statement. Keating responded by excluding the critics from the government's discussions and consulting only with those who could be relied upon to support his proposals.[34]

Labor tabled its Native Title Bill in parliament in November 1993. It was a complete betrayal of the hopes of many Aborigines. Its very basis, the concept of native title, was not much more than an illusion, a legally inferior category of land ownership, indeed, the weakest possible legal title. Native title could, the government believed, be over-ridden by pastoral leases and only coexisted with mining leases. In this latter respect the Bill was much weaker than the *Aboriginal Land Rights (Northern Territory) Act 1976*, which had been passed by the Fraser government. No provision was made under Labor's Bill to compensate those whose land had been stolen prior to 1975. Some Aboriginal figures, such as Mick Dodson, slammed it and called for serious land rights legislation such as that promised by Labor 10 years previously. Others went along with it, fearing something worse at the hands of state governments. The National Farmers' Federation and Jeff Kennett's Liberal government in Victoria welcomed it, indicating that most sections of business, despite the histrionics of the mining industry, realised that it had a friend in Canberra when it came to fending off the demand for genuine land rights.[35] The Native Title Act was passed on 21 December 1993.

On a different front, activists had been campaigning for years for justice around Indigenous deaths in custody. Aborigines continued, whether under Labor or Liberal governments, to suffer one of the highest incarceration rates in the world and one of the highest rates of deaths in police and prison custody. For years the police and warders had acted as a law unto themselves, safe in the knowledge that neither the politicians nor the media cared about the fate of locked up Aborigines. Agitation by the newly formed Committee to Defend Black Rights and annual street marches to commemorate the deaths in custody during the early 1980s of John Pat and Eddie Murray, aged 16 and 21 respectively, in Western Australia and New South Wales, brought the issue to national attention. Under pressure from this campaign and also to deflect growing criticism of its bicentennial celebrations, the Hawke government established the Royal Commission into Black Deaths in Custody in 1987. Over the following three years the Commission took evidence on 99 cases of black deaths in custody, the first time that any judicial body had ever systematically collected data on this national disgrace. The hearings revealed only too clearly the endemic nature of institutionalised racism in the police stations and jails of Australia.

In May 1991, the Royal Commission handed down its report that included 339 recommendations; in March 1992 the Keating government

tabled its response in parliament. The result was a fiasco. Not a single pros-
ecution of a police or prison officer resulted. Little changed in the watch
houses and jails. Fifteen years after the report was handed down, criminol-
ogist Chris Cuneen wrote that

> Despite the Royal Commission, indigenous people remain dramatically over-
> represented in the criminal justice system. Deaths in custody still occur at
> unacceptably high levels and the recommendations of the Royal Commission
> are often ignored. Rather than a reform of the criminal justice system, we
> have seen the development of more punitive approaches to law and order,
> giving rise to expanding reliance on penal sanctions.[36]

Once again the political process and Labor had failed Indigenous
Australians.

Deterring asylum seekers

In the late 1980s and early 1990s a series of geopolitical factors led a few
hundred refugees, chiefly from Cambodia, to head for Australian shores by
boat. But, just as they had with Aboriginal affairs, the Hawke government's
fine words about racial harmony and multiculturalism were not matched
by its actual policies on asylum seekers. The government responded with
ever tighter restrictions. Its Migration Legislation Amendment Act of 1989
greatly reduced room for discretion by migration officers and sought to
remove the potential for unsuccessful applicants to appeal a rejection of
their application for refugee status in the courts. The Act also included
provisions for mandatory deportation of 'illegal entrants' and granted the
Department of Immigration the power to sell asylum seekers' possessions
to cover the costs of their detention and deportation.[37] In 1992, by means
of its Migration Reform Act, Labor introduced automatic detention of any-
one arriving without a visa, in what were prisons in all but name. Only a
fraction of the mandatory detainees could be housed at the Villawood and
Maribyrnong centres in Sydney and Melbourne respectively, and Labor had
already sold off the old migrant hostels. So the government transported asylum seekers to a new detention centre at remote and desolate Port Hedland
in Western Australia where shocking conditions prevailed and temperatures
reached the mid 40s in summer.

Very few Western countries forcibly detained migrants beyond their initial reception, and most had limits on how long people could be kept in custody. The Keating government had no such compunctions – 14 of the 104 Cambodian 'boat people' detained at Port Hedland in October 1991 were still there five years later. The Labor government's policy on the boat people quickly became an international scandal. The United Nations High Commissioner for Human Rights said that Australia's detention of children was 'in serious danger of breaching international covenants protecting children's rights'.

During the summer of 1994–5, when 500 boat people arrived on the shores of the Northern Territory, yellow peril hysteria reached a crescendo. The Brisbane *Courier Mail* led with headlines warning of a 'Refugee Invasion'. But hostility came not just from the usual suspects. The Labor government, too, weighed in. Evoking the arguments of the extreme right, Immigration Minister Nick Bolkus simply ignored the (in any case harsh) processes established by his own department and warned the boat people 'Our message to you is that you won't have a chance'. The minister insisted that 'these people have got no right to come and impose themselves on Australian shores in the way that they have',[38] despite the internationally acknowledged legal right of asylum seekers to do just that.

The government and willing media attempted to discredit the boat people; the prime minister described them as 'economic migrants', not genuine victims of persecution.[39] One recurring theme was that asylum seekers arriving by boat were 'queue jumpers'. This charge had no basis in fact. Many of those fleeing hardship or war were leaving countries or regions in which Australia had no facilities to process any application for refugee status. If thousands of proven refugees were left rotting in offshore refugee centres it was not because a grand total of 2500 boat people washed up in Australia as 'unauthorised arrivals' between 1989–90 and 1995–6 but because Labor limited the annual refugee and humanitarian intake to 12 000, and in some years to less than 8000. This was a tiny fraction of the number of refugees taken in by several much poorer countries ranging from the Ivory Coast and Guinea to Pakistan and Thailand, and a drop in the ocean compared to the global total of 15 million refugees.[40] The Labor government's policies on refugees paved the way for the even more callous actions of its successor.

In the case of Aborigines, there was a direct explanation for racist policies in terms of class interests: securing business control over Indigenous land.

Scapegoating asylum seekers helped weld workers to the project of Australian nationalism by reinforcing the notion that 'we' all had a common interest in protecting our borders against external threats, that Australians, rich and poor, were bound together by a common interest in repelling maritime invasion by a few thousand bedraggled asylum seekers. Thus class interests operated here too: nationalism gave credibility to calls for the nation's workers to sacrifice wages, even lives, in the pursuit of an edge in economic and military competition with rival powers. Further, day to day resentments about the cost of housing, lack of jobs or paucity of public services, could be directed at asylum seekers and migrants more generally who were, allegedly, taking Australian jobs, driving up house prices and draining the public purse.

The Hawke government also tightened up the broader migration program and placed a greater focus on bringing people with skills in demand on the labour market to Australia, pandering to the racist argument that migrants took the jobs of Australians. Racist attitudes towards migrants suited the interests of the capitalist class, which was keen to ensure that those who produced the wealth in society were distracted into fighting among themselves rather than uniting against it.

The new Australian militarism

The Hawke government's defence and foreign policies were designed to enable Australia to play a more aggressive role in the southwestern Pacific and southeast Asia. What was soon dubbed a 'new Australian militarism' emerged.[41] In 1985 the government announced plans to spend billions of dollars to update Australia's armed forces with 75 F18 fighter bombers, six Collins class submarines, 100 helicopters and a range of destroyers. The Hawke government also subsidised the domestic operations of arms producers. Arms exports from Australian increased apace. In 1991, AIDEX, the largest ever arms sales expo held in Australia, took place in Canberra.

The Keating government initiated the Asia Pacific Economic Cooperation Process (APEC) as a multinational multiplier of Australian influence and made systematic efforts to boost trade with Asia and to increase Australia's own direct influence in the region. There was also greater emphasis on using aid projects to encourage trade. The interpenetration of commerce and foreign policy was particularly evident in Australian interventions in Bougainville, Cambodia and East Timor.

The Whitlam government had granted independence to Papua New Guinea in 1975 but the country essentially remained a neocolony. A stable PNG under Australian hegemony was a crucial component of Australian geopolitical interests in the region. Australian business dominated the commanding heights of the PNG economy, the mining sector in particular. For years Bougainville Copper, a subsidiary of Conzinc Riotinto Australia (CRA), had been operating a giant copper mine, Panguna, on the island of Bougainville. The Panguna mine operations had devastating consequences for the island, not the least being environmental degradation. The PNG government, anxious not to cut off the royalties that it earned from the mine, turned a blind eye to the villagers' suffering. For its part, the Hawke government championed the company's operations. Driven to desperation, the local people organised an armed resistance movement, the Bougainville Revolutionary Army, that attacked the mine operations in 1989, drove out forces sent from PNG to Bougainville to reassert control, and then declared independence. The Australian government reacted violently – it could not let villagers shut down a vital Australian asset with impunity, not only because of the economic consequences for CRA but also because of the threat of contagion. If local villagers could seize a mine in Bougainville, Australian imperial interests throughout the region could also be threatened. Labor rushed the PNG government four Iroquois helicopter gunships, four patrol boats, 55 military trainers and provided $400 million annually in military aid to wage war on the Bougainvilleans.[42] Armed to the teeth by Australia, the PNG armed forces blockaded the island and eventually crushed the resistance. 'Order' was restored.

The Australian government also participated in the outside interference in the more serious situation in Cambodia, where conflict had been raging for years between the Hun Sen government and the Khmer Rouge guerrillas.[43] In the early 1990s the Australian government took a leading role in the United Nations peace initiative that sought to engineer a settlement that increased western influence in Indochina. The Labor government's intervention had little effect on Cambodian politics but did raise Australia's economic and political profile. The Australian government also initiated aid projects in southeast Asia, notably, the Friendship Bridge between Thailand and Laos, which proved to be very lucrative for Australian companies.

More important than either PNG or Cambodia, however, was Indonesia, still under the iron fist of President Suharto. Labor, as much as the Coalition, was determined to back Suharto's stable conservative regime in Indonesia as the best guarantor of Australian interests. The Hawke government provided training for soldiers from Indonesia's *Kopassus* special forces, notorious for human rights abuses wherever they operated. On becoming prime minister, Keating's first state visit was to Indonesia, where he effusively praised the dictator. In 1993, he suggested that the Clinton administration tone down its criticism of human rights abuses in Indonesia,[44] and in December 1995, in one of its final foreign policy initiatives, the Labor government signed a pact with Indonesia that provided for regular consultation at ministerial level on 'matters affecting ... common security'.[45]

The human rights of those who rejected Suharto's New Order, most notably the East Timorese, were quite dispensable.[46] Labor continued the Fraser government's policy of recognising Indonesia's incorporation of East Timor; Australia was one of the very few countries to do so. Labor opposed East Timorese independence, fearing that it would spark autonomy movements elsewhere in the archipelago and threaten the stability of the government in Jakarta. But there was also money to be made. In 1989, without even the pretence of consulting the East Timorese, the Hawke government signed the Timor Gap Treaty with Indonesia, which divided oil exploration rights in the seas between Australia and Timor. In November 1991, after the Indonesian army massacred 150 people during a funeral at Santa Cruz cemetery in Dili and the US government imposed a ban on arms sales, the Australian government seized the opportunity to become a major military supplier to the Indonesian armed forces.

Outside what Australian governments have traditionally regarded as our neighbourhood, Labor sought to influence the world order after the fall of the Berlin Wall. In August 1990 the Hawke government enthusiastically supported the decision by President George H. W. Bush to dispatch a small armada to blockade Iraq following its invasion of Kuwait. Labor was as keen as the United States to dispel the Vietnam Syndrome that had crimped US imperialism since the mid 1970s. In a reprise of the Menzies government volunteering to dispatch troops to Vietnam before being asked to do so, the Hawke government sent two Royal Australian Navy frigates to enforce sanctions on Iraq without waiting for a direct request from the US government.[47] The frigates were of little military significance but reminded the US of the public relations and diplomatic value of the relationship with Australia. The US communication base at Nurrungar in Western Australia, which guided US bombers to their targets in Iraq once air raids began in January 1991, had greater military importance. Following the cessation of the hot war on Iraq at the end of February 1991, the frigates maintained UN sanctions on Iraq, contributing to the deaths of hundreds of thousands of Iraqis over succeeding years, due to shortages of medicines, food and other necessities.

In line with Labor's policy since the state's formation in 1948, the Hawke government was also an unabashed champion of Israel. Hawke did not flinch from his support during the first *Intifada* (mass uprising of 1987–93) when Israeli forces killed 1100 Palestinians, a level of brutality condemned by many governments around the world.

The Left drifts right

A feature of the Hawke and Keating years that was particularly demor-alising for many Labor supporters was the fact that ministers from the Left faction[48] were coopted and often called upon to sell right wing poli-cies for the government. Even before Labor took office, Bob Hogg was instrumental in watering down a range of Labor's more radical policies at the 1982 Party conference. Once in office, the opportunities for betrayal of traditional left principles escalated.[49] It was the Left's Brian Howe who scrapped the dole for under 18 year olds in 1989. It was the Left's Gerry Hand who, as Minister for Immigration, initiated mandatory detention of refugees in 1992, a policy continued by his successor Nick Bolkus, also from the Party's Left. It was George Campbell of the metalworkers union and Peter Robson of the Commonwealth Public Sector Union, influen-tial figures in the Party's Left, who championed the further enfeeblement of the award system in favour of enterprise bargaining at the 1994 Party conference.

Some ministers publicly dissented from specific government decisions. Stewart West, the Left's only minister in the first Hawke Cabinet, opposed the resumption of uranium mining at Roxby Downs in 1983 and paid for it with his position in Cabinet.[50] Senator Susan Ryan, education minister for the first four years of the Hawke government and member of the small

Centre Left faction, expressed opposition to the reintroduction of university fees and was demoted following the 1987 election; she resigned from Cabinet six months later.

On one occasion, the Left had a victory, albeit with cross-factional support. In February 1985 following discussions with just six other Cabinet ministers, Hawke announced that Australia would facilitate US testing of the new MX nuclear missile off the Australian coast, in clear defiance of the Party's anti-nuclear policy. Opposition to the content of the decision and the way in which it was made spread across all factions. Within four days Hawke backtracked. Trenchant opposition from the Left was, however, rare. More typical was the Left's response to the Keating government's sale of Qantas in 1992, in breach of Party policy. The Left announced that it would fight the decision but within a matter of weeks it had capitulated. According to *Age* journalist Michelle Grattan, Hogg, now national secretary of the Party, told Keating that 'the Government had no choice but to proceed with the sale and the Party would come to grips with the problem of the platform later'.[51]

Even where there was no evident and sacrosanct budgetary constraint to justify their stance, Left ministers were, for the most part, unstinting in their defence of Cabinet decisions. When tens of thousands demonstrated across the country in January 1991 against Australian involvement in the first Gulf War, the Left faction leaders, including Brian Howe, formerly a Methodist clergyman and urban environmental activist, loyally defended the Hawke government's dispatch of armed forces to the conflict.

There was a variety of reasons why the Left capitulated to the Hawke and Keating programs. The left reformist project, using the resources of the state to usher in changes that benefit the working class, to which most of the left subscribed, was undermined by falling profit rates since the 1970s. During the postwar boom – from the 1940s to the early 1970s – there had been sufficient economic leeway for the system to afford an expansion of social spending and working class living standards while still providing healthy profits for business. In the years following the end of the boom in 1974, the space for reforms was severely constrained. A left reformist program would quickly have run up against what business was now willing to tolerate, a limit that had already been demonstrated in 1975. Further, the collapse of the Eastern Bloc in 1989 and the dissolution of the CPA in 1991 removed important ideological reference points of the ALP left. The disastrous experiments in State Bank funded economic development in South Australia and Victoria seemed to confirm the international experience: 'socialism', at least as represented by state intervention, was dead. Former advocates of state planning now lauded the market. Social democracy was left without a strategy, and economic rationalism, the term for neoliberalism used in Australia during the 1980s and 1990s, filled the vacuum.

Another factor that explained the behaviour of the Left ministers was that they were under little left wing pressure from outside parliament. The strike rate was low and falling. Union coverage was declining rapidly. Social movements of the early 1970s had disappeared or were in decay. The Nuclear Disarmament Party, which gave the ALP a shock at the 1984 election, fell apart in acrimony quickly thereafter. The campaign against the Gulf War kicked life into peace activism for a while but its internal weaknesses prevented it from sustaining a new opposition movement. The environmental movement and the nascent Greens were at this stage still promoting themselves as 'neither left nor right but ahead'. Finally, the lure of Cabinet positions and other career opportunities made the capitulation of many leading left figures easier and more attractive.

The result of all these processes was that by the early 1990s, the ALP Left could not field a single figure who commanded widespread loyalty or respect among those who wanted to resist the government on any front, whether on student fees, union rights, uranium mining, foreign policy or Aboriginal land rights. If Whitlam had Jim Cairns, who was a thorn in his leader's side on occasion, Hawke and Keating were untroubled by any such irritants on their left.

From the sweetest victory to Keating's last stand

Recognising the ALP's pro-business economic agenda and the benefits of its Accord relationship with the unions, the majority of the capitalist class had initially backed the Hawke government. Once Labor had shown its willingness to accommodate business demands on a range of fronts, employers became more aggressive. With the onset of a deep recession in 1990–1, the capitalist class began to promote a bolder assault on the working class and unions. The Coalition moved in step and released *Fightback*, a document that promised an attack on unions, a goods and services tax (GST), extensive privatisation, reduced youth wages, lower unemployment benefits and gutting of the public health system.[52]

Labor was in a weak position to resist this right wing attack. The Hawke government had survived its first two elections after taking office with only minor swings against it. At the 1990 election, however, its unpopularity was brought home sharply when, with a primary vote of less than 40 per cent, the ALP suffered its worst result since 1931. The solid front between Hawke and Keating, which had underpinned stability in caucus, now crumbled. Keating challenged for the leadership, lost and retired to the back bench. He came back for a second tilt at Christmas 1991 and defeated his former boss.

There was no particular reason to believe that Keating could save the Labor government. As treasurer, he had been responsible for many of the policies that had undermined Labor's working class support base. It was, rather, the conservative offensive led by the new Liberal leader, John Hewson, that galvanised the working class to rally behind Labor. The first site of struggle was Victoria where Hewson's *Fightback* policies had undergone a trial run under the recently elected Liberal government of Jeff Kennett. Unions mobilised and called mass demonstrations and rolling strikes. Within a month of the Liberals' victory, 150 000 workers marched on the streets of Melbourne to protest Kennett's cuts. While the union campaign was subsequently wound back by the Victorian Trades Hall Council, the impressive scale of the demonstrations and widespread revulsion at the federal Liberal Party's *Fightback* package encouraged the Keating Labor government to deploy a populist class rhetoric in the 1993 election campaign, depicting its opponents as representatives of the privileged and wealthy. In particular Keating targeted the Liberals' proposed GST as a threat to the working class. The strategy worked. Against all expectations, Labor came home with a 5.5 per cent swing in its favour, with working class voters in particular falling in behind the government. On election night, Keating called it 'the sweetest victory' and 'one for the True Believers'.

Even though the unions had played a crucial role in defeating the right wing challenge at the 1993 federal election, they were not exempt from a fresh round of attacks by the re-elected Keating government. At an Institute of Directors dinner in April 1993 Keating announced his intention to dismantle the system of industrial awards. In July Laurie Brereton, his industrial relations minister, released the details of Labor's Industrial Relations

Reform Bill, which foreshadowed the wholesale replacement of the award system by enterprise bargaining; awards would be reduced to the role of a safety net.

Union leaders were taken aback by Labor's plans to adopt what had up until this point been Coalition policy. Maintaining the system of industrial awards, not as a safety net but as the very foundation of the entire industrial relations system, was an item of faith for most union leaders. They responded in an unprecedented fashion, booing Brereton at the 1993 ACTU Congress in August. Never before had an ALP minister been treated in such a manner at an ACTU Congress. But, having vented their anger, the union leaders soon gave in, which enabled the government to press ahead with its industrial relations changes after a few cosmetic changes.

Following the 1993 election, the prime minister promised to 'bring home the bacon' for workers who had suffered during the recession. In 1994, after two years of jobless recovery, new jobs started to appear in large numbers and real wages began to rise. But unemployment remained above 8 per cent; they started to rise again in the second half of 1995. As for the new jobs, half of them were part time, real wages for low paid blue collar males were less than they had been 20 years previously, and 'reform fatigue' was widespread among workers, who were suffering from years of redundancies and work intensification.

Six months before the 1996 election warning signs were flashing for Labor. A survey by the *Bulletin* and the Morgan organisation in September 1995 found that a significant portion of Labor's blue collar base had deserted the Party since 1993 – the Coalition was picking up support not because of any great fondness for the new Liberal leader John Howard but because workers were sick of Labor.[53] Keating appeared at the September 1995 ACTU congress and was warmly received but, as the *Bulletin* put it, 'Keating's rallying call to workers at last week's ACTU Congress to keep the faith is falling on deaf ears, given the 10 years of low-wage growth workers have endured for the national good'.[54]

Indeed, with its right wing economic program, Labor had created the space in which the Liberals could attack the government, tendentiously, from the left: Liberal frontbencher Tony Abbott noted that when Keating asked Labor voters to 'keep the faith', the prime minister's faith 'is nothing but privatisation – privatisation whatever the cost, privatisation whatever the pain, privatisation whatever the electoral discomfort it causes his own people'. Howard had learnt from the mistakes of his predecessor, Hewson. In 1996, the Coalition ran a campaign promising a 'comfortable and relaxed' Australia, and the Opposition leader offered a 'rock-solid guarantee that no worker would be worse off' if the Coalition won office. In so doing, the conservatives were able to tap into a broad vein of anger against the Keating government, even among many of its working class supporters. With the exception of 1993, Labor's vote had fallen at each successive election since 1983. At the March 1996 election Labor was tossed out of office with a primary vote of 38.7 per cent, yet another post-Depression low. The Accord had partly anaesthetised the working class over a 13 year period. The incoming Coalition surgeon could now continue the operation, which benefited capital rather than labour, with a larger, blunter scalpel.

Chapter 8

LABOR IN THE WILDERNESS

The Howard government quickly put aside the comforting words it had used to win the 1996 election. Public service jobs were slashed. New industrial relations laws were passed to wind back the award system, attack union rights, and introduce statutory individual contracts. Public sympathy for the Coalition dropped sharply; its primary support, according to Newspoll, fell from 55 per cent in May 1996 to 40 per cent one year later. Yet Labor failed to capitalise on the Coalition's slide, its poll results rising from 36 per cent to only 39 per cent.

As had occurred during the Fraser government, the trade unions were initially the real opposition to the conservatives. They mounted a series of one day strikes and rallies to protest against the government's harsh budget cuts and anti-union legislation that culminated in a large and angry demonstration outside Parliament House in Canberra on 19 August 1996. Militant unionists and Aborigines forced their way into the building. Labor and trade union leaders turned this impressive demonstration of widespread outrage against the Coalition's policies into a rout by tailing the government and conservative media in denouncing damage to the building's doors and souvenir shop. Even left wing union leaders distanced themselves from the event.[1]

Although the government prevailed against the unions in 1996, it was pushed back on the nation's waterfront two years later when many thousands of workers and union supporters joined the Maritime Union of Australia's (MUA) picket lines all around the country, shutting down the operations of Patrick Stevedores, which had sacked its entire unionised workforce of 1400 and replaced it with scabs.[2] As the containers piled high, the government and Patrick, working hand in glove, saw their vision of a smashing victory evaporate. Sustained mass action forced the Federal Court to order Patrick to reinstate the wharfies, although the latter paid a heavy price in the subsequent negotiations. Labor was no help to the MUA. For the first two weeks after the sackings, ALP parliamentary leaders kept well clear of the picket lines and refused to make any public statements in support of the MUA, preferring to position the Party as the mediator between the two warring sides. Kim Beazley, by now Party leader, condemned the International Transport Workers Federation for organising a boycott of Australian produce in the United States and not once did he promise to repeal the secondary boycott provisions, which made solidarity action with the MUA illegal, if Labor won office.

The Coalition had begun to campaign against Aboriginal land rights and the Aboriginal and Torres Strait Islander Commission even before the 1996 election, just as it had agitated against the MUA. But its attempt in government to mobilise racism against Aborigines was only partially successful. Following the High Court's December 1996 Wik decision on land rights, which determined that pastoral leases and native title could coexist, the Coalition responded with its Native Title Amendment Bill, which guaranteed pastoralists ongoing rights to occupy and use the land free from Aboriginal claims. The ALP was in a quandary.[3] The leadership wanted to ensure that the challenge to pastoral leases posed by the Wik decision was eliminated by legislation, but it was also keen to avoid seeming to endorse Howard's position. So Beazley and his shadow ministers tried to have it both ways: they labelled the Bill 'discriminatory and divisive' while also criticising the lack of certainty it provided for the pastoralists.[4] Labor blocked the Bill's passage through the Senate but did not defend land rights in principle. Once the Bill was passed in July 1998, without Labor support, Beazley announced that the ALP would not repeal it if returned to office at the forthcoming federal election.[5]

The government's anti-Aboriginal stance tied the ALP up in knots but did not give the Coalition an electoral boost because many of its supporters had decamped to Pauline Hanson's racist One Nation Party. According to Newspoll, Coalition support slumped to 34 per cent in the winter of 1998. The ALP was ahead by 11 points. Howard looked like a oncer. But in the months leading up to the election, the Coalition clawed back Labor's lead. The government promised substantial income tax cuts as a trade off for a new goods and services tax. Labor moved to the left when, in an echo of the 1993 campaign against Hewson, it took a stand against the GST and promised to extend capital gains tax. The election was close run. Having come to power in March 1996 with a primary vote of 47.2 per cent, the Coalition crept back into office in October 1998 on 39.5 per cent, and 700 000 fewer votes. The ALP garnered an extra 200 000 votes and won 50.1 per cent of the two party preferred vote but not a majority of seats. The ALP's failure to effectively promote and, in some cases, its willingness to attack, militant protests and industrial action against Howard's policies, together with the voters' all too fresh memories of the Hawke and Keating governments, prevented Labor from tipping out the conservatives after one term in office.

Coalition ascendancy

The 1998 election result was a high water mark for the ALP. The Coalition won the 2001 and 2004 elections convincingly; Labor's primary vote sank to its lowest levels since the 1931 split. Many commentators put the Coalition's success in this period down to two factors: its successful management of the economy, and its ability to tap into and manipulate the social and political attitudes of blue collar and lower white collar voters, the so-called Howard battlers. The 2004 election outcome in particular was held to indicate a conservative cultural shift. According to this interpretation, widespread among conservative commentators, Australia had become an 'aspirational' society full of self-employed tradespeople and small business owners who valued hard work and were dismissive of 'bludgers' and 'special interest groups'.[6]

Small-l liberal commentators essentially agreed. Clive Hamilton declared that the conservative victory in 2004 'reflects nothing more than the narrow-mindedness and preoccupation with self that characterises modern Australia after two decades of market ideology and sustained growth. Private greed always drives out the social good'.[7] In what follows, we challenge this argument. While economic growth did provide a basis for Coalition support, the situation was rather more complex than the conventional wisdom suggested. In particular, it ignored the important role played by Labor's own strategies in its successive defeats.

It was the Coalition's good fortune to be in government during a period of economic expansion. Other than during a brief interruption in US growth in 2001–2, the world economy as a whole grew consistently from the early 1990s until the global financial crisis of 2008. As a commodity exporter to the big industrial economies, Australia surfed the wave, its economy growing consistently faster than other rich countries.[8]

The boom provided the Howard government with a reputation for superior economic management. Economic growth lowered unemployment and thus the call on social security; it also generated tens of billions of dollars in additional tax revenue that Howard used to consolidate his middle class support base with tax cuts and big subsidies for private health insurance and private education. For those who owned their own homes outright and those in steady work, particularly professionals, managers and a number of people with a trade or skills that were in strong demand, living standards rose strongly in the early to mid 2000s. After the capital gains tax rate was reduced in 1999, speculation in property and shares escalated, generating a substantial wealth effect. Home equity rose rapidly, which enabled households to borrow more. Rising house prices benefited working class people who already owned their homes, and the various family allowances introduced in the run up to the 2004 election boosted the spending power of poorer families. As a result of falling unemployment, the labour market became particularly tight in Western Australia and Queensland where, in the mid 2000s, the mining industry boomed. But the main impact of the government's economic agenda was to consolidate the Coalition's core middle and upper class voters. Profitability and CEO remuneration continued their upward trajectory that had started during the Hawke government.[9] In 2004 the share of profits in national income reached the highest proportion ever recorded.[10] Strong profits encouraged business to invest and further stimulated the economy.[11]

Labor's economic policy

Labor failed to capitalise on the fact that millions of workers benefited very little from the sustained boom. Based on interviews with 'middle

Australians' in the early 2000s, sociologist Michael Pusey observed that many believed that 'this has been the only boom in living memory where the broad mass of the population gets nothing or as little as possible'.[12] They were right. Between 1998 and 2004, median incomes for full time non-managerial workers rose by a marginal 3.6 per cent in real terms, and by only 1.2 per cent for the bottom 20 per cent.[13] The proportion of Australians living in poverty rose from 7.6 per cent in 1994 to 9.9 per cent in 2004.[14] Further, the notion that Australia was becoming a nation of self-reliant 'tradies' and entrepreneurs was completely false: the proportion of employers and self-employed in the total workforce fell from 13 to 10 per cent during the Howard years.[15]

These factors help explain why Howard failed to win over the majority of Australian workers to his vision of an aspirational society. Popular sentiment actually shifted to the left. By 2004, Australians were substantially more in favour of government intervention to boost social spending, less attracted by tax cuts, more opposed to further widening of the income gap and privatisation, and significantly less open to union bashing than they had been when Howard was elected.[16]

Labor did not mobilise this sentiment because, with few exceptions, it agreed with the Coalition's economic program, in many respects a continuation of the policies initiated by Hawke and Keating. After opposing the GST and proposing an extension of capital gains tax at the 1998 election, Labor's leaders ditched these policies that appealed to the ALP's working class base and promoted the Party as an efficient economic manager, a supporter of balanced budgets, international competitiveness and a 'new productivity revolution'. Labor supported Howard's handouts to the private health insurance industry and boasted of its own record in cracking down on welfare spending.[17] Despite widespread union opposition, the ALP supported new laws in 1999 to entrench cut price youth wages. After the GST was introduced, the ALP accepted that this regressive tax would be permanent. Following the 2003 election of Mark Latham as leader, the ALP's rightward drift in economic policy accelerated. Latham regularly pronounced on the benefits of hard work and against 'welfare dependency'. His proposal to provide a 'ladder of opportunity' for those at the bottom of society essentially boiled down to blaming the poor for their supposed idleness or lack of initiative.

Labor's defeat at the 2004 election is often put down to the Howard government's decision to run a scare campaign on interest rates. There is an element of truth here. Fear of high interest rates under Labor played well to many blue collar workers in the outer suburbs who had taken on big mortgages and switched to the Coalition in 2004.[18] Many remembered the high mortgage interest rates – up to 17 per cent – under Labor in the early 1990s. The reason the issue resonated so strongly with voters was not that the Howard battlers were prospering but that they were scared – debt to income ratios soared during the Howard years. What could have been a point of vulnerability for the Coalition – the anxiety that many low to middle income earners felt about their precarious grip on home ownership – was turned into an advantage for the government because Labor had supported the entire program of financial deregulation and tax breaks for speculation on residential property that had underpinned the housing bubble. Labor was in no position, then, to criticise the government. Far from it: the Party continued to advocate these policies, and when Beazley returned to the Labor leadership in January 2005 he packed his shadow front bench with noted economic conservatives: Lindsay Tanner, Stephen Smith, Craig Emerson and Wayne Swan.

Labor's economic record at the state level did not inspire confidence that a federal Labor government would offer those suffering from Howard's economic policies much relief. The New South Wales Labor governments of Bob Carr and, subsequently, Morris Iemma ran down public transport, particularly the railways. They failed to sufficiently fund the health system, with the result that there were too few hospital beds, long waits, reduced hygiene and lower quality care, as staff were pressured to push patients through at minimum cost.[19] In 1998 the Carr government sold off the TAB, a cash cow, and it was only a union mobilisation that stopped it from selling off the state electricity industry in 1997. Changes to the workers' compensation system in New South Wales in 2001 were designed to cut payments to injured employees.

In Victoria, teachers and health workers repeatedly struck for higher wages and better conditions against the penny pinching Labor governments of Steve Bracks and John Brumby. Anti-union emergency powers were strengthened,[20] while business was granted $400 million in cuts to land and payroll taxes in April 2004.[21] None of the state assets privatised by the

Kennett government was renationalised, and public–private partnerships poured hundreds of millions of dollars into the coffers of construction companies, and toll road and tunnel operators.[22] In August 2005 Bracks released a 'reform blueprint' promising still lower taxation and more relaxed business regulation, to the delight of the Business Council.[23]

Brown paper bags full of cash may have gone, but, if anything, the Queensland Labor governments of Wayne Goss (1988–96) and Peter Beattie (1998–2007) were more ruthless public sector economic managers than their corrupt National Party predecessors. Beattie boosted public infrastructure for business but the Queensland welfare system continued to lag behind the southern states. Queensland continued to suffer among the worst social, educational and health indicators in the country.[24] While stinting on public sector pay, the Beattie government spent tens of millions of dollars of public money to lure companies, such as Citicorp and Virgin Blue, to Queensland, in 'commercial-in-confidence' deals,[25] and sold off the TAB and the port of Gladstone to the private sector.

Foreign and refugee policies

Labor passed up a significant opportunity to mobilise and expand its support base during the campaign against the US led invasion of Iraq in early 2003. The ALP was as enthusiastic as the Howard government about the value of the US alliance, the US invasion of Afghanistan and the need to boost military spending. Iraq, however, was different. Labor declared its opposition to the invasion plans of President George W. Bush because they lacked the constitutional fig leaf – sanction by the UN Security Council – often demanded by Labor as a condition for supporting US led wars. The ALP also wanted to capitalise on the surge of popular opposition to the impending war in the summer of that year. Compared to the deployment of Australian troops to Afghanistan, which was supported in October 2001 by 66 per cent of Australians, exactly the same proportion opposed a US invasion of Iraq in February 2003. On the weekend of 15–16 February, 800 000 protested across the country, the biggest demonstrations in Australian history. Labor leaders saw an opportunity but failed to seize it. They repeated every lie about Saddam Hussein's supposed possession of weapons of mass destruction[26] and expressed their willingness to endorse the war if it was backed by the UN Security Council. They appeared at anti-war events but actually opposed one of the movement's most basic demands: no war. The result was that Labor antagonised pro-war hawks but appeared prevaricating to those who were furious about Australian participation in the pending US attack.

Economic policy and foreign policy were two clear areas in which there were large constituencies critical of important features of the Coalition government's agenda, out of which Labor might have forged election winning margins during the early 2000s. But because its commitment to managing capitalism and its support for the US alliance prevented it from adopting clear cut, principled and consistent positions favourable to the working class, the ALP failed to do so. There were other areas where such a large potential constituency was not so obvious but where Labor could have built support if it had taken a stand. These included Aboriginal land rights, national security legislation and asylum seekers. In what follows we focus on the last of these.

The Howard government's approach to refugees built on the Keating government's strategy of mandatory detention and refined it into a policy of more extreme psychological and physical abuse. As the number of boats carrying asylum seekers fleeing persecution at home rose from 13 in 1997–8 to 42 in 1998–9, to a still paltry 75 in 1999–2000, the government issued press releases designed to create alarm about 'the biggest assault on our borders ever'. The media chimed in with increasingly hysterical warnings about 'invasions'. The government passed legislation and introduced regulations to criminalise 'people smuggling', vested the Commonwealth and states with powers to intercept boats at sea and introduced the notorious temporary protection visas, which kept their holders in a state of permanent anxiety.[27] Existing detention centres were expanded and new ones opened, forming Australia's own desert-based Gulag Archipelago, including the Woomera, then Baxter, centres in South Australia, and the Curtin and Port Hedland centres in Western Australia. The ALP, which had created the precedent of locking up asylum seekers, backed these measures. In June 1999, Shadow Immigration Minister Con Sciacca boasted that the ALP was 'as tough as, if not tougher than, the government when it comes to illegal immigrants'.[28] Labor limply condemned the government for playing wedge politics and stoking racism, but itself gave credibility to racism by passing the Coalition's legislation.[29]

There was resistance to the racist offensive against asylum seekers. In cities and country towns, supporters of the refugees mobilised, but it was the actions of the asylum seekers in the detention centres that did most to highlight their appalling plight. Their protests ranged from hunger strikes and sewing their lips together to a mass breakout from the Woomera detention centre in 2000. ALP leaders turned their backs on their desperate plight.

Labor's capitulation to racism reached its nadir in the last week of August 2001 when Captain Arne Rinnan of the Norwegian freighter, the *MV Tampa*, headed to Christmas Island intending to land 433 asylum seekers picked up from an Indonesian fishing vessel that had broken down in international waters. Captain Rinnan never made it to Australian soil: on 29 August, on the orders of the Howard government, Special Air Services (SAS) commandos boarded the *Tampa* and turned it back. Parliament was in session and the issue dominated proceedings that day and for days afterwards. Beazley had already backed the government in opposing the entry of the *Tampa* prior to the SAS operation. On hearing that the SAS had effectively hijacked the *Tampa*, Beazley defended the Howard government's actions, saying that 'In these circumstances, this country and this Parliament do not need a carping Opposition'.[30]

With the Democrats, Greens and independents, Labor blocked the government's Border Protection Bill in the Senate on the night of the *Tampa* hijack. The Bill would have retrospectively validated the government's actions and denied those on board the right to claim asylum.[31] More than that, it empowered the government to direct police, customs officials, public servants or members of the armed forces to seize 'any vessel', using force if necessary to remove the ship and its crew and passengers 'outside the territorial sea of Australia'.[32] Less than four weeks later, Labor dropped its opposition and voted for an amended version of the Bill and other government measures that underpinned what the prime minister called the 'Pacific Solution'. Labor therefore supported the removal of Christmas Island and other important landfalls for refugees from Australia's immigration zone. This reduced the refugees' access to the Australian legal system.[33]

The November 2001 election took place in the aftermath of the *Tampa* incident and the attacks on the World Trade Center and Pentagon. During the election campaign, the government stirred up anti-Muslim racism and hysteria about terrorists arriving in boats, while Labor boasted of its tough position on asylum seekers. When in early October the government denounced a group of asylum seekers for throwing their children overboard, a claim later proven to be untrue, Beazley joined in the condemnation.[34] Not even the sinking of the *SIEV-X* and the drowning of 353 of its 397 passengers on 19 October was enough to shift the ALP from its support for the government's drastic measures.[35] Only months later did the ALP, with the support of the minor parties, move to establish a Senate select committee to examine the 'children overboard' incident and the sinking of the *SIEV-X*.

Did the ALP have any alternative if it wished to avoid electoral annihilation? Years of racist propaganda about asylum seekers, sponsored by both Labor and the Coalition, had had their effect. Surveys by the ALP and the AWU at the time of the *Tampa* incident demonstrated that a large majority of the public supported a hard line stance against asylum seekers.[36] Yet, contrary to some despairing liberal commentary at the time, the public was not inherently racist. Two years earlier most people had welcomed the arrival, on safe haven visas, of 4000 Kosovars and nearly 2000 East Timorese fleeing war and persecution in their homelands.[37] In 2001 Labor controlled every state and territory government, had guaranteed access to the media, hundreds of parliamentarians in state, territory and federal parliaments, tens of thousands of members and a mass base in the trade unions. Had the Party defended the rights of asylum seekers in the late 1990s and early 2000s, it is possible that Labor could have swung the public debate. It was not as if there was no audience inside the Party and among a broader activist layer for the ALP to build upon. In November 2001, two Young Labor activists, Matt Collins and Siobhan Keating, set up Labor for Refugees, which quickly drew support from many in the Party, including Carmen Lawrence on the left and the right's John Robertson, secretary of the New South Wales Labor Council. A combination of speeches and press releases from the Party leadership condemning the government's treatment of asylum seekers, together with support for Labor for Refugees and the broader refugee solidarity movement, could have opened up the space for much more powerful opposition to the government's policies.

Labor did the opposite: the Party leaders promoted public hostility towards boat people through its current rhetoric and by invoking Labor's own record in office in opposition. Instead, it was the Greens, a party with only one senator, 2000 members and a primary vote of only 2 per cent at the 1998 election, who took the fight to the government over the *Tampa*, helped create a debate in society and gave heart to the hundreds of thousands of Labor supporters dismayed by their own leader's capitulation to the government. The Greens were rewarded with an additional 330 000 votes at the 2001 elections. Beazley's stance, by contrast, disgusted thousands of Labor supporters. Former Whitlam ministers Tom Uren and Moss Cass were only the most prominent Labor figures to endorse the Greens at the 2001 election. Other lesser known Labor activists helped by handing out how to vote cards for the Greens on election day.

Attempting to neutralise refugees as an election issue by surrendering to the government only shifted political debate in Australia to the right. Even if Labor had not convinced a majority of the electorate to oppose the government's demonisation of refugees, a firm stand against it would at least have given voters a reason to vote for the ALP and served the Party well in the future, as opposition to conscription had in 1966. Instead, voters were left with a choice between two parties, each vowing a hard line on 'illegals'. The only difference was that the one in government and implementing these draconian measures had greater credibility on the issue. What incentive was there to vote for the carbon copy when you could have the original?

WorkChoices and the Your Rights at Work campaign

After Labor's fourth consecutive federal election loss in 2004, morale in the Party plummeted. The strategy of tailing the government on the most important questions of the day and failing to campaign seriously on the issues on which it had established some differentiation had failed. The ALP finally broke through in 2007 under circumstances it had avoided for years, namely, in a political struggle that drew hundreds of thousands of people onto the streets around working class interests. Throughout the long years of Coalition domination, Labor had condemned, stood aloof from or, at best, offered lukewarm support for mass action against the Howard government, whether for the 1996 Parliament House demonstration, the MUA picket lines in 1998 or the massive antiwar mobilisations of 2003. So in 2005, when the Coalition government rammed through WorkChoices, its drastic anti-union legislation, the trade unions, rather than the politicians, again took the lead.[38]

On the face of it, the circumstances of the union campaign were not auspicious. With the exception of the momentous waterfront dispute, the employers and federal government had generally been successful in their efforts to reduce the role of unions, which, in many cases, simply refused to engage in any serious resistance. Union membership, already substantially lower in 1996 than 13 years earlier, declined further under the Howard government. But with WorkChoices, the government painted the union leaders into a corner. They now had to fight or face being entirely marginalised.

And so, after some initial hesitation, and nudged along by pressure from left wing unions in Victoria and Western Australia, the ACTU launched the Your Rights at Work campaign. Its centrepiece was an extensive advertising campaign to highlight the damage caused by WorkChoices, supplemented by community focused publicity events. Although they did not feature in the ACTU's original plan, mass demonstrations also became an important element of the campaign. Initially called by individual labour councils, the first day of action in 2005, over 30 June and 1 July, was a big success. Across the country, more than a quarter of a million marched. The success encouraged the ACTU to back further demonstrations in late 2005 and in 2006. These were the largest union mobilisations in Australian history. Hostility to WorkChoices saw, according to Newspoll, Coalition support fall from 48 per cent in February 2005 soon after its re-election to 37 per cent in October.

The ALP leadership initially shuffled as awkwardly around WorkChoices as it had around the 1998 waterfront battle. For several months Beazley would not commit to scrapping the legislation if Labor won power. Sensing that public opposition to WorkChoices was growing in the first half of 2005, however, Labor eventually jumped on board the Your Rights at Work bandwagon. Beazley spoke at the first union rally in June 2005 and promised to 'rip up' WorkChoices. Labor's regular repetition of this promise thereafter significantly boosted the Party's appeal. Here at last was Labor doing what many of its followers believed it should have done for years: taking a determined stand against the Howard government on an important issue. Labor governments in Victoria and New South Wales used hostility to WorkChoices to win re-election in 2006 and 2007. Labor leaders nevertheless emphasised to business that they were not opposed to labour market reform as such. Beazley argued that

> The Prime Minister's industrial relations attack is not about reform. It is not about the long-term interests of the Australian economy or its people. He says we suffer from reform fatigue; we do not. We just understand what reform is now needed.[39]

Instead of continuing Howard's frontal assault on the trade unions, Labor promised to resume and extend the Hawke and Keating 'reform' agenda, which had done so much to weaken trade unions and undermine long established working conditions.

After nearly 18 months of mass mobilisation, the ACTU switched the focus of the Your Rights at Work campaign to a 'vote Labor' strategy, with a particular focus on the Coalition's marginal seats. The slogan 'Your rights at work: worth fighting for' was replaced in November 2006 by 'worth voting for' and the national days of action were brought to an end. But as Labor rode high in the opinion polls following the elevation of Kevin Rudd to the Labor leadership in December 2006, the ACTU allowed the new leadership team of Rudd and his deputy Julia Gillard to push Labor's industrial relations policies steadily to the right and offered the unions less and less in return for their unstinting support.

The ALP's industrial relations platform, entitled *Forward with Fairness*, was released in two stages during 2007. While promising a series of improvements to industrial relations laws, it retained many elements of WorkChoices and was particularly strict on strikes and union rights. Any industrial action taking place outside very narrowly prescribed limits would be met 'with the full force of the law'. Pattern bargaining (joint action by workers employed by different enterprises) was prohibited, and union officials' right of entry to workplaces was highly restricted. Closed shop or union preference arrangements were banned. Where strikes threatened to 'cause significant harm to the wider economy or to the safety or welfare of the community', a new institution, Fair Work Australia, could 'end the industrial action and determine a settlement between the parties'.[40] Labor promised to extend the life of the Howard government's union-bashing Australian Building and Construction Commission (ABCC), before replacing it in 2010 with an institution that had the same brief and powers. Militant unionists dubbed Labor's industrial relations platform WorkChoices Lite.

Forward with Fairness demonstrated a change in relations between the ALP's parliamentary leadership and the union leaders. The senior politicians appreciated the effort that the unions were putting into campaigning for Labor in 2007 but they did not return the favour. What is more, the union leaders approached the parliamentary leadership as supplicants, believing that if Labor lost the election, unionism would be dead in Australia. Rudd and Gillard made sure that the union leaders understood their subordinate position. In a painful snub on election eve, Rudd declared that trade unions would not enjoy any special relationship with a Labor government, that rebuilding union membership would never become his government's responsibility and that if pursuing 'the national interest . . . means having a fight with any trade union in the future about any matter, I am more than prepared to do so'.[41]

The situation in the lead up to the 2007 election was very different from those when Labor took office in 1972 and 1983. In 1972, rank and file union militants were on the attack and the political and business establishment was in retreat, which gave union leaders considerable influence in shaping Labor policy and forcing it to the left. In 1983, the militants were still capable of mounting strikes on their own initiative, and business was looking for an alternative to Fraser. Union leaders could persuade business and the ALP that they were a force capable of disciplining workers in the name of consensus. By 2007, however, union activists had been in retreat for 25 years, strike levels and union coverage were at historic lows, and business was confident and eager to further unwind past industrial gains. The union leaders were in a weak position to make demands on the ALP's parliamentary leadership.

Kevin 07

What were Labor supporters to make of the Party's new leader, Rudd, who was clearly cut from the same right wing cloth as his predecessors? After becoming leader, he quickly emphasised the three pillars of his politics: support for 'mainstream' and 'conservative' economics, 'rock solid' adherence to the US alliance, and a 'hard-line stance' on national security.[42] None of this was any surprise to those who had followed his career. Rudd's reputation as an economic conservative had been established in the early 1990s when he was the head of the Queensland Cabinet Office under the Goss government. For his efforts in cutting back the public service, he earned the nickname 'Dr Death'. Rudd's ambition was to have the ALP adopt an agenda like that of the British Labour Party under Tony Blair. He pitched the Party's message squarely at 'aspirationals', 'working families' and small business owners, with a firm emphasis on reward for individual effort.

Rudd was, with Beazley, one of the most ardently pro-American of Labor's leading politicians. In 1993 he had attended the first US–Australian

Leadership Dialogue along with senior figures in Washington policy circles, such as Dick Cheney, Richard Armitage, Paul Wolfowitz and Bob Zoellick. In the run up to the 2003 US invasion of Iraq, Rudd repeated George W. Bush and Tony Blair's claims that the Iraqi government possessed weapons of mass destruction, the main pretext used to justify the war.[43]

Business leaders knew that they could sleep easily with Rudd in charge. His first overseas visit as Party leader was to New York where Rupert Murdoch declared that the new Labor leader would make a good prime minister.[44] During 2007, the media's attitude to Howard steadily cooled and warmed to Rudd. Labor promised to retain much of WorkChoices, giving business most of what it wanted but without the attendant union opposition. The ALP vowed to improve the nation's creaking infrastructure – ports, roads and railways – which was hampering exports and international competitiveness. With Labor in power in all states and territories, the federal leadership appealed to business on the grounds that an ALP government in Canberra could reduce antagonisms between state and federal jurisdictions. Labor's Education Revolution was aimed squarely at developing skills as inputs for business rather than the capacities and critical abilities of young people so they could enjoy and understand the world.

While firmly on the right of the ALP, Rudd also had to appeal to those fed up with the right wing agenda of the Howard government. Before being elected leader he had sought to establish his caring credentials by expressing his admiration for the anti-Nazi Lutheran priest Dietrich Bonhoeffer, his commitment to 'the marginalised, the vulnerable and the oppressed', and his hostility to the Howard government's worship of the market.[45] In an implicit criticism of Beazley's 'small target' strategy, Rudd promised, on taking the leadership, that Labor would offer 'an alternative not an echo'.[46] The Party, including the left from which Julia Gillard had emerged, rallied around the new leader and his agenda. Backed by the media, Labor opened up a commanding lead over the Coalition in the polls.

But there was rather less to Rudd's alternative than met the eye. Two of his first decisions as Party leader were to abandon Mark Latham's 2004 election promises to protect old growth forests in Tasmania and to cut funding for wealthy private schools. Labor backed Gunns Limited's proposal for an environmentally destructive pulp mill in northern Tasmania and, at its 2007 national conference in further testimony to the Party's weak commitment to environmental concerns, overturned its three mines policy on uranium mining. This had been one of the few ALP policies that, however watered down, still bore the stamp of the struggles of the 1970s.

Labor also backed the Howard government's July 2007 Northern Territory Emergency Response. This drastic intervention used a scare about child abuse, manufactured by the media, to introduce compulsory acquisition of Aboriginal land and assets, welfare quarantining – to restrict Aborigines' decisions about how they spent their pensions and other government payments – and the termination of Aborigines' right to determine who could enter their land through the permit system. Many Aborigines justifiably damned the Northern Territory Intervention from the start as a harsh, racist and paternalist act. Among other protests, 400 participants at the August Garma Festival in Arnhem Land signed a resolution denouncing the government's land grab.[47] They found no support among national ALP leaders: Labor opposed only the abolition of permits on the spurious grounds that this might give free rein to paedophiles.

In July it was left to the media to take up the cudgels on behalf of Indian-born Gold Coast doctor Muhamed Haneef who was imprisoned, and then deported at the behest of the Howard government on the unfounded charge of providing support to a terrorist organisation. In October, Rudd confirmed his opposition to same sex marriage.[48] And, at Labor's campaign launch, Rudd emphasised once again his conservative economic credentials, telling the Party faithful to loud acclaim that

> I have no intention today of repeating Mr Howard's irresponsible spending spree. Today I am saying loud and clear that this sort of reckless spending has to stop.[49]

Little wonder then that the Melbourne *Herald Sun* could write of Rudd:

> By out-Howarding Howard, he can slot into Howard's job and go on as things were before the PM got too smart with WorkChoices and the war in Iraq. Despite promising on his elevation to the ALP leadership... to be 'an alternative not an echo', there is not a sliver of difference between the Government and Opposition on many key issues.[50]

Nor did Gillard, as Rudd's deputy, give any indication that the ALP's policies in office would depart from this agenda.

Labor's response to global warming was indicative of its attempt to appear to be doing something progressive without in any way challenging business. The Howard government's refusal to ratify the Kyoto Protocol, its long years of climate change denial and its tardy and half-hearted commitment to emissions trading – widely (if erroneously) considered to be essential to arresting global warming – were matters of public concern that also worried business leaders. Howard was an obstacle to any serious policy on climate change in Australia. Rudd's promise of a full blooded market-based emissions trading scheme gave the appearance of action while committing Labor to subsidies for polluters.

At the November 2007 federal election, Labor – campaigning with the slogan Kevin 07 – tapped into a widespread perception that it was time for a change. The Party was backed by most of the mass media; even arch conservative columnists such as the *Australian*'s Janet Albrechtsen had by now given up on Howard.[51] On 24 November, the Coalition government and John Howard, MHR for the seat of Bennelong since 1974, were swept out of office: the ALP harvested 1 million more votes than it had in 2004. Twelve years of conservative rule had ended; the way was now open for Kevin 07 to demonstrate what kind of alternative his new government would pursue.

Chapter 9

THE RUDD–GILLARD GOVERNMENT

The new Labor government, elected on Rudd's promise of 'an alternative, not an echo', for the most part improvised on themes played by the Howard government over the preceding 13 years. There were some exceptions, but continuity in policy was far more evident than any clean break. Continuity, not just with the Howard government but with the Hawke and Keating governments before that. Adherence to orthodox economics, privatisation and the use of market mechanisms backed by coercive centralised control in the delivery of public services, employer friendly industrial relations reform, firm support for the US alliance, racism towards Aborigines and asylum seekers, and lack of action on climate change all characterised the Labor government of 2007–10. The interests of capitalists prevailed over those of Labor's working class supporters.

From neoliberalism to Keynesianism and back again

The exact content of Labor's economic agenda shifted dramatically during the 2008–9 global financial crisis, the defining event of the period – from neoliberalism to massive government intervention – but in both cases Labor's policy was entirely in accord with the dominant trend endorsed and promoted by the OECD. At the outset, Labor was determined to establish itself as a fiscally conservative government.[1] Shortly after Labor's first

budget in May 2008, in which Treasurer Wayne Swan projected a surplus of
$21.7 billion, Rudd told the Victorian ALP conference that

> We cut out waste and pared back the excesses of the previous Liberal gov-
> ernment. Every single dollar of new spending in this Budget was more than
> matched by savings elsewhere. As a share of GDP, we have reduced govern-
> ment spending to its lowest level since 1989. And tax as a proportion of
> GDP has also been reduced. Delegates, what the Budget demonstrated . . . is
> that the Australian Labor Party is now unmistakably the party of responsible
> economic management.[2]

According to Melbourne's *Herald Sun*, 'Wayne Swan's first Budget looks like
being the one Peter Costello always wanted to deliver'.[3]

The crash in the world financial system in September 2008 put paid
to Labor's fiscal conservatism for 18 months: its neoliberal orthodoxy was
replaced overnight by enthusiasm for large scale government intervention.
The Australian Labor government took its lead from the Bush administration, committing billions of dollars to underwrite bank deposits and
interbank lending, followed soon after by a stimulus package of $10 billion
in December and a further $42 billion in February 2009. The Reserve Bank
slashed its cash interest rate to 3 per cent.

In the face of the biggest crisis in the world economy since the Great
Depression, Rudd ramped up populist appeals. The problem, he argued, was
'extreme capitalism and unrestrained greed that have perverted so much of
the global financial system', through the activities of 'predatory speculators'.[4]
The fundamental cause did not lie in the logic of capitalist accumulation –
that is, production subordinated to profit making – or in the material world
at all, but was free market ideology that, for reasons unexplained, had
shaped economic policy for 30 years. This was akin to the populist Labor
tradition before the 1950s, when sections of the Party denounced 'the money
power' and advocated the extension of state control and ownership. Now
a section of the respectable economics profession, which included its revi-
talised Keynesian wing and pragmatic exponents of neoclassical theory, also
blamed economic problems on greedy speculators. The solution was a more
regulated, gentler form of capitalism.[5] Rudd conveniently remained silent
on Labor's own leading role in pioneering neoliberal policies in the 1980s
and 1990s.

After suffering a scare in the months after the Wall Street meltdown in late 2008, the Australian economy bounced back fairly quickly. When measured in per capita terms, GDP fell by 1.5 per cent in the year to September 2009,[6] yet, taken as whole, Australia fared rather better than any other OECD member state. Unemployment peaked at less than 6 per cent and for those who kept their jobs and full time hours, the situation was relatively benign. The combination of federal government cash handouts, first home buyers' grants, lower petrol prices and lower mortgage interest rates boosted household disposable income in the year to June 2009 by 9 per cent.[7] On the other hand, in December 2009 household debt exceeded GDP for the first time.[8] The buoyancy of the Australian economy owed something to the government's stimulus spending and its guarantee of bank deposits. But the ALP could hardly claim credit for the continuing boom in mineral exports to China, which played such a crucial role in sustaining growth in Australia. Nor was Labor responsible for the fact that Australian banks were just starting to expand their exposure to the market for dubious US mortgaged-backed securities when it collapsed.[9]

By the second half of 2009 the housing market was recovering, but interest rates were on their way back up. Rising house prices continued to make first home ownership difficult for many in their 20s and 30s. If the government had lurched away from the main tenets of neoliberalism during the global financial crisis, this was only a short term manoeuvre to pull capitalism back from the abyss. Very soon it was warning that a return to a balanced budget would involve 'difficult and unpopular cuts' and that economic recovery would involve 'belt tightening' and harder work, in plain language, cuts in working class living standards.[10] In February 2010 Treasurer Swan told the National Press Club of his intention to swing the axe on spending to 'improve the sustainability of government finances over the medium-term'. While trotting out wildly optimistic growth forecasts, he returned to the theme of fiscal conservatism in the May budget, establishing a theme for Labor's election campaign.[11] If the forecasts were not realised, the tightening of access to disability pensions and the elimination of the Medicare rebate for mentally ill people who see social workers made it clear that the government was prepared to cut deep to reduce the deficit, but not until after the 2010 election.

Meanwhile, Labor did not touch those who had benefited from what Rudd had called 'extreme capitalism'. At the height of the crisis, in response to widespread public dissatisfaction at sky high CEO salary packages, the government asked the Productivity Commission to prepare a report on their pay.[12] The Commission produced its report in the summer of 2010 but no action was taken by the government. It chastised banks that raised home lending rates by more than the increase in the central bank rate, generating enormous profits in the process, but did nothing to force them to cut their rates.[13] Prominent union leader and ALP member John Sutton lamented that

> Kevin Rudd's grand treatise on the failures of capitalism a few months into the global financial crisis [is] ending with a whimper rather than a roar . . . Despite the effect of the GFC [global financial crisis], tough talk of regulatory reform now looks like empty promises.[14]

The party of privatisation

Previous governments, Labor and conservative, had in the past owned vital economic assets. These included road, railway, tram, bus, postal, telephone, radio, television, water, sewerage and power networks, cattle stations, butcher shops, shipping lines and coal mines, and electronics, weapons and clothing factories. In the 1980s Labor reversed its commitment to state ownership and became a party of privatisation. Enterprises that it had not sold off before losing office in 1996, such as Telstra, were privatised by the Howard government.

Despite widespread public concern about vital industries being left to the vagaries of the market and the price gouging and fat executive salaries associated with the privatised entities, Labor under Kevin Rudd and Julia Gillard made no move to renationalise any of the privatised public assets. Instead, it continued the Howard government's approach of throwing billions of dollars at private companies or public–private partnerships. In April 2009 the Rudd government announced its decision to establish a national broadband network with an investment of up to $43 billion. This was to be a public–private partnership and sold off to the private sector after five years.[15] The state was to bear all the risk in establishing crucial infrastructure from which business was to be the main beneficiary. Likewise,

the Rudd government backed the failed 2008 attempt by the Iemma government in New South Wales to sell off electricity generation and retail-
ing, a sale that was blocked by trade unions at the ALP state conference
of that year. More successful was Queensland's Anna Bligh who, shortly
after leading Labor to a fifth consecutive election victory in February 2009,
announced a wide ranging $15 billion privatisation program that included
the sale of port facilities, timber plantations, motorways and Queensland
Rail's coal freight operations.[16] The Rudd government lent Bligh its full
support.

The Labor government's commitment to market solutions and subsidies for business was also apparent with its response to global warming.
Rudd had declared global warming to be 'the great moral challenge of our
time'.[17] To combat it, his government proposed a market-based emissions
trading scheme (ETS) like that of the European Union. This plan was flawed
from the outset. The European experience had shown that the market could
not be used to fix the very problems that it had created.[18] Business had
too much money invested in fossil fuels and related industries to let governments impose sufficiently heavy penalties to change their behaviour.[19]
So it proved in Australia. In December 2008, the government published a
White Paper in which it outlined its carbon pollution reduction scheme
(CPRS), which mandated a target of only 5 per cent reduction in emissions below 2000 levels by 2020, far below what was required. Polluting
companies were offered a range of subsidies, while households were to
be only partially compensated for the increased cost of energy and other
goods and services that would result. Environmental groups slammed the
scheme.[20] The major business groups complained that it did not offer
them enough. In May 2009 the government announced even bigger subsidies for polluting industries and, following negotiations with Coalition
leader Malcolm Turnbull in November, a still more generous scheme for
business.[21] The government's Bill never passed into law because of an internal revolt within the Coalition and Turnbull's replacement by the more
aggressive Tony Abbott. The failure of Rudd's ETS legislation was a step
forward as it would have done nothing to curb global warming and consti-
tuted only a massive transfer of taxpayer funds to the worst polluters. The
regressive nature of the ETS was confirmed in April 2010 by the Grattan
Institute, whose founding members included the Labor government and

BHP Billiton.[22] In the same month Labor decided to shelve the scheme indefinitely.[23]

Coddling the rich, squeezing the poor

Compared to the Whitlam government, which took office at the high point of working class struggle and pressure from the left, the Rudd-Gillard government had a much freer hand to pursue regressive tax and social security policies. Its much vaunted responsible economic management was only meant to apply to workers and the poor. The wealthy were to be coddled, just as they had been under Howard. The regressive income tax cuts promised by the Howard government during the 2007 election campaign, which disproportionately benefited the rich, were delivered in full in Labor's 2008 budget. In the same year the government instigated a review of the tax system chaired by Treasury Secretary Ken Henry.

The government's much anticipated response to the Henry Review in 2010 did nothing to increase the progressiveness of taxation in Australia. It maintained the policy of favouring superannuation over the age pension, while throwing crumbs into the super accounts of the low paid. The wealthy benefited disproportionately from the flat, low tax rate on superannuation fund earnings, which was not changed. Those with healthy superannuation accounts, overwhelmingly middle and upper class men, would also continue to enjoy one of the Howard government's biggest give-aways to the rich, tax free income from their super funds, once they reached the age of 60. Tax breaks for negative gearing, which allowed those with investments – evidently the better off – to claim their interest expenses against tax remained in place, thereby denying Treasury billions of dollars in foregone tax revenue.[24] Labor tried to use its distance from individual businesses and industries to redistribute from the superprofits of the mining sector to the average profits in the hand of the whole capitalist class by proposing a resources rent tax while cutting the company tax rate and promising new infrastructure spending for business. The government justified the new tax in populist terms: it would ensure that the 'Australian people' got a fair share of the returns from mining. Recognising that it mainly involved shifting income sideways rather than from top to bottom, many businesses and the International Monetary Fund welcomed this trade-off. The mining industry claimed that it would lead to large scale job losses and frozen investments.[25]

The government was committed to increasing the age pension to 27.5 per cent of average weekly earnings but also announced in its 2009 budget that the pension age would rise from 65 to 67 between 2017 and 2023, the first time that it had ever been increased. Labor also suspended welfare payments to parents of school-age children who were not attending school, a measure that was likely to have a particularly regressive impact on the most destitute of families.[26]

The Rudd government expanded spending on education and health but it maintained the same bias to the private sector and the same tendency to attack the working conditions of public sector employees evident under the Howard government. Labor increased spending on tertiary education in an effort to boost the proportion of the workforce aged between 25 and 34 with university degrees to 40 per cent, but not by enough to make up for years of neglect. Outlays on higher education were projected to rise significantly in 2009–11. But even at the end of this triennium they would still only be three-quarters of the OECD average, as a proportion of GDP, and on this measure they were projected to decline after 2011.[27] The government promised to index university funding from 2011, but the baseline had been so eroded since 1995, when indexation was terminated under Paul Keating, that this policy would only prevent the situation from deteriorating further. Thousands of new university scholarships were offered, but access to Youth Allowance, which enabled many students to gain some financial independence from their parents, was tightened at the same time.[28] The Howard government's ban on universal student unionism, designed to politically silence tertiary students, was left in place. Student control of student affairs would remain as distant under Rudd as it had been under Howard.

Massive handouts to the already privileged private schools, introduced under Howard, continued. The Scotch Colleges and Shores would continue to dip into the public purse to pay for their rifle ranges and manicured lawns, while public schools in working class suburbs lacked crucial school infrastructure, staff and resources. The public school system was projected to receive only 37 per cent of Commonwealth government school funding in 2010–11, down from 43 per cent when the Howard government took office, equivalent to a drop of $1.4 billion.[29] In January 2010 Gillard, as minister for education, launched the My School website, which laid bare the vastly different educational performances (measured by a narrow range of criteria covered by the National Assessment Program Literacy and Numeracy – NAPLAN – tests) of well resourced and poorly resourced schools, further stigmatising the latter. Promoted by the government as a means to 'empower' parents,[30] My School was better described, in the words of long time Victorian teacher unionist Tess Lee-Ack, as

> a weapon to beat up on teachers (as lazy and/or incompetent) and a cover for
> the continuing failure of governments, state and federal, to adequately fund
> and resource public schools–especially those in working class areas.[31]

It would also lead to teaching to the test and rote learning, rather than developing children's understanding and their capabilities. Gillard and the Labor premiers crushed a proposed union ban on supervising the NAPLAN tests by organising a scab workforce and threatening disciplinary action and heavy fines against teachers and principals who took part in the ban.[32] Gillard's Education Revolution rejected all serious pedagogical research. It did advance the project of drilling and ranking students to provide their end 'users', the employers, with more amenable human capital.

During the 2010 election campaign, Gillard, now prime minister, boasted that she had stood up to the teachers' unions. She also promised to retain the formula for schools funding, which had delivered large sums to rich private schools, for at least another three years.[33]

Instead of expanding Medicare into a universal, free health system, the Rudd–Gillard government maintained the Howard government's basic agenda in health policy: reliance on private provision of health services outside hospitals and market-based administrative mechanisms. The government did, however, try to introduce means testing of the health care rebate for private insurance, a progressive measure blocked by the Opposition in the Senate. But even if this measure had been passed, it would not have eliminated the waste of funds on private insurance that could otherwise have been directed to public health. The public health system had been systematically undermined by the failure of Medicare to cover the full cost of services, which forced people into private health insurance. The long term solution of abolishing the private health care rebate, complemented by more progressive taxation to provide adequate resources for a universal system, would have involved a challenge to the insurance industry and the well off, something that was anathema to Labor under Rudd and Gillard.

With the public hospital system creaking under the strain of years of underfunding, the Rudd government announced a plan in March 2010 to increase federal control and, after pressure from state governments, some extra funding. Most of the additional funding was a mirage. Dr John Deeble, architect of Medibank and Medicare under the Whitlam and Hawke governments, wrote, 'There is nothing in the plan that would improve hospital care or access to it, or inject any extra money into public hospitals over the next 10 years'.[34] The plan to generalise the system of case mix funding, pioneered by the Kennett Liberal government in Victoria, is likely to create further stresses within the system and undermine patient care, as funding is allocated to hospitals that can demonstrate the highest productivity, that is, can process patients fastest.[35]

In summary, Labor pursued a highly orthodox economic policy program, firmly focused on advancing capitalist interests, during boom, bust and recovery. Market-like mechanisms in health and education were buttressed by the government's punitive command and control framework. Major infrastructure initiatives to meet the needs of an expanding economy were introduced but in forms that maximised the opportunities for profit making by the private sector. The government sought to meet the threat of global warming with a system that was flawed from the outset and provided large subsidies to polluting industries. The interests of public sector workers and users of public services were subordinated to those of high income earners anxious for tax cuts and continued subsidies for private health services and private schools. Business priorities continued to prevail.

From WorkChoices to WorkChoices Lite

Labor's pro-business agenda was also evident in its relations with the unions. Some union leaders had held out hopes that Gillard, as minister for workplace relations, would reveal a more union-friendly industrial relations agenda than she had foreshadowed in *Forward with Fairness* in 2007. As the months progressed and as selected elements of Labor's *Fair Work Australia Bill* were released in 2008 it became clear that the Rudd government was going to hold firm to the main anti-union features of WorkChoices. Of

particular concern was its insistence on keeping the union-busting Australian Building and Construction Commission (ABCC) until 2010 when it
would be incorporated with the same powers into the Fair Work system. As
the number of deaths on construction sites rose, the Commission was more
concerned about prosecuting workers who were defending their conditions
than employers for neglecting safety.[36]

When the ABCC took legal action against Construction, Forestry, Mining
and Energy Union (CFMEU) official Noel Washington and, later, against
CFMEU member Ark Tribe for refusing to inform on their fellow unionists,
anger over the Commission's activities spread through the union movement.
Determined to see an end to its punitive investigations, construction unions
launched a Rights on Site campaign to force Labor to scrap the Commission
and its coercive powers. In 2008 the unions mobilised tens of thousands
of their members in demonstrations around the country. In this period
the argument that Labor's new legislative program was little more than
WorkChoices Lite went from the margins of the labour movement into the
mainstream. Five months after receiving a warm welcome at the Victorian
ALP state conference in May 2008, Gillard's reception at a subsequent Party
conference in Melbourne was frosty.[37] The ACTU began to ramp up its
lobbying.[38]

When the Fair Work Australia Bill was finally tabled in parliament at the
end of November 2008, ACTU lobbying had evidently extracted some minor
concessions, but the bulk of the Bill's provisions relating to trade union rights
continued to reflect WorkChoices. The continuity with Howard's legislation
was highlighted at the 2009 ACTU Congress when CFMEU (Construction
Division) National Secretary Dave Noonan told delegates about the threat
to jail Ark Tribe:

> It is a shameful reflection on this Labor government that an ordinary construc-
> tion worker now faces the possibility of six months imprisonment because
> the government has not removed the most extreme laws left behind by John
> Howard.

Gillard responded with an anti-union diatribe against workers fighting for
their jobs and conditions on Melbourne's West Gate Bridge.[39]

The ABCC wasn't the only problem. Labor maintained the Howard
government's Fair Pay Commission for fully two years after taking office

and took no action to compensate low paid workers when the Commission awarded them a zero increase by the Commission in June 2009.[40] Some months later, Gillard was to boast that Labor's industrial relations laws had resulted in the lowest rate of increase in private sector wages since 1998.[41] 'Harmonisation' of occupational health and safety (OHS) legislation across the states and territories, a key element of Labor's package designed to bring about uniform national standards, threatened to result in a race to the bottom in protection of workers' rights.[42] Labor's award modernisation process, inherited from the Howard government, tended to converge on low, rather than the highest, standards across the various awards being merged.[43]

The government was assisted in its efforts to retain much of WorkChoices by the mostly uncritical public support lent to it by the ACTU. Secretary Jeff Lawrence described Labor's Fair Work Bill as 'major steps forward for Australian workers'.[44] When the Liberals under new leader Tony Abbott announced in February 2010 that the Coalition would be seeking to restore a series of WorkChoices provisions that had been scrapped by Labor, the ACTU went into bat for the government, declaring that its new laws had 'restored many rights for workers' and that the Fair Work Act was 'light years away from WorkChoices'.[45] In so doing, the ACTU gave the government the opportunity to pose as a friend of what it called 'working families' and failed to counteract pressure from business and the Coalition with a campaign for industrial reforms that would be of real benefit to workers and their unions. The ACTU likewise backed the government's regressive emissions trading scheme and trumpeted its management of the economy at every opportunity.[46]

Labor fails the oppressed

Because the Rudd government put the needs of business first, the circumstances of oppressed groups were neglected or made worse. Thus, the ALP had promised before the 2007 election to introduce paid parental leave, which would have brought Australia into line with every other OECD member state, with the exception of the United States. The government's Bill, tabled in May 2009, demonstrated a miserly attitude to working parents, particularly women. It provided for only 18 weeks paid parental leave, to take effect in 2011, and means tested payments, set at the minimum wage.[47]

This policy was less generous than the recommendations of the Productivity Commission report commissioned by the government and, indeed, was worse than that of any other OECD country.[48] When Abbott proposed a far more generous scheme in early 2010, to be financed by a 1.7 per cent tax on business, creating a furore amongst the Coalition's business supporters, Labor attacked Abbott from the right, ridiculing him for his suggestion that employers should help pay the costs of raising the next generation of workers.[49]

The Howard government had introduced a ban on same sex marriage in 2004, with the support of the Labor Opposition. Although the Rudd government lifted a range of discriminatory legal provisions relating to gay and lesbian couples in January 2009, it maintained the homophobic ban on same sex marriage, even as the Tasmanian and Victorian state Labor conferences voted in favour of lifting it.[50] When the ACT government introduced legally binding civil union ceremonies between same sex couples, the federal government vetoed the legislation. After she became prime minister, Gillard, who, unlike Rudd, is an atheist, also endorsed the ban. During the 2010 election campaign, Australia's first openly homosexual federal minister, Penny Wong, did the same. Not that it could claim that it was held back by force of public opposition, an argument often used by Labor supporters to justify government inaction on progressive reforms. Sixty per cent of people surveyed in 2009 supported equal marriage rights.[51]

Aboriginal policy: the genocide continues

The election of the Labor government raised hopes that its predecessor's racist policies towards Aborigines would be reversed. These hopes were quickly dashed. The Rudd government, following in the steps of Hawke and Keating, undermined the progressive legacy of the Whitlam and Fraser governments in this sphere. On 13 February 2008, the first day of parliamentary business, the new prime minister did extend an apology to the Stolen Generations of Indigenous Australians. Although this was popular, as it appeared that a historical page was being turned, Indigenous activist Gary Foley's description of the apology as 'yet another fraud in the long line of historically fraudulent acts and dishonest gestures that typify the indigenous experience of all governments in Australian history' was apt.[52] Rudd ruled out compensation for Aborigines who as children had been taken from their parents,[53] although the landmark *Bringing Them Home* report of 1997 had identified reparations as one of the most important elements of redress for the Stolen Generations.

The apology served as a fig leaf to cover the fact that the new government was more interested in maintaining the Howard agenda.[54] Most importantly, the racist Northern Territory Intervention was continued with only minor tinkering. Labor restored the permit system under which Aborigines determined who could visit their land, but vigorously pursued the Intervention's main purpose, to remove Aborigines from their traditional lands and destroy communal land ownership. It used a variety of methods.

The Howard government had identified 20 'hub towns' to be the focus of Northern Territory and federal government housing, infrastructure and social services. This project was continued under Rudd. In order to drive Aborigines into these hub towns, the Northern Territory Labor government announced in May 2009 that it would freeze all funding to more than 500 homelands, or outstations, prompting the angry resignation from the ALP of former deputy Northern Territory chief minister, Marion Scrymgour.[55] The Rudd government forced Aboriginal communities to sign over land to the Northern Territory government on 40 year leases in exchange for federal government funding for housing and infrastructure, thereby eliminating land rights that had been struggled for and won over decades.[56] The housing took forever to build. By February 2010 a total of two houses had been completed, in Wadeye, southwest of Darwin.[57]

The Rudd government maintained welfare quarantining, whereby 50 per cent of Centrelink payments were provided in the form of a Basics Card. This was humiliating, requiring its holders to line up in segregated queues when paying for goods and to travel long distances from outstations to access shops that accepted the card. It made life in remote outstations increasingly difficult and increased pressure on Aborigines to move to major towns and settlements. Singling out Aborigines for welfare quarantining meant that the Howard government had to suspend the Racial Discrimination Act. The Rudd government's solution in 2010 to this embarrassing feature of the Intervention was to extend welfare quarantining, thereby penalising white and black Australians. This did not disguise the fact that its main target was still Aborigines who were much more likely to be unemployed. As if to add insult to injury, the government signed the UN Declaration on the Rights of Indigenous Peoples in April 2009, despite the fact that its Intervention breached this Declaration in several important respects.

According to the government, the Intervention was a means to improve health in Indigenous communities. The evidence was mixed at best. In March 2009 the Sunrise Health Service, which covered clients in a wide region east of Katherine, reported that health outcomes had actually deteriorated under the Intervention.[58] Standards of nutrition had declined, and anaemia was on the rise. One year later, the Australian Indigenous Doctors Association complained that 'the ways in which [the Intervention] is being introduced and is being implemented are likely to contribute to the high burden of trauma and disease already carried by Aboriginal people across generations'.[59] The number of incidents of attempted suicide and self-harm in Northern Territory communities subject to the Intervention rose from 97 in the year prior to the Intervention to 181 in 2009.[60]

The Intervention severed several purposes. It undermined Aboriginal gains from the 1976 Land Rights (Northern Territory) Act, thereby placating the mining companies and pastoralists. The idea that land should be held in common and not traded on the market was a threat to capitalist norms, challenging the notion that everything in society should be a commodity. The very existence of Aborigines on outstations, for the most part living on social security and producing no profits for employers, was also an affront to capitalist expectations. Aborigines should be *made* to work for a boss and life made hell for them if they did not because they remained on their land. The scrapping of public services for people on outstations also had a cost cutting logic for the federal and Northern Territory governments.

Aborigines fought back against the Intervention. On 12 February 2008, the day before the government's apology to the Stolen Generations, 1500 Aborigines and their supporters protested against the Intervention on the lawns of Parliament House. The community at Yuendumu near Alice Springs was at the forefront of resistance: it held off welfare quarantining for many months and then refused to sign 40 year leases. Barbara Shaw and others at the Mount Nancy town camp in Alice Springs took the government to the UN Committee on the Elimination of Racial Discrimination. In May 2009 Tangentyere Council, which oversaw the affairs of town camps in Alice Springs, rejected a government offer of $125 million in exchange for signing land over to the government on a 40 year lease.[61] Only under threat of compulsory acquisition did the Council eventually agree to the government's terms.

Three hundred and fifty kilometres northeast of Alice Springs, 150 Alyawarr people from the prescribed community of Ampilawatja walked off their settlement, which had been seized under the provisions of the Intervention, in July 2009 and established a new settlement at Honeymoon Bore, 3 kilometres away, free from government control.[62] In a revival of the links between Aboriginal struggle and the trade union movement that had characterised the land rights campaigns of the 1960s and early 1970s, Richard Downs from Ampilawatja and Harry Jakamarra Nelson from Yuen- dumu, toured the east coast in October 2009, with union support, raising awareness about the reality of the Intervention.[63] Four months later a range of unions sent volunteers to Honeymoon Bore to erect the first house there for the residents.[64]

Repelling refugees

It was not only the Labor government's treatment of Aborigines that began to cause disquiet among some Labor supporters. This was also true of its response to asylum seekers. On taking office the Rudd government made some changes to the Howard government's Pacific Solution. It closed down the Nauru and Manus Island detention centres, and abolished temporary protection visas, but mandatory detention remained, and Ashmore Reef and Christmas Island continued to be excised from Australia for the purpose of processing claims by asylum seekers.[65] Australia's refugee intake remained at the same low levels set by the Howard government. The quota of refugees to be admitted in 2010 was 13 750. The government simply replaced the G4S corporation, whose record in running detention centres became notorious during the Howard years, with another private contractor.[66]

Labor's maintenance of the Coalition's strategy of intercepting and dis- rupting refugee movements by sea and the excision of offshore islands had another tragic consequence on 16 April 2009, when asylum seekers, whose boat was being boarded by the Australian Navy, set fire to it, causing an explosion that killed five people. Rudd described people smugglers as 'the vilest form of human life' who 'should rot in jail', a tactic which, although not directly damning the asylum seekers themselves, cast aspersions on them through guilt by association.[67]

During the 2007 election campaign, Rudd told a reporter from the *Aus- tralian* that a Labor government would turn back seaworthy boats headed

for Australia, a proposal Labor had originally strongly condemned when it
was first advanced by Pauline Hanson.[68] And he went on to do precisely that.
On 13 October 2009, the prime minister rang the Indonesian president to
ask him to intercept and turn around a boat carrying 255 Sri Lankan Tamil
asylum seekers heading for Christmas Island. The Indonesian Navy towed
the boat to the port of Merak in western Java, where the Tamils demanded
resettlement in Australia or another Western country.[69] The Australian government refused to take them in. The Tamils promptly went on a hunger
strike and refused to disembark until their demands were met. In the same
week, the Australian Customs ship *Oceanic Viking* picked up another 78
Tamil asylum seekers in Indonesian waters. On being told that the captain
was taking them to an Indonesian detention centre, the Tamils on board
also started a hunger strike and refused to get off the boat. Indonesia, which
was not a signatory to the 1951 UN Convention on Refugees, already held
3000 refugees in detention centres in appalling conditions.[70] As a result of
their determination, the 78 Tamils held on the *Oceanic Viking* were eventually offered rapid assessment of their claims and the opportunity for
resettlement in Australia or another Western country. Their compatriots in
Merak were not so fortunate: after six months those who remained on their
boat eventually surrendered and were transported to an Indonesian
detention centre.

In the first four months of 2010, Rudd removed any doubt that his government's approach to asylum seekers was any more humane than Howard's.
In February, the government announced details of its Anti People Smuggling and Other Measures Bill, which criminalised those who helped asylum
seekers even if they did so unwittingly or for humanitarian reasons. It was
a measure that threatened far reaching consequences for charities or political activists involved in refugee support work. In April the government
announced a freeze on the processing of Afghan and Sri Lankan asylum
seekers, who then made up two-thirds of all those in detention. Deakin
University law professor Mirko Bagaric told the *Sydney Morning Herald*
on 14 April:

> This is probably the most repugnant refugee policy of any Western country
> that is a party to the international refugee convention. I know of no precedent
> of anything approaching a Western democracy doing anything as brutal to
> refugees as this.[71]

Days later, the government announced the re-opening of the Curtin detention centre in Western Australia, which had been closed in 2002 following a series of protests and riots by detainees angry about the appalling conditions.

Meanwhile, conditions at the Christmas Island detention centre, which had taken over the role of the now mothballed centres at Woomera, Baxter and Port Hedland, went from bad to worse. It had quickly filled to capacity and in September 2008 the UN High Commission for Refugees told the Parliamentary Joint Standing Committee on Migration that it 'has all the characteristics of a medium-security prison'.[72]

The government's own statistics told the story of the continued inhumane treatment of asylum seekers under Labor. Immigration Minister Chris Evans had declared in July 2008 that detention was to be used 'as a last resort and for the shortest practicable time'.[73] In June 2010, the number of asylum seekers held in detention – 3760 – was identical to that at the height of the Howard Government's harsh refugee crackdown in 2000–1. More than 500 asylum seekers had been detained for more than six months, and 55 for more than a year.[74] The minister had promised to end the imprisonment of children in detention centres but, in June 2010, 240 children were being kept in 'alternative temporary detention in the community' on Christmas Island under circumstances, including strict curfews and barbed wire, that were similar to those in the detention centres.

Labor in combat fatigues

Although there were minor changes to Australia's foreign policy, there was fundamental continuity between the periods before and after the 2007 election. The Rudd government was just as committed as the Howard government to the US war on terror – the attempt by the US to impose its domination over the world by using its still unmatched military power. Rudd withdrew combat troops from Iraq in 2008, but this was by no means a radical step. It followed Britain's decision to pull out its forces and President Bush's declaration that 30 000 troops would be withdrawn after the US troop surge in 2007. The situation in Afghanistan was different. Labor had been as enthusiastic as the Coalition about sending troops to fight there.[75] For the ALP, the conflict in Afghanistan was the 'good war' sanctioned by the United Nations. Iraq was a sideshow; Afghanistan was 'Terrorism Central'.[76]

So, when the US's puppet government in Kabul, a collection of warlords, drug traffickers and corrupt politicians united only in their desire to enrich themselves with US funds, faced rising popular resistance, Rudd turned recruiting sergeant to prop it up. In April 2008, following his first state visit to the US, Rudd attended a NATO summit on Afghanistan in Bucharest and urged member countries to increase their troop deployments to sustain the US led occupation.[77] One year later, the Labor government dispatched its own little surge of 450 military personnel, and in its May 2008 budget doubled spending on the occupation to $1.2 billion.[78]

Contrary to the conventional left nationalist wisdom on these matters, Australia was not supporting the US occupation of Afghanistan because it was in any way a lapdog of the United States. Both Labor and Coalition governments wanted the US to secure its control over the Middle East and Central Asia: a strong US meant a strong Australia. Rudd saw in the alliance between the two countries, as much as Curtin and Menzies did, a means to boost Australia's own diplomatic clout within the southwest Pacific and southeast Asia. Defeat in Vietnam had weakened the power of the US and its allies. The first Gulf War of 1990–1 had gone some way to remedying that. The 9/11 attacks had given the US the opportunity to recover more lost ground. Australia shared with the US a keen desire for victory in Afghanistan to continue that process.

Israel was also crucial for US power in the Middle East, and the Rudd government maintained Australia's long standing support for this country, even as its international reputation soured following attacks on Lebanon in 2006, Gaza in 2009, and an aid flotilla in 2010. Australian support for Israel was rooted in its desire to see the country remain a watchdog for US (and, by extension, Australian) imperialist interests in the Middle East. Rudd frequently declared his 'lifelong friendship' with Israel, and on the 60th anniversary of its foundation, on 12 March 2008, the prime minister moved a motion in Parliament, with bipartisan support, to 'celebrate and commend the achievements of the state of Israel'.[79] There was no sympathy offered to the millions of Palestinians left to mourn *Al Nakba* (the catastrophe) in foreign countries, cast out from their homeland and barred from ever returning, or to those living under Israel's apartheid regime.

The Rudd government was acutely aware of challenges to US and Australian domination closer to home, in particular the threat posed by the rise of China. The US still retained overwhelmingly the biggest military arsenal in the world but was increasingly concerned about China's attempts to expand its own influence in the Asia–Pacific region. Chinese military force, although still weak compared to the US, was growing at a rapid rate,[80] and China was seeking to extend its influence in the region through aid and trade relations with countries hitherto regarded as lying within the Australian domain, including Fiji, East Timor and Papua New Guinea. A central feature of imperialist competition during the 20th century was now being replayed in the 21st. Changes in the relative strength of national economies and the pursuit of strategic advantage by each increased the chances of military conflicts.

These developments were the background to the Rudd government's May 2009 Defence White Paper, *Force 2030: Defending Australia in the Asia Pacific Century*, which identified China as a threat to Australian security interests. With a commitment of $100 billion, and a 21 per cent expansion of defence outlays in 2009–10, the White Paper ushered in the biggest boost to military spending in the country's peacetime history. The government announced that it would buy 12 new submarines armed with Tomahawk cruise missiles, a new fleet of 11 frigates and air warfare destroyers, and 100 new F35 Joint Strike Fighters capable of hitting targets at a great distance. This was Australian militarism on steroids. Globalisation, far from ushering in an age of peace, was simply remaking the military tensions of the 1930s and 1940s in the Asia–Pacific, but with a slightly different cast of characters. The Rudd government was determined that Australian imperialism would not be left behind in the competition for influence in the region.

From honeymoon to assassination

During the global financial crisis, the Rudd government's policies of under-writing the banks, pushing down interest rates and pumping billions of dollars into the economy, in the context of strong demand for Australian commodity exports, a relatively stable domestic banking sector and a resilient housing market, helped Australian business ride out the crisis with far less pain than its counterparts in most other countries.[81] Its positions on a series of important issues, from tax to industry policy, from foreign policy to Aboriginal rights, indicated that it was pursuing a conservative political agenda.

As a result, the Rudd government was very popular with business during its first two years in office. Business Council (BCA) President Graham Bradley remarked shortly before the government's second anniversary that 'There is . . . considerable alignment between the BCA's priorities and agenda and the government's priorities and agendas'.[82] The *Australian* named Rudd its Australian of the Year in January 2010.[83] Just as Hawke had worked closely with the BCA, the Rudd government had close links with the Australian Industry Group and its boss Heather Ridout, who was frequently consulted by the Rudd government on a wide range of matters,[84] leading some union leaders to note bitterly that she appeared to be a *de facto* member of Cabinet, whereas they had been left out in the cold.

Rudd may have denounced 'extreme capitalism' during the economic crisis but had no compunction about associating with some of its leading representatives. In February 2009, before an audience that included Telstra chief Sol Trujillo, Visy Industries CEO Dick Pratt and Rupert Murdoch, Rudd praised the largest owner of shopping malls in the world and Australia's richest man, Frank Lowy, for his 'courage' and 'resilience' in building his business empire.[85] Two months later, as Pratt, facing charges for illegal price fixing in the cardboard box industry, lay dying at Raheen, his mansion in Kew, Rudd and other senior Labor figures paid tribute to him and praised his contribution to Australian society.[86]

Although the prime minister and business formed something of a mutual admiration society for a period, Rudd's support base within the ALP was relatively fragile. He came to the leadership without a strong factional power base within the parliamentary Labor Party, the machine or the trade unions. Nor did Rudd enjoy the kind of loyalty that Whitlam or Hawke could count on among rank and file ALP members, while progressives became increasingly uneasy about his social conservatism. Apart from anything else, Rudd just did not appear to be a Labor man: he and his wife Therese Rein were by far the richest Labor family to have ever occupied the Lodge.[87] His conservative religious beliefs and his regular church going habits also jarred in some Labor circles. Rudd was supported within the Party because he had led the ALP to victory and was popular in opinion polls.

One significant asset that Rudd did have was the continued capitulation of the left of the Party to the government's right wing agenda. Just as Deputy Leader Brian Howe had provided Bob Hawke with left cover when the Hawke government was pursuing right wing policies in the 1980s, so Deputy

Leader Gillard provided the same service for Rudd. It was Gillard who was responsible for promoting Labor's Fair Work laws, who attacked militant unions and enthusiastically promoted the government's market agenda in education. Likewise, Finance Minister Lindsay Tanner was at the forefront of calls for cuts in public spending.[88] Defence Minister John Faulkner endorsed the deployment of an extra 30 000 US troops to Afghanistan in 2009. In the run up to the 2009 Party conference Martin Ferguson, like Gillard from the soft left subfaction, criticised the unions for their timid criticisms of Labor's industrial relations laws,[89] and as resources minister was a keen advocate for the uranium industry. Industry Minister Kim Carr, from the hard left, was responsible for dishing out hundreds of millions of dollars in subsidies to manufacturing companies,[90] while fellow faction member Jenny Macklin aggressively promoted the Northern Territory Intervention.

As for Labor's working class voters, Rudd initially enjoyed their support because he appeared to be someone who could defeat Howard, and then did. The usual post-election honeymoon followed for several months, while the Liberals were in disarray. His popularity was subsequently buoyed by the government's apparent success in managing the economy during the global financial crisis of 2008–9. Even in this period, however, leaders of blue collar unions regularly lambasted the prime minister at mass meetings of workers for his industrial relations policies and were applauded by their members for doing so. No rank and file workers insisted on defending Rudd as once they would have rallied around Hawke. Rudd was tolerated but not liked within the working class – when Labor won office in 2007 there was no evident increase in Party membership such as had occurred after Whitlam and Hawke first took office. Labor clubs on university campuses remained as inactive outside election periods as they had been in the last years of the Howard government.

Labor's continuation of Howard government policies, especially Work-Choices Lite and the Northern Territory Intervention, was compounded by its backflip on climate change and indefinite detention of Afghan and Sri Lankan refugees in early 2010. The ALP's constituency among militant workers and on the left, already eroded by Labor's decades long pursuit of conservative policies, became even more disillusioned. The government's decision to postpone any action on climate change, at first indefinitely and then until 2013, directly contradicted Rudd's identification of the issue as a major priority before the 2007 election and created wider concerns about

Labor's effectiveness in office. Business also complained about continued lack of certainty in this area.

From early 2010, sections of the mass media were increasingly critical of the Rudd government. As media support declined, Rudd's hold on office became vulnerable. Then, in response to the proposal for a mining superprofits tax, large mining corporations launched an hysterical and expensive advertising campaign, and attempted, as the banks had during the late 1940s, to involve the industry's workforce and other sections of the capitalist class in a mobilisation against the government. Labor was not prepared to conduct its own tough and consistent campaign against the mining companies by stoking populist, let alone working class, hostility to mining industry executives. Because Rudd would not fight, other sections of business were unwilling to stick their necks out to defend the new tax and the concomitant cut in the general company tax rate. At the same time the swing in mainstream economic thinking around the world, away from the need to stimulate the economy to prioritising cuts in public spending as the best means to restore profits, reinforced the Opposition's arguments that Labor was not moving far or fast enough to reduce government outlays.

During the first half of 2010, opinion polls indicated a slide in support for the ALP, and particularly for Kevin Rudd. His authority in the government and cabinet quickly drained away. The *Australian* encouraged speculation that Gillard would replace Rudd.[91] Sensing defeat at the coming federal election, right wing faction leaders moved quickly. On the night of 23 June 2010, they got the numbers to oust Rudd in favour of Gillard. Caucus confirmed the change the following morning, the first time that the Party had ever dumped a sitting prime minister during his first term in office.[92]

As they had under Whitlam from 1974, key Party leaders decided that the ALP could not improve its popular support by acting in the interests of its working class base, because this would alienate business. In the hope of salvaging a Labor victory at the impending federal election, they tried to refurbish the Party's brand image while shifting its policies to the right. Gillard seemed more saleable: they thought she had better people skills than Rudd. She also had much deeper factional ties in the ALP.

Australia's first woman prime minister was by no means a clean-skin. As Rudd's deputy, Gillard had been involved in all the major decisions taken by his government. As Minister for Workplace Relations she had responsibility for WorkChoices Lite and the ABCC. As Minister for Education, she had successfully stared down the teachers' unions and introduced My School. Earlier, she had fought to maintain Labor's policy of mandatory detention when it came under attack from Labor for Refugees at the 2004 national conference. In office, she was as enthusiastic a refugee baiter as Rudd. When she was acting prime minister in December 2008, Gillard had defended Israel's attack on Gaza. She retained not a shred of the left wing principles with which she had apparently entered politics.[93]

In her first public statement after taking office, the new leader acknowledged the positive contributions of John Howard and Peter Costello in continuing the economic reform program of the Hawke and Keating governments. Within two weeks she watered down the proposed new tax on mining profits, in the face of the mining corporations' campaign. She appeased racists by denouncing their critics, as John Howard had, for being politically correct. In this spirit, Gillard indicated her desire to limit population growth and migration, and intensified the government's brutal treatment of people seeking political asylum. Instead of blackmailing impoverished island states in the western Pacific to warehouse refugees arrested by Australian authorities, she sought to impose their imprisonment on East Timor.[94] Her commitment to putting a price on carbon emissions in 2013 had the same regressive implications for income distribution as Rudd's or, for that matter, Howard's proposals for dealing with global warming by means of market mechanisms.

The transition from Rudd to Gillard was a case of 'Meet the new boss, same as the old boss' on all substantive issues. By dumping Rudd, Labor achieved a boost in the polls. Hoping to capitalise on this honeymoon, Gillard called an election for 21 August.

The election campaign was mainly a contest over the images of Gillard and Abbott; the policy differences between Labor and the Coalition were minor.[95] Both leaders were committed to a right wing agenda that put the needs of business first. Their campaigns had an air of other worldliness in the common assumption that Australia could indefinitely withstand the ongoing turmoil of the world economy. Labor and the Coalition made predictions about a rapid return to a budget surplus and the paying down of debt; neither side promised any substantial new social programs.[96] Labor sought to position itself as more generous to business, slamming Abbott as an irresponsible high tax and spend politician for his plans to levy large corporations to pay for his parental leave scheme.[97]

Gillard and Abbott were unequivocal about their commitment to the war on Afghanistan.[98] When Abbott promised to reintroduce temporary protection visas for refugees, he faced no substantive opposition on the issue from Labor, which also sought to be tough on asylum seekers, for which both were condemned by Human Rights Watch.[99] Neither the ALP nor the Coalition advanced any firm plans to deal with global warming.

Both parties were adamant that the restrictions on unions, introduced by WorkChoices and maintained under Labor's Fair Work legislation, would stay. Gillard was under no pressure from trade union officials: when they were not heaping praise on the government's economic record, ACTU media releases focused on the threat posed by the Liberals to bring back Work-Choices, as if large parts of it were not still in effect.[100] While spending millions of dollars on electronic advertising, in a reprise of the Your Rights at Work campaign, the unions placed no serious pressure on Labor to improve its industrial legislation in its second term in office.[101] To disarm the issue, Abbott promised not to reinstate WorkChoices.

Committed to a conservative agenda, the ALP could not rouse any enthusiasm among its supporters. Labor's improved popularity in the wake of Gillard's elevation to the leadership was short lived. The Party's primary support in opinion polls slumped to the mid 30s, well below that of the Coalition.[102] By the third week of the campaign, what had seemed impossible six months previously – a Labor loss after only one term in office – had become a distinct possibility.[103] Gillard thrashed about, promising to reveal a 'new Julia', whose public appearances would not be scripted down to the last comma, semicolon and dash. But this involved no change in policy direction. Rudd, so recently booted out of the tent, was invited back in to join the election campaign in order to avoid the appearance of disunity in the ALP.[104]

Outdoing its 2007 effort by running the most right wing campaign in the Party's history, Labor lost its majority in the House of Representatives. The Party's share of the primary vote fell by over five per cent and its initial two party preferred vote dropped below fifty per cent.[105] But there was no sharp turn to the right in the electorate: most of the voters who abandoned the ALP went to the Greens and their preferences mainly flowed back to Labor. The ALP retained office only with the support of a Green, a liberal independent and two ex-National Party independents. But there was no hint that Labor would rethink the fundamental orientation of its policies in the ALP's responses to the election result. The first lesson Gillard drew was that 'our process of explaining our priorities and what we were doing simply broke down'.[106]

Business, despite the fickleness of its relationship with Labor, had benefited from the continuity from Howard to Rudd and Gillard. On the other hand Labor's working class supporters were left to ponder how, in voting out Howard, they had ended up with a government committed to the same basic policies on virtually every score.

Chapter 10

THE LABOR PARTY TODAY: WHAT'S LEFT

In this book we have argued that the Australian Labor Party can best be understood as a capitalist workers' party, working class in its supporters and union origins, capitalist in the policies that it has pursued. In chapter 5 we reviewed the material constitution of the ALP as it stood 70 years after its formation. We concluded that the party was still very much a capitalist workers' party at that time, but, alongside a fundamental continuity, there were also changes. Over the following 50 years further major changes have become apparent. The Party is obviously much older and has greater experience of holding office and, as a result, has become much more integrated into Australian capitalism.

These changes have to be situated within changes in the broader political economy. Capital itself has undergone substantial restructuring. The competitiveness and viability of Australian capitalism today depend much more on closer integration with international flows of finance and production than was the case five decades ago. Most importantly, the end of the postwar global boom in the early 1970s has affected the long term economic dynamism of Australian capitalism. Labor's approach to managing the economy has contributed and adjusted to these changes. Furthermore, the working class is more urban and larger than ever before. White collar workers are now a larger proportion of the working class, as industries such as education, hospitality, tourism, retail, and banking and finance have become much more significant employers. Union coverage has slumped, as has union militancy. These developments have all had an impact on the ALP.

Is the ALP, despite changes in its environment and its own characteristics, still a capitalist workers' party, or have these changes transformed the party? To answer this question we deal first with Labor's material constitution – the relationships among union leaders, parliamentarians, Party machines, members and voters that define the organisation. We then consider continuity and change in the Party's policies. The final sections of this chapter assess alternatives to the ALP as it has been for 120 years, for those seeking fundamental, progressive social change.

Union leaders a weakened force in the Party

The Rudd government's continuation of many aspects of WorkChoices, and the generally dismissive approach taken by Rudd and Gillard to trade union leaders, illustrate the decline in the influence of union officials within the ALP in recent decades. This decline has its origins in the deep downturn in working class struggle since the early 1980s.[1] Not only has union membership slumped from one-half of the workforce to one-fifth, but the strike rate and other indicators of industrial combativity are at all time lows. Workplace militancy has virtually dried up in many of unionism's earlier strongholds. A capitalist class that is much more aggressively anti-union than in previous decades, backed in many cases by governments, has inflicted a series of defeats on trade unions, codified in Coalition and Labor legislation. The consequences are work intensification, loss of conditions, job insecurity and a plague of unpaid overtime. The industrial courts are able to levy fines on unions at will, notably in the building and construction industry since the formation of the ABCC, and the unions have complied without serious resistance.

Even the union movement's successes, most notably the blows struck against the Howard government during the MUA dispute in 1998 and the Your Rights at Work campaign of 2005–7, had limited effects, as union leaders failed to press home their advantage, squandering the MUA victory in a mess of damaging concessions and diverting Your Rights at Work into a campaign to return the Labor Party to office, committed as it was only to minor amendments to WorkChoices.

From a confident force able and willing to challenge bosses, courts, industrial tribunals and governments in the late 1960s and early 1970s, the trade union movement has become a weak reed. This was not inevitable and is reversible. The Prices and Incomes Accord with the Hawke and Keating Labor governments played the main part in this transformation. The damage inflicted then has not subsequently been repaired, only compounded.

The result is defeatism within the unions, which is apparent everywhere from the ACTU leadership to the workplace delegate. Demoralised by their own failures, and experiencing no serious pressure from working class militants, the union leaders are generally preoccupied with survival on the most modest and defensive basis and lack a program for rebuilding the union movement. Nor is there a consistent and distinctive left current among them willing to fight it out with the more conservative elements. In addition, trade unions have become more centralised and bureaucratic as a result of the decline of members' self-confidence and the round of union amalgamations in the early 1990s.

The reluctance of ordinary unionists to take militant action on their own initiative, compounded by the unwillingness of their full time officials to rebuild working class self-confidence through industrial struggle, explains the weakness of the trade union leaders in the councils of the ALP. The parliamentary leaders understand this well and take full advantage of it. Union officials complain about their marginalisation within the Party but when a serious fight could be waged, as over Labor's maintenance of the union busting ABCC, they sound the charge, and then retreat before even joining battle. This is not because they have no clout within the Party, as they demonstrated in June 2010 when right wing union power brokers such as Paul Howes of the AWU led the operation that brought down Rudd, in alliance with leaders of the right faction in the federal caucus. Furthermore, ten of the 21 members of the ALP's national executive with voting rights in 2010 were union officials. Union representatives, even if their share of delegates has been cut to 50 per cent, and their factional allies still dominate most state conferences.

Yet there are few signs that they are willing to use this power for the defence of working class interests. The union officials' unwillingness to confront the parliamentarians when they attack workers is not least because they agree that effectively managing Australian capitalism is the fundamental priority for Labor governments.

On occasion, union officials have taken a stand, though only half-heartedly, and shifted Labor government policy. At the 2008 New South

Wales state conference, trade union officials combined with the chiefs of the factional machines to defeat attempts by the state government to privatise electricity generation, eventually bringing down Premier Morris Iemma and Treasurer Michael Costa. This success, worrying though it was for business (and the Rudd government) at the time, quickly gave way to the usual backroom dealing. The champion of the union movement in its fight with the premier and treasurer, Unions NSW Secretary John Robertson, was appointed to succeed Costa in the Legislative Council and soon became the minister responsible for privatising prisons and selling off parts of the power industry.

The New South Wales battle over electricity privatisation demonstrated the continuing potential for union leaders to resist attempts by Labor's parliamentary leaders to ride roughshod over them but also their lack of determination to do so in a consistent fashion. Other examples, such as the refusal of the left unions to vote against Premier Anna Bligh's privatisation program at the Queensland state conference in June 2009, demonstrated their reluctance to conduct a fight within the Party.

In addition to the lack of counterpressure from below and their agreement about the need to manage Australian capitalism responsibly, personal opportunism also helps explain the preparedness of senior union officials to allow ALP politicians to get their own way. Many have future careers to consider, whether as parliamentarians, paid members of government advisory bodies, industrial commissioners, directors of superannuation funds or human resource advisers. No such posts are likely to come their way if they have a reputation for rocking the boat. The final factor holding them back is their desire to avoid a severe schism inside the Party. Since the three major splits of 1916, 1931 and 1955, union leaders have been very wary of taking action that might precipitate a fourth.

The politicians gain weight

As the power of the union officials in the ALP has shrunk, that of the politicians and, in particular, the Labor leadership has grown. Compared with the union officials, the resources available to the politicians have expanded dramatically. Since the 1960s, there has been a huge publicly funded expansion in the number of employees in MPs' offices. Each federal parliamentarian is allowed a minimum of four full time staff, which, following the 2007 election, gave Labor at least 460. Federal ministers and other Labor parliamentary office holders had a further 352 staffers. Federal ALP parliamentarians now have 70 per cent more staff than when Labor last won office in 1983.[2] State MPs and ministers also have their legions of staffers. Then there is the small army of students working for parliamentarians on a part-time or ad hoc basis. In addition, there are the public service advisers in Labor ministers' offices who can be deployed to advance their cause. It is difficult to count all personnel dependent entirely or largely on the goodwill of federal, state and territory ALP politicians, but the figure would be in the thousands. This enormous resource has significantly increased the political weight of the politicians inside the ALP, compared with union and also Party officials. Furthermore, parliamentarians are entitled to office expenses, a proportion of which can be used to promote their own interests within the Party.

The power of Labor leaders in the Party has expanded because of changes in political campaigning. The electronic media have become the main means to spread the ALP message. This in turn is increasingly focused on the personality of the leader who is presented as the embodiment of the values and image that the Party wants to project. Consequently, leaders have additional leverage to get their way inside the Party. Thus, in the euphoria after the 2007 election, Rudd simply nominated his cabinet, breaking more than 100 years of democratic tradition whereby the Caucus elected the ministry. The new cabinet quickly acceded to Rudd's request to change Caucus rules to make this a permanent arrangement. Bligh did the same in Queensland after the 2009 state election.

The social origins of Labor's parliamentary representatives increasingly diverged from those of its voting base during the last decades of the 20th century. Until the 1950s, most Labor politicians came from relatively plebeian or skilled working class backgrounds. By 2005, two-thirds of federal Labor parliamentarians had been employed by a politician, union or the ALP itself immediately prior to their election.[3] Staffers have become increasingly important, not just as a resource for incumbents but also as a pool of future parliamentarians. Rudd and Gillard are perhaps the best known former staffers. He was chief of staff for Queensland Opposition leader and later premier, Wayne Goss. She was chief of staff for Victorian Opposition leader John Brumby, a leader of the right wing of the Party. Other ex-staffers on Labor's front bench before the 2010 election included Anthony Albanese, Jenny Macklin, Stephen Smith and Wayne Swan.[4] At the state level, premiers Morris Iemma and Nathan Rees (New South Wales), Steve Bracks (Victoria), David Bartlett (Tasmania) and Mike Rann (South Australia) had all been staffers for Labor politicians.

Trade union leaders continue to find their way into Labor caucuses. National Secretary of the Community and Public Sector Union Stephen Jones engineered the affiliation of his union to the ALP in every state and territory in the late 2000s and was rewarded in 2010 with preselection for the safe seat of Throsby (New South Wales) for the forthcoming federal election. Those who preceded him included many Rudd ministers and parliamentary secretaries, including Simon Crean, Martin Ferguson, Lindsay Tanner, Greg Combet, Bill Shorten, Richard Marles and Mark Butler. While the transfer of such figures from unions to the parliamentary Caucus might appear to maintain the ALP's strong working class linkages, this is much less true than previously. With some important exceptions, most contemporary union officials have little or no experience as workers in the industry or occupation that they cover. More common is their appointment to union positions as political operatives soon after leaving university, sometimes after a stint as a political staffer.[5] The gene pool from which parliamentarians are preselected is thus becoming increasingly narrow, with much intermingling of positions within the restricted circles of staffers, union officials and Party functionaries.

The life experiences of most Labor politicians and their working class constituents are very different. Regardless of their family circumstances, all Labor leaders since Whitlam, with the exception of Keating, graduated with at least a bachelor's degree from one of the nation's top universities. Seventy-eight per cent of all ALP federal parliamentarians in 2005 possessed a university degree, far in excess of the figure for the Australian population.[6] Labor parliamentarians and Party leaders generally have to reach a very long way back in their memories to recall what the daily work experience of the majority of people in Australia is like: doing a routine job, being bossed around by a supervisor on a building site, in a factory, mine, supermarket, school or hospital. This is certainly the case for Rudd and Gillard, despite their plebeian origins. Rudd attended the Australian National University and went on to be an elite recruit in the Department of Foreign Affairs and Trade, a political staffer, top Queensland public servant and consultant to big businesses before entering parliament. He was the first Labor leader with a wealthy spouse, Therese Rein, a member of the capitalist class in her own right.[7] Gillard studied at the Universities of Adelaide and Melbourne and became a partner in a large law firm in 1990 before working for Brumby and then entering the federal parliament as the member for Lalor.

Politicians' pay also distances them from the workers that they represent. The prime minister's basic salary in 2010 was almost seven times average earnings.[8] Although the basic pay of junior federal MPs remains around three times average earnings, a level that has been fairly constant since 1950,[9] the various allowances available to the politicians have expanded. These include funds for postage, printing, phone calls, other office resources, a car and travel expenses.

In terms of gender, ALP MPs have become more representative of the Party's membership and electorate. By 2009, women had made it as Labor chief ministers or premiers in every state and territory, with the exception of Tasmania and South Australia, and 40 per cent of all Labor politicians in federal, state and territory jurisdictions were female.[10] In 2010 Gillard became Australia's first female prime minister. Other changes have included a decline in the proportion of Labor parliamentarians with British and Irish backgrounds and an increasing number from families with non-English speaking origins. They are not, for the most part, first generation migrants – 88 per cent of ALP candidates at the 2007 federal election were born in Australia[11] – but second or later generation migrants who had left behind their family's manual or shopkeeper origins. Bracks, for example, came from a Lebanese, Iemma from an Italian and Bolkus from a Greek family background. In municipal politics, ALP figures from the Vietnamese community have won positions in migrant-dominated blue collar working class electorates in Sydney and Melbourne. Demographically, Labor politicians have become rather more representative of their electorates; in terms of class, rather more dissimilar.

Machine power

Labor's formal and factional machines remain a crucial mechanism for exercising power within the ALP. Even so, the distinctiveness of the factions has sharply declined in recent decades.

From the Party's foundation, the left and, at least occasionally, sections of the Party's right talked about socialism. Especially after the defeat of Chifley's bank nationalisation, and even more so after the election of the Whitlam government, the right cooled on this kind of language. Electoral pragmatism, that is, the enthusiastic abandonment of ALP policies, was its reflex strategy for winning votes. The right now invoked Chifley's light on the hill support for social welfare, fairness and, especially from the 1970s, equality of opportunity as the sum total of its aspirations. The left continued to be distinguished in the postwar decades by references to socialism, commitment to social equality and a greater willingness to promote and participate in extra parliamentary struggles. It still had illusions about the virtues of state ownership and regulation, and many Labor leftists shared the Communist Party's sympathies with the 'socialist', that is, state capitalist, states in eastern Europe and China. The left voiced the concerns of more militant workers and helped to harness them to Labor's project of managing Australian capitalism. While the discipline of cabinet solidarity meant that the practical – as opposed to rhetorical – differences between the left and right were small when Labor was in office, there were some quite important points of ideological cleavage between the two sides.

This changed during the long decade of the Hawke and Keating governments, when most of the distinctiveness of the left's formal policies, let alone its actions, evaporated. The left was complicit in these governments' most significant policies and was responsible for carrying out many of them, including toughening access to social security and locking up asylum seekers.

Despite the waning of ideological conflict within the Party, the 1980s marked the emergence of formal national factions out of the previous ad hoc alliances of the still powerful state branch-based factions. With Labor in office, the spoils of victory in factional battles at the federal level were much greater, necessitating tighter coordination.

While the main left factions in New South Wales and Victoria had 'socialist' in their names, by the 2000s, anti-capitalism hardly featured in public utterances by their leaders. More significant than rhetoric, however, was the virtual abandonment of extra parliamentary activism by the Party's left. There was a huge contrast between the role played by the Labor left in the movements against the Vietnam War and against the 2003 invasion of Iraq. In the late 1960s and early 1970s the Labor left was a crucial element in the antiwar movement. In 2003, individuals such as Carmen Lawrence (and the right's Harry Quick) had some prominence, but as organising forces in the movement the ALP and its left factions had virtually disappeared. The main business of factions now was the advancement of their members in preselections and caucus appointments. Sometimes factions have helped hoist into the leadership, politicians who seemed capable of saving Labor's electoral skin, regardless of their factional backgrounds. The New South Wales right replaced premier Iemma, one of their own, with the left's Rees in September 2008. The national right, in June 2010, dumped factional colleague Rudd and handed the post of prime minister to Julia Gillard. No questions of principle or ideological demarcation were at issue: simply an assessment of who was most likely to lead the Party to victory in the upcoming election. As Dick Gross, former Labor Mayor of Port Phillip in Melbourne, told the authors in 2009, today 'a faction is just a preselection machine with an ideological vacuum at its heart'.

Former Carr government minister Rodney Cavalier identified a 'standing army' within the Party, which includes ministerial staffers, members' staffers, university educated union officials and Party employees who owed their jobs, and thus their loyalty, to the heads of the factions.[12] Former Hawke minister John Button likewise condemned 'The domination of the Party hierarchy by a new class of labour movement professionals who rely on factions and unions affiliated to the Party for their career advancement.'[13] Local branches and the activities of dedicated amateurs have not been entirely displaced by this expanded bureaucratic layer in the Party, but they have become less important.

The ALP's federal structure still means that national leaders are more insulated than are state and territory leaders from pressure from workers in local branches or the unions, and there has also been a long term trend towards the centralisation of power within the Party, going back at least to the formation of the federal executive in 1915. During the Rudd era, the process accelerated, as the selection of candidates for federal seats by the national executive (NE) became more routine. The 2007 national conference gave the NE the right to determine outstanding preselections in New South Wales. In 2009 the NE vested the five person national executive committee, made up of factional heavyweights and Kevin Rudd, with the power to supervise federal preselections. And in 2010, the national executive, at Rudd's behest, overturned the preselection of a leading union official for the top Senate spot in Tasmania and arrogated to itself the power to determine the dates of state conferences, in the hope of avoiding embarrassing stoushes during an election year.[14]

Membership and local branches

With a claimed membership of 50 000, the ALP today supposedly has as many members as it had at the time the Hawke government was elected in 1983, and somewhat more than it did when Whitlam became prime minister 11 years earlier.[15] By way of comparison, this is 10 per cent less than the membership of the Collingwood Football Club in 2010.[16] Compared to Labor's federal vote, membership has shrunk drastically – whereas in the late 1940s one in every 33 ALP voters was a Party member, by 2007 the ratio had fallen to one in every 108.[17]

The occupational makeup of the Party's membership has also changed markedly. Three trends stand out. The first is the growing importance of professionals. In the late 1980s, Andrew Scott claimed that 'a professional [was] more than three times as likely as a manual worker, and five times more likely than a salesperson, personal service employee or clerk, to participate at the ALP's most basic levels'. The percentage of professionals in the Party membership became much higher than in the population at large.[18] The second major change is the much greater weight of what Button described as labour movement professionals – parliamentarians (whose number has grown as parliaments have become larger), union officials and staffers.[19] The largest category of members is those who paid concessional dues, as retirees, recipients of social security benefits, students and so forth. These comprised 71 per cent of Victorian members in 2005 and more than half of the financial members in New South Wales in 2009.[20] It is almost certain that many of them were stackees, whose sponsors saved money by buying concessional membership tickets for them. Labour movement professionals and stackees complement each other. Stackees are numbers for office holders and aspirant office holders, who can use their connections to do favours for their supporters.

Cavalier estimated in 2005 that the New South Wales branch had only 1000 active members outside the apparatus and that the number of local branches that had a real life was not much over 100.[21] This may have been an exaggeration. There are certainly many branches with a vigorous internal life and committed members, although their political energies are seldom directed outwards, beyond the confines of the Party.[22] Some branches still have discussions and presentations about important issues of the day, but the impact of resolutions arising from them on Party policy is small.[23] As federal front bencher Lindsay Tanner pointed out in 2002, 'For those without political ambitions who simply wish to make a contribution, rank-and-file membership of the ALP is profoundly unappealing'.[24]

While the Party leadership occasionally laments the loss of branch vitality and membership, the use of television, market research and the internet mean that Labor leaders no longer require an active membership to spread the word or get feedback from the electorate. Since the 1960s, television commercials, polling and email have supplemented radio and press advertising, and further reduced the role of public meetings, leafleting, putting up posters, door to door canvassing and local branch meetings.[25] During the 2007 federal election it was the trade unions that did most local work promoting Labor, not the local branches.

Working class votes

The ALP's abandonment of a broad program of working class reforms, most evident since the election of the Hawke government in 1983, has done damage to the Party's primary vote (figure 1). Only in the disastrous 1931 election, soon after the splits of the Depression, and back before 1910, when the Party was still establishing its national electoral presence, was the ALP's proportion of the primary vote as low as that in 2001 (37.8 per cent) and 2004 (37.6 per cent).[26] In 2007, when Labor formed a new federal government for the seventh time in its history, it did so with a primary vote of 43 per cent, far lower than the 48 to 50 per cent it attained on the previous six occasions.

Decades of Labor governments attacking the Party's base, jettisoning basic social democratic ideas and capitulating to the right, along with declines in trade union and Party membership, reduced both the size and the enthusiasm of the ALP's core constituency in the working class. Labor has become increasingly dependent on backing from the capitalist class and the vagaries of public opinion. The fragility of Rudd's and the Party's popularity

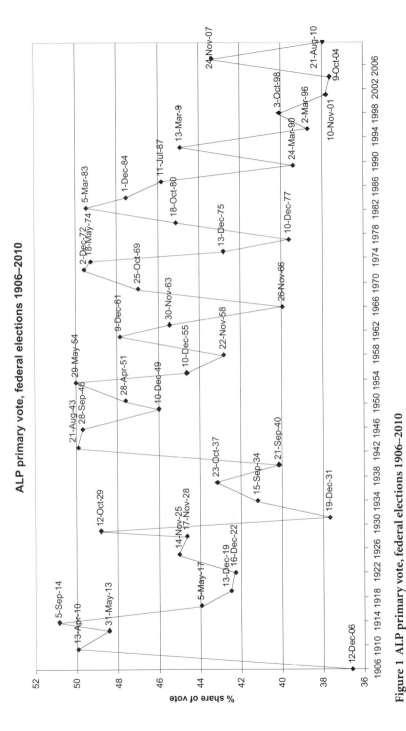

Figure 1 ALP primary vote, federal elections 1906–2010

Source: Australian Government and Politics Database, accessed at http://elections.uwa.edu.au/partysearcha.lasso,
8 September 2010.

was demonstrated by the rapid collapse in support for them in the polls during the autumn of 2010. The switch in leadership to Gillard offered only temporary respite. The subsequent drop in Labor's support indicated that the problem was not so much dissatisfaction with the cold and colourless figure of Kevin Rudd as a more profound disenchantment with the Party.

Labor's support among the working class has been hard but not irreparably hit. While the Party has traditionally won the majority of working class votes, this was not the case in the 1996, 2001 and 2004 elections, when the Coalition matched or narrowly outpolled the ALP among workers. The Your Rights At Work campaign and the general fear of WorkChoices saw many workers move back into Labor's camp at the 2007 election, with the ALP winning 50 per cent of workers' votes as opposed to the 38 per cent of workers who backed the Coalition.[27] Among trade unionists, Labor still retains a substantial margin over the Coalition. For the entire period from 1966 to 2007, the proportion of unionists voting Labor exceeded 50 per cent at every federal election, with the exception of 1990 and 2001. During this period, Labor always outpolled the Coalition among unionists, and this was particularly marked at in 2007. Support for Labor is also high among the more oppressed sections of the working class, those from non-English speaking backgrounds. In the 1996 and 2001 federal elections, when a small majority of white workers from English speaking backgrounds voted for the Coalition, a large majority of workers from non-English speaking backgrounds voted for Labor.[28] Labor also retains strong support among Aborigines.

More important in assessing Labor's material constitution is the class composition of its own electoral support. Figure 2 shows that the proportion of Labor's voters who were workers has consistently been much higher than the proportion of workers' among the Coalition's supporters.[29]

Another demonstration of the class bias in Labor's vote is with reference to workers' class enemy, those who defined themselves in the 2006 Census as 'managers'. At the 2007 federal election, Labor's vote was strongly negatively correlated with the proportion of managers in each electorate. For every 1 per cent increase in this section of the electorate, Labor's vote declined, on average, by 2.3 per cent.[30]

One final method of illustrating the continuing salience of Labor's working class vote is by reference to the class character of its safest seats. Once these were to be found overwhelmingly in the inner city and port areas of the state capitals, for example, Sydney and Grayndler (in Sydney's inner

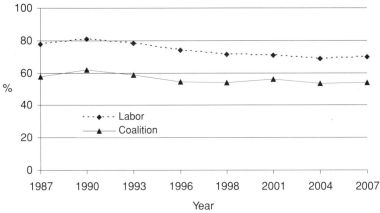

Figure 2 **Workers as proportion of party primary vote, 1987–2007**
Source: Ian McAllister et al., *Australian Election Survey, 1987*; Ian McAllister et al.,
Australian Election Study, 1990, 1993, 1996, 1998, 2001, 2004, 2007, all accessed at
http://assda-nesstar.anu.edu.au/webview.

west), Port Melbourne, Port Adelaide and Fremantle. As gentrification has
reduced the working class character of these inner city and wharf areas, they
have become less secure for the ALP. At the 2007 federal election, none of
Labor's 10 safest seats, where it received more than 60 per cent of the primary vote, were inner city electorates. Apart from the very safest, Throsby,
on the unfashionable south side of Wollongong, all of Labor's safest seats
encompassed working class suburbs further out, towards the edges of Melbourne and Sydney. State seats provide a higher resolution picture that
confirms an electoral geography of class. In Sydney, for example, the results
of the 2007 New South Wales election showed a broad north–south divide.
North of the harbour and Parramatta River the electorates were, apart from
red Ryde, blue Liberal seats. The predominantly working class south and
west were red, falling to Labor, except for the wealthier blue seats of Vau-
cluse and Cronulla and the city centre, which was held by independent
Clover Moore.[31]

The distinctiveness of the Labor Party's electoral base has been slowly
declining over the period for which we have comparable survey data. Furthermore, the Coalition (and the Greens) have attracted working class

votes, while the ALP continues to attract some middle class support, as
it has always done. But Labor voters are still more likely to be working
class than voters for the Coalition, and this is especially the case when
the issue of class is posed sharply during elections, as it was in 1993
and 2007.

In summary, the ALP's distinctive connections with the unions, the electorate and to a lesser extent its membership mean that it can still accurately,
although not without qualification, be labelled a workers' party.

Still a capitalist party

If the evidence suggests that the ALP is still a workers' party, it is even clearer
that it also remains a capitalist party. This is apparent in its approaches to
foreign policy, race, economic management and industrial relations.

Labor has been loyal to the security of Australian imperialist interests in the Asia–Pacific region since the colonial era and to the US
alliance since it began under Curtin in the 1940s. In modern times
Labor has endorsed or prosecuted virtually every major military ven-
ture by Australian armed forces since World War II. These include the
Korean War, the naval blockade, sanctions and war on Iraq in the 1990s
and the occupation of Afghanistan. The two important exceptions were
Vietnam and the second war on Iraq in 2003. Labor's opposition to
these bloody campaigns was based on the accurate assessment that they
would undermine US and consequently Australian strategic interests. The
ALP backed Australian involvement in UN operations in fields ranging from Yugoslavia, Israel and Lebanon, Pakistan and Afghanistan, to
Cambodia, East Timor, Bougainville and Serbia. The Party also supported
the establishment of US controlled spy bases at Pine Gap, Nurrungar and
Geraldton.

Associated with Labor's support for the capitalist state's strategic interests
overseas has been the Party's promotion of nationalism and its complement,
racism. The ALP may have played a role in ending the White Australia policy in the 1960s and 1970s but its substitute, multiculturalism, was equally
attuned to the interests of the capitalist class in maintaining good relations
with Australia's main trade partners and in ensuring that migrant workers did not undermine political stability at home. That the Party could

simultaneously be for multiculturalism and promote racism is demonstrated in its treatment of asylum seekers. Racism has also been embedded in the ALP's response to demands for Indigenous land rights since the 1960s. Under pressure from campaigns by Aborigines and their supporters, Labor gave ground to the call for land rights during the early 1970s. From the early 1980s, however, Labor first betrayed the demand for national land rights legislation, and then did its utmost to dilute the progressive impact of the Mabo High Court case, substituting limited native title for comprehensive land rights. It opposed the Howard government's further dilution of native title in 1998, but on the most hesitant basis. Its support for, then implementation of, the Northern Territory Intervention only demonstrated Labor's desire to wind back the land rights that had been won as a result of earlier struggles.

As for Labor's economic policies, their specific content changed substantially between the 1950s and the 2000s (just as the economic policies of the conservative parties changed) but the general bias has remained the same. In the earlier period Labor was more supportive of greater regulation of product, commodity and financial markets. It established a variety of state run enterprises in the first half century and also attempted to nationalise the private banks. The onset of economic crisis in the mid 1970s was the catalyst for a dramatic change, which took effect in the 1980s with wholesale privatisation, deregulation and reduced tariffs. In both periods Labor followed the economic orthodoxy of the day, while favouring somewhat greater state intervention than the conservatives. The Party was just as keen to use the machinery of the state to promote the interests of Australian capitalism in the more integrated world economy under Hawke, Keating, Rudd and Gillard as it had been in the postwar decades when it supported tariffs to help develop Australian business. With the onset of the global financial crisis in 2008, Labor again rushed to rescue Australian capitalism with a substantial injection of funds, which was warmly welcomed by most business organisations.

The changes in the ALP's economic policies reflect less a transition from radicalism to moderation or from true belief to betrayal, than shifts in the requirements of Australian capitalism and changes in the balance of pressure on the Party from the working and capitalist classes. There have been significant differences between Labor and its conservative opponents, and both sides have had an interest in rhetorically magnifying their disagreements about details for the purpose of electoral product differentiation. These differences can still, in some circumstances, allow the ALP to advance capitalist interests more effectively than the Coalition. During and after World War II and under the Accord, Labor was able to cut real wages, thanks to the Party's connections with the working class. The parliamentary leadership was able to rely on the top union officials' loyalty, and workers' support or acquiescence, when it adopted anti-working class measures. There were isolated protests and acts of disobedience against the Accord, but no organised opposition. The continuing commitment of union leaders to the ALP explains their willingness to endorse Rudd and Gillard's WorkChoices Lite, even though life was more difficult for trade unions under Labor's legislation than the Howard Government's 1996 Workplace Relations Act.

On the other hand, because the ALP has a base independent of business, it has sometimes been braver than the conservatives about introducing reforms that hurt specific sectors but served the interests of the capitalist class as a whole. Hence the shift away from traditional protectionist policies under Hawke and Keating. The Rudd government's plan to tax mining industry profits in order to reduce company tax was another example of this mechanism. Gillard's capitulation to the mining industry's scare campaign, when she slashed the proposed resources tax and halved the cut in the company tax rate, suggests that the ALP's ability to operate in this way has declined. The Party today has less of a base in the working class that it can use as a counterweight to a section of the capitalist class mobilising against particular government policies.

Despite these differences between the main forces in Australian electoral politics, Labor and the Coalition are agreed on a fundamental task: to serve the needs of Australian capitalism. In periods of economic expansion, there has been scope for reforms that benefited the working class; in periods of retrenchment, conservative and Labor governments alike have withdrawn at least some of these reforms. Hence Labor's approach to social security, whose expansion it supported during the postwar boom, but which it has done its best to rein in since the boom ended, and to health and education, where Labor has encouraged the growth of the private sector and the offloading of costs onto workers through user pays mechanisms. ALP governments have also done their best to curb public sector pay.

Finally, Labor has been just as keen as the conservative parties to use the machinery of the state to discipline the working class. In 1949 Chifley sent the troops in to break the coal miners' strike. In 1989, Hawke used the airforce to break a strike by domestic airline pilots. In 2009 Gillard sooled the ABCC onto building sites to break the construction union. Industrial arbitration, which for many decades had played an important role in disciplining trade unions, was supplanted in the 1990s by enterprise bargaining. The rhetoric of centralised wage determination gave way to the language of labour market flexibility, which has enabled employers to impose even more of the uncertainties of capitalist production onto workers and seriously weakened the trade unions. But in both periods, Labor's goal was to maintain employer prerogatives and the subordination of labour to the logic of competitive accumulation.

The Party once rhetorically supported socialism. Now, the Labor leadership openly denounces it. But the shift has been more apparent than real. For Labor's earlier leaders, the socialisation objective was only ever window dressing to attract idealistic young recruits, never operational policy for governments. Today, the ALP no longer suggests – not even rhetorically – that a systemic alternative to the capitalist status quo is possible.

In pursuing a more explicitly right wing agenda ALP leaders have faced little resistance from the Labor left. As the Labor Party has moved to the right over the past 30 years, the left has moved rightwards too. In most cases it has been as complicit, occasionally after gnashing of teeth, as has the right of the Party, in betrayals of ALP policy and workers' interests.

The past three or four decades have seen significant changes in the material constitution of the ALP. First, its working class membership is much smaller proportionately than during the first half of the 20th century. Second, the membership at large, other than those employed by the Party, the politicians and the unions, plays a diminished role within the organisation. The job of promoting Labor's messages is now largely undertaken by media and public relations professionals, although members, through the branches and the unions, are still useful distributors of how to vote cards on election day. The role of union officials within the Party has shrunk in line with their diminished role in society as the level of working class struggle has declined. Decades of running governments at state and federal levels have domesticated the Party – it is much more integrated into the capitalist state and its horizons for social change are consequently lower. By the same token, it is no longer seen as any kind of threat by the capitalist class whose members, although they may owe their primary loyalty to the Coalition parties, are usually quite relaxed at the prospect of Labor holding office.

The ALP is a much wealthier institution now, with far greater resources, courtesy of years of accumulating property but, most importantly, because of public funding and, to a lesser extent, business donations. Union funding is, as a corollary, significantly less important. The federal Labor leadership is now much stronger compared to the state branches, in line with the centralisation of power in the Party more generally. The Party's ability to rely on a solid primary vote of 45–50 per cent has passed into history. Finally, the earlier ideological divisions in the organisation have more or less vanished, to be replaced by a factional system based on little more than the allocation of jobs.

So the ALP has undergone significant change. It is no longer the party it once was. Despite this, its character is still determined by the continuing, albeit reduced, role of the trade union leaders in the constitutional structures of the Party and in its daily operations. Parliamentarians and trade union leaders remain interdependent, although the exact nature of the relationship has shifted. Trade unions continue to be affiliated, which very much shapes the character of the ALP – the more class conscious workers are, as measured by union membership, the more they support the Party. Class conscious workers, furthermore, tend to regard Labor as their party, even if they may not share the illusions of their grandparents or great grandparents that Labor might usher in major and progressive social changes. Even after years of sellouts have eliminated any hope of substantial reforms, class conscious workers still perceive Labor as qualitatively different to the Coalition parties – Labor is supposed to be on their side. Hence their hopes when Labor is elected, followed very often by their disillusionment when Labor attacks them. Whether reforming or retrenching, however, the ALP is a steadfast defender of the capitalist system. Labor is still a capitalist workers' party, which distinguishes it not just from the conservative, even more explicitly pro-business, parties, but also from the Greens.

What's the alternative?

The fact that Labor is a capitalist workers' party and acts accordingly when in office has repeatedly generated bewilderment, resentment and active opposition among workers. Isn't Labor supposed to be their party? This is not a new phenomenon by any means. Less than two years after the formation and early electoral successes of the Labor Electoral Leagues in New South Wales, Arthur Desmond, a leading activist in the Active Service Brigade, an unemployed group, slammed Labor's legislators in a poem entitled 'Backing Down', which reads in part:

> We placed you there to fight for us, to free us from the bale
> Of those who would our rights subvert, our Liberties assail.
> And now instead of royal deeds your grovel shames the town,
> Our hopes are stranded once again, our chiefs are 'backing down'.
> No wonder that the people turn, they are so oft betrayed
> By means of mighty promises whom danger makes afraid.
> O what's the use of choosing chiefs to smash the Evil down,
> If when they get in the van they end by 'backing down'.[32]

We conclude this book by considering four alternatives for those, like Arthur Desmond, who wish to fight for a better world but are dissatisfied with Labor's betrayals: reforming the ALP from within, joining the Greens, forming a new social democratic party or building a revolutionary organisation.

Reform from within

Perhaps the most common response to the failures of the ALP has been to try to change it from within – to drag it leftwards so that it really will fight for socialism. The many attempts to do so since the 1890s have all failed.[33] Their failure is rooted in the fact that Labor governments have never been interested in socialist transformation, not because of the personal failings of the leaders and not because right wing factions dominate caucus, but for the simple reason that the Party is an integral part of the capitalist system rather than a threat to it. Far from the Party acting as a representative of workers in the capitalist system to improve things for those who do the labour in our society, the ALP works full time as a representative of the capitalist system in the field of working class politics to improve things for those who reap the profits. It is not a mechanism for achieving social progress but an obstacle to it.

Richard Crossman, a British Labour Cabinet minister in the 1960s, explained how the British party was structured so as to attract and abuse left wing activists. To hold militants, who do useful work but 'tended to be "extremists"', the party needed to appear democratic by, for example, granting conference supreme power. In practice, the disciplined votes of union delegations and the autonomy of the parliamentary party prevented militants from exercising any effective power within the party.[34] Labor parliamentary caucuses in Australia likewise ignore Party policy when it suits. There are seldom serious consequences. In his memoir, former Victorian Premier John Cain junior described how, in the face of opposition from rank and file members and the state conference, he rammed through legislation to destroy the Builders' Labourers' Federation in the mid 1980s:

> despite the oft-repeated phrase that Conference is supreme and decides policy, in effect, when the crunch comes, if the government is right and has popular support in the community and significant support in the Party, it can hold sway against Conference.[35]

The belief that they can bend the parliamentary leaders to their will traps genuine socialists in the ALP. Those who attempt to change the Party from within do not change the ALP: they are digested and in turn become part of the problem, or are spat out. The power of the politicians and union officials is at the core of the Labor Party, responsible for its fundamental orientations and policies. It is not possible to destroy that power without destroying the Party itself.

The Greens

What about the Greens? In the period from the 2001 election, the Greens established themselves as a clear left alternative to Labor. In some electorates the Greens began to pose a serious threat to Labor. This was particularly the case in the inner cities.[36] By 2007, they had clearly displaced Labor as the party with most appeal to idealistic young workers and students. Membership of the Greens more than quadrupled from 2200 in 2000 to 9000 in 2007.[37] They won their first House of Representatives seat in a general election in August 2010 and increased their numbers in the Senate to nine, which gave them the balance of power in the upper house.

During the Howard years, the Greens took a wide range of traditionally left stances. For example, they supported free tertiary education, the end of mandatory detention of refugees and the Pacific Solution, the lifting of any restrictions on abortion and immediately pulling troops out of Iraq and

Afghanistan.[38] The industrial relations policy that the Greens took to the 2007 election was well to Labor's left: they promised to scrap all of Howard's anti-union laws. Greens were often to be found on platforms at rallies and, during the speech by President Bush to the federal parliament in September 2003 when he promoted the War on Terror, the two Greens senators heckled him.

The Party's 'leftism' has, however, definite limits. Greens supporters include not just idealistic left wing youth but also small business people and middle class professionals who provide the base for a strong conservative wing in the party. Unlike Labor, the Greens receive their support overwhelmingly from white voters, and have failed to break through in migrant communities, not least because, according to one Greens activist, 'the party *as a whole* has no . . . strategic orientation to the working class or trade unions'.[39] Most importantly, the Greens, like the ALP, are committed to capitalism and see parliament as the only effective avenue for achieving social change. So, the party opposed particular policies of the Howard government but only within the logic of nationalism and the profit system. Thus, they opposed sending troops to Afghanistan in October 2001, but only because the war was not sanctioned by the UN.[40] Six years later Greens leader Bob Brown argued against the dispatch of 300 SAS soldiers to Afghanistan on the grounds that 'they should remain in our region where instability is rife and our defence forces already stretched'.[41] Concern about this 'instability' led the Greens to support the deployment of troops and police to East Timor in 1999 and 2006, and the Solomon Islands in 2003. Brown complained only that the Howard government had been tardy in doing so. The Greens consistently demanded that the Howard government ratify the Kyoto Protocol but favoured a market-based emissions trading system to deal with global warming.

The Greens' parliamentary focus meant that while they won support among those who attended rallies for progressive causes during the Howard years they did little to build them; nor did they send large contingents to them, with the exception of the 2003 campaign against the invasion of Iraq. Their structures, likewise, are geared to winning elections rather than social activism: they have no caucuses in the trade unions, clubs on most university campuses or active local branches outside elections.

The limits of the Greens' politics became more obvious once Labor won power in 2007. They did nothing to mount campaigns against Rudd's new work laws, the ongoing occupation of Afghanistan or the continuation of mandatory detention of refugees. In March 2010 the Greens called for a cut in skilled migration,[42] feeding perceptions that migrants were responsible for a lack of jobs for Australians. Increasingly, the Greens played down their earlier association with activism and sought to position themselves as a party that would play a 'responsible' role in parliamentary affairs.[43] Following the 2010 Tasmanian election, Brown proposed a coalition government of all three parties – Liberal, Labor and Greens.[44] After three weeks of wrangling, the Greens were given two Cabinet posts as reward for their support of the government of Labor's David Bartlett, although, before the election, they had attacked his government as corrupt and in the pocket of the Gunns timber conglomerate. With an election breakthrough possible in forthcoming state and federal elections in Victoria in 2010, the Greens' state campaign manager, Szilvia Csanyi, told the *Age* in April that the party was going to pitch much more strongly to middle class professionals: 'We're trying to cut through this old image and false perception of the Greens as tree-hugging radicals – that's not what the party is about'.[45] After the 2010 election, the Greens signed an agreement to support the Gillard government but Brown secured no substantive concessions from Labor, despite his initial insistence on having discussions with both the Coalition and the ALP.[46] Commitment to capitalism and parliamentary reform is conservatising the Greens just as it conservatised the ALP.

Left social democratic parties

If the Greens and Labor are committed to capitalism and moderation, is there potential for a genuinely left wing social democratic party with a real base in the working class to chart a different course? While there is no evidence in Australia on which to base an answer to this question, observation of such parties internationally suggests that they will fall at the same hurdles.

In several countries, new social democratic organisations have formed in the past two decades through splits in the existing parties and fusions with other forces, in the context of disillusionment with the traditional social democratic parties. Two important cases are Italy's *Rifondazione Comunista* (RC, Communist Refoundation) and *Die Linke* (The Left) in Germany. Both achieved electoral support of around 10 per cent in the first decade of the 21st century. Having won support in the early 2000s for their role in building mass demonstrations against neoliberalism and the war in Iraq,[47] RC parliamentarians joined the social democratic Prodi government in 2006. Very quickly, they began to scandalise their supporters by agreeing to maintain the Italian troop deployment in Afghanistan, backing the dispatch of additional soldiers to Lebanon and voting for the expansion of an American military base in the face of huge public opposition.[48] RC was reduced to a rump at the 2008 general election.

In Germany, *Die Linke* was formed in a merger in 2006–7 between the former ruling communist party in the East (the Party of Democratic Socialism, PDS), a bloc of left social democrats who broke from the Social Democratic Party (SPD) in 2005 and radical leftists in the West. With the SPD in a coalition government with the Greens between 1997 and 2005 and as part of a Grand Coalition with the conservative Christian Democratic Union (CDU) until 2008, a space opened up to its left, which the PDS, and then an electoral alliance between the PDS and the western leftists, quickly filled.[49] As in Italy, *Die Linke* joined the social democrats in coalition governments in the states of Berlin and Brandenburg, which pursued neoliberal policies: cutting back public services and employment, and privatising public assets. The dominant wing of the party, based in the east, has its heart set on a national coalition with the SPD and possibly the Greens, which, if it eventuates, will draw *Die Linke* into the same compromises in federal politics that it has made in the states.[50]

The tendency for left social democratic parties to follow the same trajectory as their mainstream cousins is apparent even when such parties are formed from scratch in countries with limited social democratic traditions. Thus, the *Partido dos Trabalhadores* (PT, the Workers Party) was formed in Brazil in 1980 out of a wave of impressive working class struggles in the late 1970s. In 2002 the PT won the presidency under Luiz Inácio Lula da Silva, a former militant metal worker and union leader, who was elected on a platform of resisting an IMF austerity program. Within 18 months, Lula had diverted resources tagged for poverty relief to debt repayment. By 2005 Lula's administration seemed 'able to impose neoliberal policies more consistently and successfully than any other government, however right-wing or ideologically committed to neoliberal interests'.[51]

All three parties – RC, *Die Linke* and PT – shared the same basic flaw, the belief that radical social change can come through parliament. They all suffered the same fate: rather than changing parliament, parliament, and the broader capitalist system in which it was embedded, changed them.

The revolutionary alternative

Any genuine socialist alternative to the ALP has to start from a very different premise to all parliamentary parties. It must be based on the conviction that socialism cannot be bestowed on the working class from on high but can only be achieved through the struggles of the working class itself, a basic principle of Marxism. Struggle can win genuine reforms under capitalism and prepare the working class, politically and organisationally, to seize power. A party formed on this basic principle evidently has to be hostile to the capitalist order and any strategic compromise with it. It has to fight for the interests of the working class as the social force capable of conducting the most advanced and powerful struggles, while drawing behind it other classes and social groups antagonistic to or oppressed by the capitalist order. If it is to be successful in challenging the ALP, it has to be a mass working class party of some tens of thousands of members, including the most militant and class conscious sections of the working class. Such a party has to be an activist organisation that imbues its members with a fighting spirit rather than reducing them to the role of passive observers, the norm in the ALP. In other words, such a party has to be a revolutionary socialist workers' party dedicated to overthrowing, rather than serving, capitalism.

The success of the CPA in recruiting thousands of workers in the 1930s, even with politics heavily tainted by Stalinism, suggests that the construction of a revolutionary alternative to Labor is possible in Australia. Furthermore, the task facing revolutionaries is less arduous today because the ALP can no longer count on a mass base within the working class eager to defend Labor from left-wing criticism.

Even though the ALP's base in the working class is weaker and it no longer advocates serious social reform, Labor is not going to be easily pushed aside. Millions of workers still vote Labor and in some senses still see it as their party. Further, Labor can rely on the support of the trade union leaders and capitalists to help repel attacks from its left. And, more generally, reformist ideas have deep roots in the working class, arising out of the basic conditions of life that foster a dual and contradictory consciousness – of resistance on the one hand, and powerlessness on the other. The ALP appeals to this dual consciousness. A serious challenge to Labor can, therefore, only emerge from a wave of working class struggle and the confidence that this can bring.

A series of major class battles involving a resurgent working class will be necessary before large numbers of workers break from reformism. At present such a prospect seems remote. But the way capitalism gives rise to economic crises, wars and oppression means that it necessarily, if irregularly, generates major class struggles. The task of a revolutionary socialist party is to win the working class away from loyalty to the ALP in the course of these struggles. Yet the work to build the basis of such a party cannot wait until such struggles break out. It has to be started now or socialist politics will be swept aside by the tide of events when the struggle gathers pace.

NOTES

Introduction

1 'Crashing through', *Stateline*, ABC Television, 9 May 2008, at www.abc.net.au/stateline/nsw/content/2006/s2240777.htm, accessed 24 September 2009; Brad Norington, 'Dr Evil blows fuse amid calls to resign', *Australian*, 5 May 2008, p. 4; Emma Griffiths 'The latest from the New South Wales Labor Conference', *Insiders*, ABC TV, 4 May 2008, www.abc.net.au/insiders/content/2007/s2234680.htm, accessed 24 September 2009.

2 Unless otherwise stated, the following account draws on articles by Michael Easson, 'Politics: An Agent for Change', Barrie Unsworth, 'History: A Proud Tradition', Chris Christodoulou, 'Seduction: Michael and Me', Michael Costa with Peter Lewis, 'Exit Interview', from a tribute issue of *Workers Online*, 21 September 2001, at http://workers.labor.net.au/112; Brad Norington, 'The Costa Politics', *Sydney Morning Herald*, 17 April 1999, p. 35; Marilyn Dodkin, *Brothers: Eight Leaders of the Labor Council of New South Wales*, UNSW Press, Sydney, 2001; Michael Costa inaugural speech, New South Wales Legislative Council 5:58 pm, 19 September 2001; Mark Riley, 'Costa's blues', 3 August 2002, p. 23; Imre Salusinszky, 'Michael Costa: the free radical', *Australian Magazine*, 12 April 2008, p. 26.

3 Tracey Aubin, *Peter Costello: A biography, the full and unauthorised story of the man who wants to be PM*, HarperCollins, Sydney, 1999, p. 58.

4 Personal communications from Stuart Rosewarne, 25 September 2009, and Frank Stilwell, 21 October 2009.

5 Michael Costa and Mark Duffy, *Labor, Prosperity and the Nineties: Beyond the Bonsai Economy*, Federation Press, Sydney, 1991, pp. 180–94.

6 Michael Costa, 'Being Michael Costa', interview with Peter Lewis, *Workers Online*, 20 December 2000, at http://workers.labor.net.au/82/a_interview_costa.html, accessed 1 October 2009.

7 'Costa defends Police actions at Homebush', *PM*, ABC Radio National, 15 November 2002, www.abc.net.au/pm/stories/s728096.htm, accessed 2 October 2009.

8 Andrew West, 'Union sell-off protest, but Costa powers on', *Sydney Morning Herald*, 26 February 2008 p. 4; Imre Salusinszky, 'Iemma set for showdown on power sell-off', *Australian*, 3 May 2008, p. 4.

9 Michael Costa, 'Centrist formula best bet for NSW Labor', *Australian*, 21 November 2008, p. 12; Brian Robins, ' "Failed" treasurer Costa warns on health budget', *Sydney Morning Herald*, 1 October 2009, p. 4.

Chapter 1: Labor's love's lost?

1 The name 'Australian Labor Party' was not officially adopted by the Party until 1912. Prior to that time the various colonial and state parties had various names. We use the 'ALP', or 'Labor' or 'the Party' to denote the organisation in all periods.

2 Michael Keating, *The Australian Workforce 1910–11 to 1960–61*, Australian National University Press, Canberra, 1973; Australian Bureau of Statistics, *2008 Labour Statistics In Brief*, Catalogue 6104.0.

3 Commonwealth of Australia, *Parliamentary Debates, House of Representatives, Hansard*, 5 December 2006, p. 43, www.aph.gov.au/Hansard/reps/dailys/dr051206.pdf, 1 February 2009.

4 Kevin Rudd, 'A Labor manifesto for the modern age', *Age*, 7 July 2002, accessed at www.theage.com.au/articles/2002/07/06/1025667073518.html, 19 January 2009.

5 For a good starting point, see Rick Kuhn (ed.), *Class and Struggle in Australia*, Pearson, Sydney, 2005.

6 Australian Bureau of Statistics, *E08_aug96 – Employed Persons by Sex, Occupation, State, Status in Employment, August 1996 onwards*, data cube.

7 Ben Chifley, 'The Light on the Hill', 12 June 1949, at www.nswalp.com/light-on-the-hill, accessed 31 January 2009.

8 W. K. Hancock, *Australia*, Jacaranda, Brisbane, 1961 [1930], p. 182; Bede Nairn, *Civilising Capitalism: The Beginning of the Australian Labor Party*, Melbourne University Press, Melbourne, 1989 [1973].

9 John Howard, doorstop interview, Paralympics Dinner, 1 November 2000, accessed at http://pandora.nla.gov.au/pan/10052/20010821-0000/www.pm.gov.au/news/interviews/2000/interview528.htm; http://pandora.nla.gov.au/pan/10052/20010821–0000/www.pm.gov.au/news/interviews/2000/interview528.htm, 29 December 2009.

10 Verity Burgmann, *'In Our Time': Socialism and the Rise of Labor, 1885–1905*, George Allen & Unwin, Sydney, p. 82; Raymond Markey, *The Making of the Labor Party in New South Wales 1890–1900*, UNSW Press, Sydney, 1988, p. 175.

11 The dual and contradictory nature of working class consciousness is explored in Antonio Gramsci, *Selections from the Prison Notebooks*, Lawrence & Wishart, London, 1971, p. 333; see also Georg Lukács, *History and Class Consciousness*, Merlin, London, 1971.

12 See Rick Kuhn, 'Class analysis and the left in Australian history', in Rick Kuhn and Tom O'Lincoln (eds), *Class and Class Conflict in Australia*, Longman, Melbourne, 1996, pp. 145–62.

13 William Morris Hughes, *The Case for Labor*, University of Sydney Press, Sydney, 1970 [1910], p. 140.

14 Humphrey McQueen, 'Glory without power', in J. Playford and D. Kirsner (eds), *Australian Capitalism: Towards a Socialist Critique*, Penguin, Ringwood, 1972, p. 360.

15 W. R. Winspear, *Economic Warfare*, Marxian Press, Sydney, 1914, p. 3.

16 Vladimir Ilyich Lenin, 'Affiliation to the British Labour Party', speech to the Second Congress of the Communist International, 6 August 1920, accessed at www.marxists.org/archive/lenin/works/1920/jul/x03.htm, 7 May 2007; see also Lenin's 'Imperialism and the split in socialism', December 1916, accessed at www.marxists.org/archive/lenin/works/1916/oct/x01.htm, 7 May 2007.

17 Cited in McQueen 'Glory without power', p. 351.
18 See Tony Cliff and Donny Gluckstein, *The Labour Party – A Marxist History*, Bookmarks, London, 1988, p. 390.
19 Vere Gordon Childe, *How Labour Governs*, Melbourne University Press, Melbourne, 1964 [1923].
20 Winspear, *Economic Warfare*, pp. 47–8.
21 Ibid.
22 Karl Marx, *Value, Price and Profit*, 1865, www.marxists.org/archive/marx/works/1865/value-price-profit/ch03.htm, accessed 21 April 2010.
23 Antonio Gramsci, 'Unions and councils', from *L'Ordine Nuovo*, 12 June 1920, cited in David Forgacs (ed.), *An Antonio Gramsci Reader: Selected Writings, 1916–35*, Schocken Books, New York, 1988, pp. 92–6.
24 C. Wright Mills, *The New Men of Power: America's Labor Leaders*, Harcourt Brace, New York, 1948, pp. 8–9.
25 Richard Hyman, *The Workers Union*, Blackwell, Oxford, 1971, p. 223.
26 Sidney and Beatrice Webb, *The History of Trade Unionism*, Longmans Green, London, 1920 [1898], p. 594. Tom Bramble, 'A portrait of Australian trade union officials', *British Journal of Industrial Relations*, 39 (4), 529–37.
27 Sidney and Beatrice Webb, *Industrial Democracy*, self-published, London, 1902 [1898], pp. 12, 59.
28 Vladimir Ilyich Lenin, 'In Australia', in Appendix, Lance Sharkey, *Australia Marches On*, Communist Party of Australia, Sydney, 1942.
29 Karl Marx and Friedrich Engels, *The Manifesto of the Communist Party*, accessed at www.marxists.org/archive/marx/works/1848/communist-manifesto/ch04.htm, 25 April 2010.
30 Jim Hagan, *The History of the ACTU*, Longman Cheshire, Melbourne, 1981, pp. 108–9; Commonwealth of Australia, *Digest of Decisions and Announcements*, 18, 1943, pp. 15–16.
31 Cited in McQueen, 'Glory without power', p. 353.
32 Lance Sharkey, *Australia Marches On*, Communist Party of Australia, Sydney, 1943, p. 26; Tom Bramble and Rick Kuhn, 'Social democracy after the long boom: economic restructuring under Australian Labor, 1983 to 1996', in Martin Upchurch (ed.), *The State and 'Globalisation': Comparative Studies of Labour and Capital in National Economies*, Mansell, London, 1999, pp. 20–55.
33 McQueen, 'Glory without power', pp. 346, 358.
34 Kelvin Rowley, 'Bob Hawke: capital for Labor?', *Arena*, 25, 1971, pp. 9–17; Robert Catley and Bruce McFarlane, *From Tweedledum to Tweedledee: The New Labor Government in Australia*, Australia and New Zealand Book Company, Sydney, 1974, pp. 4, 14–36; see also Bob Catley and Bruce McFarlane, 'Technocratic Laborism – the Whitlam Government', in E. L. Wheelwright and Ken Buckley (eds), *Essays in the Political Economy of Australian Capitalism Volume One*, Australia and New Zealand Book Company, Sydney, 1975, pp. 242–69.
35 Melanie Beresford, 'The Technocratic Labor thesis: a critique', *Arena* 39, 1975, p. 65.
36 For more detailed summaries of arguments about the Labor Party during the late 1980s and early 1990s see Peter Beilharz, *Transforming Labor: Labour Tradition and the Labor Decade in Australia*, Cambridge University Press, Melbourne, 1994.

37 D. A. Kemp, *Society and Electoral Behaviour in Australia: A Study of Three Decades*, University of Queensland Press, St Lucia, 1978.

38 See Murray Goot, 'Class Voting, Issue Voting and Electoral Volatility', in Judith Brett, James Gillespie and Murray Goot (eds), *Developments in Australian Politics*, Macmillan, Melbourne, 1994, pp. 153–81.

39 Dean Jaensch, *The Hawke–Keating Hijack*, Allen & Unwin, Sydney, 1989, pp. 20, 96, 154, 157–8, 165, 177.

40 Paul Kelly, *The End of Certainty*, Allen & Unwin, Sydney, 1994 [1992], pp. xxv, 9, 15.

41 Humphrey McQueen, 'Struggles over settlements', 'The Review', *Australian Financial Review*, 2 November 2007, pp. 6–8; see also http://home.alphalink.com.au/ ~loge27/aus_hist/aus_hist_harvester.htm, accessed 31 January 2009.

42 Graham Maddox, *The Hawke Government and Labor Tradition*, Penguin, Ringwood, 1989, pp. 4, 13, 65, 66, 138–53, 1801; see also Frank Stilwell, *The Accord and Beyond: The Political Economy of the Labor Government*, Pluto Press, Sydney, 1986, especially p. 120; Michael Pusey, *Economic Rationalism in Canberra: A Nation Building State Changes Its Mind*, Cambridge University Press, Melbourne, 1991.

43 Peter Beilharz, 'Labor: the new conservatives', in Brian Costar (ed.), *For Better or For Worse: The Federal Coalition*, Melbourne University Press, Melbourne, 1994, p. 43 (41–6); see also Beilharz, *Transforming Labor*.

44 Peter Fairbrother, Stuart Svensen and Julian Teicher, 'The ascendancy of neo-liberalism in Australia', *Capital & Class*, 63, Fall 1997, pp. 1–12.

45 Tom Bramble, *Trade Unionism in Australia: A History from Flood to Ebb Tide*, Cambridge University Press, Melbourne, 2008, pp. 125–80.

46 Gary Johns, 'Party organisations and resources', in Ian Marsh (ed.) *Political Parties in Transition?*, The Federation Press, Sydney, 2006, p. 66; Ian Ward, 'Cartel parties and election campaigns in Australia', in Ian Marsh (ed.), *Political Parties in Transition?*, p. 89; Ian Marsh, 'Policy convergence between the major parties and the representation gap in Australian politics', in Ian Marsh (ed.), *Political Parties in Transition?*, pp. 131, 135–7; see also Ian Marsh, 'Australia's political cartel? The major parties and the party system in an era of globalisation', in Ian Marsh, *Political Parties in Transition?*, p. 13.

47 Ashley Lavelle, *The Death of Social Democracy: Political Consequences in the 21st Century*, Ashgate, Aldershot, 2008, pp. 8, 11, 15, 49–63.

48 Tony Cliff, 'Economic roots of reformism', in Tony Cliff, *Neither Washington nor Moscow: Essays on Revolutionary Socialism*, Bookmarks, London, 1982 [1957], p. 117.

49 Neville Wran, 'The great tradition-Labor reform from Curtin to Hawke', John Curtin Memorial Lecture 1986, accessed at http://john.curtin.edu.au/jcmemlect/wran1986.html, 19 February 2009; see also Paul Keating, 'One Nation' ministerial statement, Commonwealth of Australia, *Parliamentary Debates, House of Representatives, Hansard*, 26 February 1992, pp. 264–71.

50 Carole Johnson, *The Labor Legacy* Sydney, Allen & Unwin, 1989; Haydon Manning, 'The ALP and the union movement', *Australian Journal of Political Science*, 27 (1), 1992, pp. 12–30.

51 Andrew Scott, *Fading Loyalties: The Australian Labor Party and the Working Class*, Pluto Press, Sydney, 1991; Andrew Scott, *Running on Empty: 'Modernising' the British and Australian Labour Parties*, Pluto Press, Sydney, 2000, pp. 256–8.

52 Greg Patmore and David Coates, 'Labour parties and the state in Australia and the UK', *Labour History*, 88, May 2005, p. 138.

Chapter 2: In the beginning: Labor's first quarter century

 1 Raymond Markey, *The Making of the Labor Party in New South Wales: 1880–1900*, UNSW Press, Sydney, 1988, p. 32.
 2 Ibid., pp. 137–40, 318.
 3 Ibid. p. 5.
 4 Stuart Svensen, *The Sinews of War: Hard Cash and the 1890 Maritime Strike*, UNSW Press, Sydney, 1995.
 5 Stuart Svensen, *The Shearers' War: The Story of the 1891 Shearers' Strike*, 2nd edn, Hesperian Press, Perth, 2008.
 6 This peak body went through various incarnations and names during the 1890s and early 20th century, with varying levels of authority in New South Wales beyond Sydney.
 7 Bede Nairn, *Civilising Capitalism: The Beginning of the Australian Labor Party*, Melbourne University Press, Melbourne, 1989 [1973], pp. 68–9; see also pp. 126–7.
 8 Lynn Lovelock and John Evans, *New South Wales Legislative Council Practice*, The Federation Press, Sydney, 2008, p. 186; Glen Withers, Anthony M. Endres and Len Parry, 'Labor', in Wray Vamplew (ed.), *Australian Historical Statistics*, Fairfax, Syme and Weldon, Sydney, 1987, p. 160.
 9 Dennis J. Murphy, 'Queensland', in Dennis J. Murphy (ed.) *Labor in Politics: The State Labor Parties in Australia 1880–1920*, University of Queensland Press, St Lucia, 1975, p. 155.
10 John Merritt, *The Making of the AWU*, Oxford University Press, Melbourne, 1986, p. 264.
11 Dennis Murphy, *T. J. Ryan: A Political Biography*, University of Queensland Press, St Lucia, 1975, p. 48.
12 Peter Love, *Labour and the Money Power*, Melbourne University Press, Melbourne, p. 35.
13 Markey, *The Making of the Labor Party*, pp. 211, 280; Nairn, *Civilising Capitalism*, p. 162.
14 See Verity Burgmann, *'In Our Time': Socialism and the Rise of Labor, 1885–1905*, George Allen & Unwin, Sydney, 1985; Markey, *The Making of the Labor Party*, pp. 243–4.
15 Ian Turner, *Industrial Labour and Politics: The Dynamics of the Labour Movement in Eastern Australia, 1900–1921*, Hale & Iremonger, Sydney, 1979 [1965], p. 48.
16 Humphrey McQueen, 'Victoria', in Murphy, *Labor in Politics*, p. 308 (pp. 291–340); Brian Dickey 'South Australia', in Murphy, *Labor in Politics*, p. 252–3 (pp. 231–89).
17 For the arrangements in New South Wales in 1895, see Nairn, *Civilising Capitalism*, p. 136; for Queensland in 1901, see Murphy 'Queensland', p. 167.
18 Nairn, *Civilising Capitalism*, p. 210.
19 H. J. Gibney, *Labor in Print: A Guide to the People Who Created a Labor Press in Australia Between 1850 and 1939*, ANU Press, Canberra 1975; Murphy, *T. J. Ryan* p. 43.

20 Michael Hogan, 'Reid, George (later Sir George) Houstoun', in David Clune and Ken Turner (eds), *The Premiers of New South Wales, 1856–2005: 1856–1901*, The Federation Press, Sydney, 2006, p. 200; Nairn, *Civilising Capitalism*, pp. 176–7; H. V. Evatt, *William Holman: Australian Labour Leader*, Angus & Robertson, Sydney, abridged 1979 [1940], pp. 94–5.

21 Phil Griffiths, 'Labor's tortured path to protectionism', Sixth Biennial National Labour History conference, Wollongong, October 1999, at http://members.optusnet. com.au/~griff52/LaborProtectionism.rtf, accessed 23 July 2009; Rick Kuhn, 'Workers, capital and the protection racket', in Verity Burgmann and Jenny Lee (eds), *A Most Valuable Acquisition*, Penguin, Ringwood, 1988, pp. 123–36.

22 Ross Fitzgerald, *'Red Ted': The Life of E. G. Theodore*, University of Queensland Press, St Lucia, 1994, p. 61.

23 Verity Burgmann, *Revolutionary Industrial Unionism: The Industrial Workers of the World in Australia*, Cambridge University Press, Melbourne, 1995, p. 16.

24 Turner, *Industrial Labour and Politics*, p. 53.

25 Albert Metin, *Socialism Without Doctrine*, Alternative Publishing Co-operative, Sydney, 1977 [1910]; Frederic William Eggleston, *State Socialism in Victoria*, King & Son, London, 1932; Noel G. Butlin, 'Colonial socialism in Australia 1860–1900', in H. G. J. Aitken (ed.), *The State and Economic Growth*, Social Science Research Council, New York, 1959.

26 Peter Loveday, 'New South Wales', in Murphy, *Labor in Politics*, p. 80–1; H. J. Gibbney 'Western Australia', in Murphy, *Labor in Politics*, pp. 365–6; D. J. Murphy, 'State enterprises', in D. J. Murphy, R. B. Joyce and Colin A. Hughes (eds), *Labor in Power: The Labor Party and Governments in Queensland 1915–1957*, University of Queensland Press, St Lucia, 1980, pp. 138–56.

27 Helen Hughes, *The Australian Iron and Steel Industry*, Melbourne University Press, Melbourne, 1964, pp. 65–8.

28 Hawkins, 'John Forrest', p. 147.

29 Julie P. Smith, *Taxing Popularity: The Story of Taxation in Australia*, Federalism Research Centre, ANU Press, 1993, pp. 43–5; Jim Longley, *Land Tax Review: Report of the Government Treasury Advisory Committee*, Sydney, 1990, p. 15; B. Dickey, 'The introduction of direct taxation in New South Wales, 1892–1898', *Journal of the Royal Australian Historical Society*, 74 (4), April 1989, p. 335; McQueen, *A New Britannia*, p. 168; Sam Reinhardt and Lee Steel 'A brief history of Australia's tax system', 22nd APEC Finance Ministers' Technical Working Group Meeting in Khanh Hoa, Vietnam, 15 June 2006.

30 Love, *Labour and the Money Power*, passim., on the Commonwealth Bank, pp. 50–5.

31 L. F. Giblin, *The Growth of a Central Bank: The Development of the Commonwealth Bank of Australia, 1924–1945*, Melbourne University Press, Melbourne, 1951.

32 John Barrett, *Falling In: Australians and 'Boy Conscription', 1911–1915*, Hale & Iremonger, Sydney, 1979, pp. 67–70, 215.

33 Turner, *Industrial Labour and Politics*, pp. 37–40; Burgmann, *Revolutionary Industrial Unionism*, pp. 21–2; Graeme Osborne, 'Town and Country', in John Iremonger, John Merritt and Graeme Osborne (eds), *Strikes: Studies in Twentieth Century Australian Social History*, Angus & Robertson, 1973, pp. 26–50.

34 Turner, *Industrial Labour and Politics*, pp. 38, 40; Evatt, *William Holman*, p. 239.

35 Turner, *Industrial Labour and Politics*, p. 87.
36 The definitive account of the general strike of 1917 is Robert Bollard's ' "The Active Chorus": The Mass Strike of 1917 in Eastern Australia', PhD thesis, School of Social Sciences, Faculty of Arts Education and Human Development, Victoria University, Melbourne, September 2007, at http://eprints.vu.edu.au/1472/, accessed 18 November 2009; see also Robert Bollard, ' "Rank and fileism" revisited: trade union bureaucracy and the Great Strike', *Marxist Interventions*, 2, 2010, at www.anu.edu.au/polsci/mi/2/.
37 Turner, *Industrial Labour and Politics*, p. 150.
38 Ibid., p. 157.

Chapter 3: Between the wars

1 Verity Burgmann, *Revolutionary Industrial Unionism: The Industrial Workers of the World in Australia*, Cambridge University Press, Melbourne, 1995, pp. 216–17.
2 The full texts of the socialisation objective and the Blackburn Declaration are cited in Andrew Scott, *Running on Empty: 'Modernising' the British and Australian Labour Parties*, Pluto Press, Sydney, 2000, pp. 50–60.
3 D. J. Murphy, 'State enterprises', in D. J. Murphy, R. B. Joyce and Colin A. Hughes (eds), *Labor in Power: The Labor Party and Governments in Queensland 1915–57*, University of Queensland Press, St Lucia, 1980, p. 138.
4 Unless otherwise indicated, accounts of developments in Queensland in this chapter draw on Ross Fitzgerald and Harold Thornton, *Labor in Queensland from the 1880s to 1988*, University of Queensland Press, St Lucia, 1989, pp. 100–4 and 108–13 and Tom Cochrane, *Blockade: the Queensland loans affair 1920 to 1924*, University of Queensland Press, St Lucia, 1989.
5 K. H. Kennedy, 'The South Johnstone strike and railway lockout', *Labour History*, 31, November 1976, pp. 1–13; Margaret Bridson Cribb, 'Ideological conflict: the 1927 and 1948 strikes', in Murphy, Joyce and Hughes, *Labor in Power*, pp. 383–405.
6 Miriam Dixon, *Greater Than Lenin*, Melbourne Politics Monograph, University of Melbourne, Melbourne, 1977, p. 126.
7 Unless otherwise indicated, the account of the Lang government draws on essays in Heather Radi and Peter Spearritt, *Jack Lang*, Hale & Iremonger, Sydney, 1977; Robinson, *When the Labor Party Dreams* and Bede Nairn, *The 'Big Fella': Jack Lang and the Australian Labor Party 1891–1949*, Melbourne University Press, Melbourne, 1986, pp. 213, 259.
8 'Mr. Lang's policy speech: 44-hour week promised: states' agreement attacked: will restore service salaries', *Argus*, 23 September 1930, p. 9.
9 See Peter Sheldon, 'State-level Basic Wages in Australia during the Depression, 1929–35: Institutions and Politics over Markets', *Australian Economic History Review*, 47 (3), November 2007, pp. 249–77.
10 'Rationing and 44 hours', *Sydney Morning Herald*, 5 January 1931, p. 8; 'Unemployment growing', *Sydney Morning Herald*, 7 January 1931, p. 12.
11 Ross McMullin, *The Light on the Hill: The Australian Labor Party, 1891–1991*, Oxford University Press, Melbourne, 1991, p. 175.
12 R. B. Walker, 'The fall of the *Labor Daily*', *Labour History*, 38, May 1980, pp. 67–75.
13 The following account draws on Robert Cooksey, *Lang and Socialism: A Study in the Great Depression*, ANU Press, Canberra, 1976.

14 Cited in Cooksey, *Lang and Socialism*, p. 54.

15 For example, Oscar Schreiber, 'Remedies for unemployment: Labor's view', *Labor Call*, 9 April 1936, p. 14.

16 Alex Millmow, 'W. Brian Reddaway – Keynes' emissary to Australia, 1913–2002' *Economic Record*, 79 (244), March 2003, pp. 136–8.

Chapter 4: Hot war, cold war, split

1 Peter Stanley, *Invading Australia: Japan and the Battle for Australia, 1942*, Viking, Melbourne, 2008, p. 158; Tom O'Lincoln, *Australia's Pacific War: Critical essays*, forthcoming.

2 Rob Watts, 'The origins of the Australian welfare state', in Richard Kennedy (ed.), *Australian Welfare History: Critical Essays*, Macmillan, Melbourne, 1982, pp. 141–9.

3 See Dean Ashenden, 'Evatt and the origins of the Cold War', *Journal of Australian Studies*, 4 (7), November 1980, pp. 73–95.

4 See Daniel Mandel, *H V Evatt and the Establishment of Israel: The Undercover Zionist*, Frank Cass, London, 2004, particularly pp. 273–5.

5 E. R. Walker, *The Australian Economy in War and Reconstruction*, Oxford University Press, Oxford, 1947, pp. 15–16, 72; Commonwealth of Australia, *Digest of Decisions and Announcements and Important Speeches by the Prime Minister*, 18, 1942, pp. 15–16, and *Digest of Decisions and Announcements*, 35, 1942, p. 5.

6 H. V. Evatt, *Post-war Reconstruction: A Case for Greater Commonwealth Powers*, Government Printer, Canberra, November 1942, p. 57.

7 Jim Hagan, *The History of the ACTU*, Longman Cheshire, Melbourne, 1981, pp. 108–9; *Digest of Decisions and Announcements*, 18, 1942, pp. 15–16.

8 See Tom Sheridan, *Division of Labour: Industrial Relations in the Chifley Years*, Oxford University Press, Melbourne, 1989, p. 57.

9 Ibid., pp. 95–114; George Petersen, 'The Labor movement and World War II', lecture, 7 December 1980, transcript held by Eric Petersen, p. 16.

10 Douglas Blackmur, 'The ALP Industrial Groups in Queensland', *Labour History*, 46, May 1984, pp. 88–108.

11 D. M. Hocking and C. P. Haddon-Cave, *Air Transport in Australia*, Angus & Robertson, Sydney, 1951, pp. 79–80.

12 For developments in the federal public service, see Rick Kuhn, 'Class struggle in the public service', *International Socialist*, 10, 1980.

13 S. J. Butlin and C. B. Schedvin, *War Economy 1942–1945*, Australian War Memorial, Canberra, 1977, p. 747.

14 A. G. L. Shaw and G. R. Bruns, *The Australian Coal Industry*, Melbourne University Press, Melbourne, 1947, p. 170.

15 *Joint Coal Board Annual Report 1947–8*, pp. 6, 12, 18–19, 21, 26.

16 Jock Collins, 'The political economy of post-war immigration', in E. L. Wheelwright and Ken Buckley, *Essays in the Political Economy of Australian Capitalism, Volume One*, Australia and New Zealand Book Company, Sydney, 1975, pp. 109, 110, 118.

17 L. F. Crisp, *Ben Chifley*, Angus & Robertson, Sydney, 1977, p. 320; Rick Kuhn, 'Paradise on the Installment Plan: The economic thought of the Australian labour movement between the Depression and the long boom', PhD thesis, Sydney University, Sydney, 1985, pp. 122–51.

18 This account draws on the work of Rob Watts, especially *The Foundations of the National Welfare State*, Allen & Unwin, Sydney, 1987.

19 J. B. Chifley, *Banking Bill 1947: Second Reading Speech Delivered on 15th October, 1947* Government Printer, Canberra, 1947, p. 7.

20 For more details see A. L. May, *The Battle for the Banks*, Sydney University Press, Sydney, 1968; Rick Kuhn, 'Paradise on the Instalment Plan: The Economic Thought of the Australian Labour Movement Between the Depression and the Long Boom', PhD thesis, Sydney University, Sydney, 1985, pp. 138–40.

21 Edgar Ross, *Of Storm and Struggle: Pages from Labour History*, Alternative Publishing Co-operative, Sydney, 1982, p. 104.

22 Andrew Scott, 'Fading Loyalties: Working-Class Participation in, and Electoral Support for, the Australian Labor Party since World War Two', BA honours thesis in History, University of Melbourne, Melbourne, 1990, Appendix 3, Table 2.

23 Gough Whitlam, *The Whitlam Government: 1972–1975*, Penguin, Ringwood, 1985, p. 184.

24 David Clune, 'The Labor Government in NSW 1941–1965: A Study in Longevity in Government', PhD thesis, University of Sydney, Sydney, 1991, p. 73.

25 Arthur Calwell, *Commonwealth Parliamentary Debates (House of Representatives)*, 45, 23 March 1965, p. 242.

Chapter 5: Labor after 70 years

1 Ross M. Martin, 'Australian professional and white-collar unions', *Industrial Relations*, 5 (1) 1965, pp. 93–102.

2 Haydon Manning, 'The ALP and the union movement: beyond 2000', in John Warhurst and Andrew Parkin (eds), *The Machine: Labor Confronts the Future*, Allen & Unwin, Sydney, 2000, p. 240 (pp. 231–49). Only in Tasmania, with a small population and puny union movement, were union delegates outnumbered by those from local branches; see Richard Davis, *Eighty Years' Labor: The ALP in Tasmania, 1903–1983*, Sassafras Books, Hobart, 1983, p. 89.

3 Don Rawson, *Labor in Vain: A Survey of the Australian Labor Party*, Longman, Melbourne, 1966, pp. 22–3.

4 Jim Hagan and Ken Turner, *A History of the Labor Party in New South Wales: 1891–1991*, Longman Cheshire, Melbourne, 1991, p. 164.

5 Bobby Oliver, 'The formation and role of an independent trades and labor council in Western Australia', in Bradon Ellem, Raymond Markey and John Shields (eds), *Peak Unions in Australia: Origins, Purpose, Power, Agency*, The Federation Press, Sydney, 2004, pp. 116–32.

6 Ross Fitzgerald and Harold Thornton, *Labor in Queensland: from the 1880s to 1988*, University of Queensland Press, St Lucia, 1989, pp. 231–2, 285.

7 David Clune, 'The Labor Government in New South Wales 1941–1965: A Study in Longevity in Government', PhD thesis, University of Sydney, Sydney, 1991, pp. 17–18.

8 Manning, 'The ALP and the union movement', p. 234.

9 *Australian Dictionary of Biography*, accessed at http://adbonline.anu.edu.au, 22 February 2010.

10 L. F. Crisp and B. Atkinson, *Australian Labour Party: Federal parliamentarians, 1901–1981*, mimeo, ANU Press, Canberra, p. 57 and extracted from relevant profiles for 1962.

11 See Andrew Leigh's calculations, 2010, accessed at http://people.anu.edu.au/andrew.leigh/pdf/TopIncomesAustralia.xls, 9 April 2010.

12 These data are drawn from Margaret Reynolds, *The Last Bastion: Labor Women Working Towards Equality in the Parliaments of Australia*, Business and Professional Publishing, Sydney, 1995, pp. 20, 41, 223–5.

13 Rawson, *Labor in Vain*, p. 23.

14 The following account of factions and machines draws on the essays about the state branches of the Party in Parkin and Warhurst, *Machine Politics*.

15 The exception was the executive's instruction that the Communist Party Dissolution Bill should be passed by the Labor controlled Senate in 1950. Bron Stevens and Pat Weller (eds), *The Australian Labor Party and Federal Politics: A Documentary Survey*, Melbourne University Press, Melbourne, 1976, p. 56; Rawson, *Labor in Vain*, p. 25.

16 Andrew Scott, 'Fading Loyalties: Working-Class Participation in, and Electoral Support for, the Australian Labor Party since World War Two', BA honours thesis in History, University of Melbourne, Melbourne, 1990, Appendix 3, Table 2; Geoff Robinson, *When the Labor Party Dreams: Class, Politics and Policy in NSW 1930–32*, Australian Scholarly Publishing, Melbourne, 2008, p. 25; ratio of members to voters calculated for the 1929 federal election.

17 Cyril S. Wyndham, *Australian Labor Party, Party reorganisation: Recommendations of the General Secretary*, mimeo, 1965, p. 16.

18 Andrew Scott, 'Fading Loyalties', Appendix 3, Table 2.

19 There were still departments in the Commonwealth and some state public services in which it was a distinct advantage to be a Freemason or a Catholic at this time.

20 Ian Wilson, *The 1958 Federal Election in Yarra*, Monograph 1, Australian Political Studies Association, Sydney, 1959, p. 2.

21 R. B. Walker, 'The fall of the *Labor Daily*', *Labour History*, 38, May 1980, pp. 67–75.

22 Ian Ward, 'The early use of radio for political communication in Australia and Canada: John Henry Austral, Mr Sage and the Man from Mars', *Australian Journal of Politics and History*, 45 (3), 1999, pp. 311–329.

23 On political advertising see Sally Young, 'A century of political communication in Australia, 1901–2001', *Journal of Australian Studies*, 27 (78), 2003, pp. 97–110.

24 Rawson, *Labor in Vain*, pp. 22–3.

25 Janet McCalman, *Struggletown: Public and Private Life in Richmond 1900–1965*, Hyland House, Melbourne, 1998, p. 281.

26 The following account draws extensively on Michael Hogan, *Local Labor: A History of the Labor Party in Glebe 1891–2003*, The Federation Press, Sydney, 2004, especially pp. 156–72; Rodney Cavalier, 'The Australian Labor Party at branch level: Guildford, Hunters Hill and Panania Branches in the 1950s', in Gough Whitlam et al., *A Century of Social Change*, Pluto Press, Sydney, 1992, pp. 92–133.

Chapter 6: The Whitlam era

1 Tom O'Lincoln, *Into the Mainstream: The Decline of Australian Communism*, Stained Wattle Press, Sydney, 1985 (reprinted by Vulgar Press, 2009), pp. 140–1.

2 Meredith Burgmann and Verity Burgmann, *Green Bans, Red Union: Environmental Activism and the NSW Builders Labourers Federation*, UNSW Press, Sydney, 1998.

3 Phillip Bentley, 'Australian trade unionism, 1969–70', *Journal of Industrial Relations*, 12 (4), 1970, p. 379.

4 Cited in Bob Scates, *Draftmen Go Free: A History of the Anti-Conscription Movement in Australia*, self-published, Melbourne, 1989, p. 50.

5 The following account draws on Mick Armstrong, *1, 2, 3, What Are We Fighting For? The Australian Student Movement from its Origins to the 1970s*, Socialist Alternative, Melbourne, 2001, Chapter 5.

6 Andrew Scott, 'Fading Loyalties: Working-Class Participation in, and Electoral Support for, the Australian Labor Party since World War Two', BA honours thesis in History, University of Melbourne, Melbourne, 1990, Appendix 3, Table 2.

7 Malcolm Saunders, 'The trade unions in Australia and opposition to Vietnam and conscription: 1965–1973', *Labour History*, 43, 1982, 64–82.

8 Tom Wheelwright, 'New South Wales: the dominant Right', in Andrew Parkin and John Warhurst (eds), *Machine Politics in the Australian Labor Party*, George Allen & Unwin, Sydney, 1983, p. 34.

9 The following account is drawn from Declan O'Connell, 'Party reform: debates and dilemmas, 1958–1991', in Gough Whitlam et al., *A Century of Social Change*, Pluto Press, Sydney, 1992.

10 Marian Simms, 'New South Wales: The microcosm of a nation', in John Warhurst and Andrew Parkin (eds), *The Machine: Labor Confronts the Future*, Allen & Unwin, Sydney, 2000, p. 103.

11 Phillip Bentley, 'Australian trade unionism, 1970–71', p. 416; Ashley Lavelle, 'In the Wilderness: Federal Labor in Opposition', PhD thesis, Faculty of International Business and Politics, Griffith University, Brisbane, 2003, p. 83, pp. 92–3.

12 Cited in Lavelle, 'In the Wilderness', p. 80.

13 Clyde Cameron on 'Productivity and the community', *House of Representatives, Parliamentary Debates*, 1 April 1971, reproduced in *Monthly Journal*, Amalgamated Engineering Union, June 1971, p. 22.

14 The following account of Whitlam's reform program draws on Tom O'Lincoln, 'The rise and fall of Gough Whitlam', *Socialist Review*, (Melbourne) 5, Autumn 1992, pp. 126–54.

15 Tom O'Lincoln, *Years of Rage: Social Conflicts in the Fraser Era*, Bookmarks Australia, Melbourne, 1993, p. 20.

16 For the attitude of the press, see Henry Mayer, Elaine Thompson and Lyn Beatty, 'Partial partners? the Melbourne *Age* and the *Sydney Morning Herald*', in Henry Mayer (ed.), *Labor to Power*, Angus & Robertson, Sydney, 1973, pp. 216–24.

17 Cited in Carol Johnson, *The Labor Legacy: Curtin, Chifley, Whitlam, Hawke*, Allen & Unwin, Sydney, 1989, p. 56.

18 Leon Glazer, *Tariff Politics: Australian Policy-making 1960–1980*, Melbourne University Press, Melbourne, 1982, pp. 91, 272–3.

19 Denis Murphy, *Hayden, A Political Biography*, Angus & Robertson, Sydney, 1980, p. 34; Gough Whitlam, *The Whitlam Government: 1972–1975*, Penguin, Ringwood, 1985, p. 192.

20 Whitlam, *The Whitlam Government*, p. 219–20.

21 Bob Catley and Bruce McFarlane, *From Tweedledum to Tweedledee: The new Labor Government in Australia, a Critique of its Social Model*, Australia and New Zealand Book Company, Sydney, 1974, pp. 45–53.

22 Bob Catley and Bruce McFarlane, 'Labor's plan: neo-capitalism comes to Australia', *Intervention* 3, 1973, pp. 11–13.

23 Amanda Biggs, 'Medicare', Parliamentary Library, Background Brief, 9 May 2003, at www.aph.gov.au/library/intguide/SP/medicare.htm, accessed 10 August 2009; Catley and McFarlane, *From Tweedledum to Tweedledee*, p. 32.

24 Catley and McFarlane, 'Labor's plan', pp. 17–18.

25 Will Sanders, 'Decolonising Indigenous Australia: Labor's contribution?', in John Warhurst and Andrew Parkin (eds), *The Machine: Labor Confronts the Future*, Allen & Unwin, Sydney, p. 316.

26 Diane Bell, 'We are hungry for our land', in Verity Burgmann and Jenny Lee (eds), *A Most Valuable Acquisition*, McPhee Gribble, Melbourne, 1988, pp. 30–1.

27 Alec Robertson, 'Labor: what has been done?', *Tribune*, 26 February–4 March 1974, p. 5.

28 Sean Brawley, 'Long hairs and ratbags: The ALP and the abolition of the White Australia Policy', in Gough Whitlam et al., *A Century of Social Change*, Pluto Press, Sydney, 1992, p. 206.

29 Robert Tierney, 'Migrants and class in postwar Australia', in Rick Kuhn and Tom O'Lincoln (eds), *Class and Class Conflict in Australia*, Longman, Melbourne, 1996, p. 97.

30 Allen Barnes, 'All a Chipp off the old Gorton', *Age*, 5 May 1972, p. 9.

31 Phil Griffiths, 'Racism: Whitewashing the class divide', in Rick Kuhn, *Class and Struggle in Australia*, Pearson Education Australia, Sydney, 2005, p. 168.

32 Fifty-three per cent of all Australians born in Italy, Greece, Malta and Turkey indicated their support for Labor in 1973 as against only 43 per cent of those born in Australia; David Kemp, *Society and Electoral Behaviour in Australia: A Study of Three Decades*, University of Queensland Press, St Lucia, 1978, p. 191.

33 Barry York, 'Australia and Refugees, 1901–2002: An annotated chronology based on official sources', Social Policy Group, Parliamentary Library, Parliament of Australia, Table 6, accessed at www.aph.gov.au/library/pubs/online/Refugees_s9.htm#table1, 27 December 2009.

34 Gough Whitlam, *The Whitlam Government*, p. 36.

35 J. L. Richardson, 'Australian strategic and defence policies', in Gordon Greenwood and Norman Harper (eds), *Australia in World Affairs 1966–1970*, Cheshire, Melbourne, 1974, p. 262.

36 Simon Mohun, 'The Australian rate of profit, 1965–2001', *Journal of Australian Political Economy*, 52, 2003, p. 88.

37 Phillip Bentley, 'Australian trade unionism, 1973–74', *Journal of Industrial Relations*, 1974, p. 384.

38 Mohun, 'The Australian rate of profit', p. 88.

39 Bentley, 'Australian trade unionism, 1973–74', p. 384.

40 For a detailed account of the Whitlam government's macroeconomic policy, see Catley and McFarlane, *From Tweedledum to Tweedledee*, pp. 132–51.

41 Phil Griffiths, 'Strike Fraser out! The labour movement campaign against the blocking of supply and the sacking of the Whitlam Government, October–December

1975', accessed at www.anu.edu.au/polsci/marx/interventions/sacked.htm, 18 January 2010. The account that follows draws heavily from this source.

42 Ibid., p. 3.

43 Bob Carr, 'Australian trade unionism in 1975', *Journal of Industrial Relations*, December 1975, p. 422.

44 Griffiths, 'Strike Fraser out!', p. 10.

45 Gough Whitlam, *The Truth of the Matter*, Melbourne University Press, Melbourne, 2005.

46 Carr, 'Australian trade unionism in 1975', p. 422.

47 Lavelle, 'In the Wilderness', p. 128.

48 Ibid., p. 169.

49 Catley and McFarlane, *Australian Capitalism in Boom and Depression*, p. 143.

50 The following analysis is explored in more detail in Tom Bramble, *Trade Unionism in Australia: A History from Flood to Ebb Tide*, Cambridge University Press, Melbourne, 2008, pp. 109–14.

Chapter 7: Economic rationalism under Hawke and Keating

1 Neville Wran, 'The great tradition – Labor reform from Curtin to Hawke', 1986 John Curtin Memorial Lecture, accessed at http://john.curtin.edu.au/jcmemlect/wran1986.html, 30 December 2009.

2 Graham Maddox, *The Hawke Government and the Labor Tradition*, Penguin, Ringwood, 1989, p. 5.

3 Matthew Stevens 'Argus warns of complacency in dangerous times', *Australian*, 25 March 2010, p. 19.

4 For example, Max Ogden, 'The Accord: intervening to deepen the democratic process', *Australian Left Review*, 90, 1984; John Mathews 'The Politics of the Accord', in D. McKnight (ed.), *Moving Left: The Future of Socialism in Australia*, Pluto Press, Sydney, 1986.

5 Cited in Ashley Lavelle, 'In the wilderness: federal Labor in opposition', PhD thesis, Faculty of International Business and Politics, Griffith University, Brisbane, 2003, p. 170.

6 Braham Dabscheck, *Australian Industrial Relations in the 1980s*, Oxford University Press, Melbourne, 1989, p. 53.

7 National Economic Summit Conference, Communiqué, April 1983.

8 Tom Bramble *Trade Unionism in Australia: A History from Flood to Ebb Tide*, Cambridge University Press, Melbourne, 2008, pp. 131–6; 156–7.

9 John Stone, 'Let's start all over again', Proceedings of the H. R. Nicholls Society, Sydney, March 2006, accessed at www.hrnicholls.com.au/archives/vol27/vol27–3.php, 18 January 2010.

10 *Business Review Weekly*, 22 September 1989.

11 *Australian Financial Review*, 30 July 1987.

12 Bramble, *Trade Unionism in Australia*, pp. 165–8.

13 Economic Planning Advisory Council, *Future Labour Market Issues for Australia*, Commission Paper 12, Australian Government Publishing Service, Canberra, 1996, p. 99.

14 ABS, *Australian National Accounts: National Income, Expenditure and Product*, September 2007, catalogue 5206.0.

15 See Rick Kuhn, 'From one industry strategy to the next', *Politics*, 23 (2), November 1988; Ann Capling and Brian Galligan, *Beyond the Protective State: The Political Economy of Australia's Manufacturing Industry Policy*, Cambridge University Press, Melbourne, 1992.

16 Jerome Fahrer and Andrew Pease, 'International trade and the Australian labour market', in Philip Lowe and Jacqueline Dwyer (eds), *International Integration of the Australian Economy*, Reserve Bank of Australia, Sydney, 1994, p. 186.

17 Fred Gruen and Michelle Grattan, *Managing Government: Labor's Achievements and Failures*, Longman, Melbourne, 1993; Frank Stilwell, *The Accord and Beyond*, Pluto Press, Sydney, 1986.

18 Fahrer and Pease, 'International Trade', p. 200; Steering Committee on National Performance Monitoring of Government Trading Enterprises, *Second Annual Report*, Australian Government Publishing Service, Canberra, 1994.

19 Australian Council of Trade Unions/Trade Development Council, *Australia Reconstructed*, Australian Government Publishing Service, Canberra, 1987; Tom Bramble, 'Union-management co-operation in the Australian vehicle industry, 1983 to 1992', *Labour and Industry*, 5 (1 and 2), pp. 83–104.

20 Tom O'Lincoln, *Into the Mainstream: The Decline of Australian Communism*, Stained Wattle Press, Melbourne, 1985, p. 186.

21 *Australian Financial Review*, 3 March 1989.

22 Steering Committee on National Performance Monitoring, *Second Annual Report*.

23 Stephen Loosley, 'Lingering memories of illegitimacy', *Australian*, 11 November 2005, p. 16.

24 For Labor's record, see the government's publication 'Towards a Fairer Australia: Social Justice under Labor: A Summary', Australian Government Publishing Service, Canberra, 1988.

25 Ibid.

26 Keith Norris and Ben McLean, 'Changes in earnings inequality, 1975 to 1998', *Australian Bulletin of Labor*, 25 (1), March 1999, pp. 22–31.

27 Neville Wran, 'The Great Tradition'.

28 *Canberra Times*, 6 March 1986, cited in Gary Foley and Tim Anderson, 'Land rights and Aboriginal voices', *Australian Journal of Human Rights*, 12 (2), December 2006, p. 94.

29 Peter Read, *Charles Perkins: A Biography*, Penguin, Ringwood, 2001, p. 319.

30 Paul Keating, 'Redfern Park Speech', in *Indigenous Law Bulletin*, 6 (26), pp. 15–16.

31 For a critical review of the Mabo decision, see Foley and Anderson, 'Land rights and Aboriginal voices', pp. 95–6.

32 Keating, 'Redfern Park Speech', p. 16.

33 Gary Foley, 'The road to Native Title: the Aboriginal rights movement and the Australian Labor Party, 1973–1996', 2001, accessed at http://kooriweb.org/foley/essays/essay_26.html, 29 January 2010.

34 Foley and Anderson, 'Land rights', p. 97.

35 Ibid.

36 Chris Cuneen, 'Aboriginal deaths in custody: a continuing systematic abuse', *Social Justice*, 33 (4), 2006, p. 39.

37 Barry York, 'Australia and Refugees, 1901–2002: An annotated chronology based on official sources', Social Policy Group, Parliamentary Library, Parliament of Australia, accessed at www.aph.gov.au/library/pubs/online/Refugees_s1.htm#from, 27 December 2009.

38 Karen Middleton, 'China "no" to boatpeople – Bolkus demands end to "racket" ', *Age*, 29 December 1994.

39 See the interview with Bob Hawke on *A Current Affair*, reproduced in Grewcock, *Border Crimes*, p. 127.

40 York, 'Australia and Refugees, 1901–2002'.

41 See Graeme Cheeseman and St John Kettle, *The New Australian Militarism*, Pluto Press, Sydney, 1990; Tom O'Lincoln, 'The new Australian Militarism', *Socialist Review* (Sydney), 4, 1991, pp. 27–47.

42 See Douglas L. Oliver, *Black Islanders: A Personal Perspective of Bougainville 1937–1991*, Hyland House, Melbourne, 1991, pp. 230–1.

43 Gareth Evans and Bruce Grant, *Australia's Foreign Relations: The World of the 1990s*, Melbourne University Press, Melbourne, 1991, pp. 200–20.

44 Tom Burton, 'Keating cools his advice on human rights in Asia', *Australian Financial Review*, 15 September 1993, p. 13.

45 Government of Indonesia and Government of Australia, 'Agreement between the Republic of Indonesia and Australia on the Framework for Security Cooperation', 1996, accessed at www.dfat.gov.au/GEO/indonesia/ind-aus-sec06.html, 31 December 2009.

46 Scott Burchill, 'Not guilty on Timor? Explain this then', *Age*, 12 March 2001, accessed at http://members.pcug.org.au/~wildwood/01marguilty.htm, 26 April 2010.

47 Milton Cockburn, 'The politics of Australian involvement', in Murray Goot and Rodney Tiffin (eds), *Australia's Gulf War*, Melbourne University Press, Melbourne, 1992, p. 44.

48 'Left', as opposed to 'left', refers to the Left faction in the federal Party.

49 Scott, *Running on Empty*, p. 198.

50 Ross McMullin, *The Light on the Hill: The Australian Labor Party, 1891–1991*, Oxford University Press, Melbourne, 1991, p. 425.

51 Michelle Grattan, 'Left bypassed as sale of Qantas goes ahead', *Age*, 13 August 1992, p. 3.

52 John Hewson and Tim Fischer, *Fightback! It's Your Australia*, Liberal and National Parties, Canberra, 1992; John Hewson and Tim Fischer, *Fightback! Fairness and Jobs*, Liberal and National Parties, Canberra, 1992.

53 Kerry-Anne Walsh, 'Blood, sweat and jeers', *Bulletin*, 10 October 1995, pp. 16–20.

54 Ibid. p. 18.

Chapter 8: Labor in the wilderness

1 See Luke Deer ' "Precisely because it was the seat of government": The Parliament House riot of 1996', *Marxist Interventions*, accessed at www.anu.edu.au/polsci/marx/interventions/riot.htm, 30 April 2010.

2 See Tom Bramble, *Trade Unionism in Australia: From Flood to Ebb Tide*, Cambridge University Press, Melbourne, 2008, pp. 189–98, for a fuller account of this important dispute.

3 Gary Johns, 'Native Title: six questions for Labor', *Courier Mail*, 12 March, 1998, accessed at www.ipa.org.au/news/779/native-title-six-questions-for-labor/pg/9, 20 October 2009.

4 Cited in David Glanz, 'Labor in election gear', *Eureka Street*, March 1998, p. 21.

5 Georgina Windsor and Dennis Shanahan, 'Labor vows to leave native title alone', *Australian*, 9 July 1998, p. 6.

6 Paul Kelly, 'PM is beyond Menzies', *Weekend Australian*, 23–24 October 2004, p. 32.

7 Clive Hamilton, 'Self-absorption wins the day', *Sydney Morning Herald*, 11 October 2004, p. 2.

8 Parliament of Australia, *Monthly Economic and Social Indicators*, 2004a, Table 8.1 Economic Growth, accessed at www.aph.gov.au/library/pubs/mesi/mesi81.htm, 27 May 2004.

9 Simon Mohun, 'The Australian rate of profit 1985–2001', *Journal of Australian Political Economy*, 52, December 2003, p. 88; Anthony Atkinson and Andrew Leigh, 'The distribution of top incomes in Australia', Discussion Paper, 514, 2006, Centre for Economic Policy Research, Australian National University, Canberra.

10 Australian Bureau of Statistics, *Australian National Accounts: National Income, Expenditure and Production, September 2004*, catalogue no. 5206.0, Table 36.

11 Parliament of Australia, *Monthly Economic and Social Indicators, Table 4.4 Business Investment*, accessed at www.aph.gov.au/library/pubs/mesi/mesi44.htm, 5 September 2004.

12 Cited in Ashley Lavelle, 'The boom, the left and capitalism', *Journal of Australian Political Economy*, 61, 2008, p. 305.

13 'Busted: Howard's 14 per cent fudge', *Workers Online*, 26 August 2005, accessed at http://workers.labor.net.au/278/news1_fudge.html, 2 March 2010. For other indicators of hardship among Labor's base, also see ACTU, 'Casual and insecure employment in Australia', ACTU Fact Sheet, 2 August 2004, accessed at www.actu.org.au/public/news/files/Factsheet0802_Casuals_final.doc, 26 March 2010; Iain Campbell, 'Pressing towards full employment? The persistence of underemployment in Australia', *Journal of Australian Political Economy*, 61, pp. 156–80; Mike Steketee and Peter Dawkins, 'Easy street hits a dead end', *Weekend Australian*, 4–5 September 2004, p. 27; Stephen Lunn, 'Income dropped, say most earners', *Australian*, 15 September 2008, p. 3.

14 Australian Council of Service figures, cited in Lavelle, 'The boom, the left and capitalism', p. 305.

15 George Megalogenis and Lauren Wilson, 'Self-employed go back to the boss', *Weekend Australian*, 25–26 April 2009, p. 4.

16 Michael Pusey and Nick Turnbull, 'Have Australians embraced economic reform?', and Shaun Wilson, Gabrielle Meagher and Trevor Breusch, 'Where to for the welfare state?', both in Shaun Wilson, Gabrielle Meagher, Rachel Gibson, David Denemark and Mark Western (eds), *Australian Social Attitudes: The First Report*, UNSW Press, Sydney, 2005; Australian Centre For Industrial Relations Research and Teaching, 'Australian employees' attitudes to trade unions', Working Paper 82, University of Sydney, Sydney, March 2003; John Robertson, 'State of the Union', Workers Online, April 2005, accessed at http://workers.labor.net.au/features/200504/b_tradeunion_auspoll.html, 12 March 2010.

17 Martin Ferguson, 'Backward steps for the jobless', *Australian*, 5 February 1999.

18 According to Andrew Scott, 47 per cent of blue collar voters supported the Coalition in 2004, compared to 42 per cent who voted Labor; Andrew Scott, 'The ALP after 2004', paper presented to the Australasian Political Studies Association conference, University of Newcastle, September, 2006, p. 3. This is not necessarily a good indicator of manual working class support because the category includes many self-employed tradespeople and proprietors of small businesses.

19 John Buchanan and Gillian Considine, 'Stop telling us to cope! NSW nurses explain why they are leaving the profession', NSW Nurses Association, Sydney, 2002.

20 Michael Bachelard, 'Anti-unionist emergency powers to be stepped up', *Australian*, 21 April 2004, p. 6.

21 Michelle Gilchrist, '$400 m is channeled to business', *Australian*, 21 April 2004, p. 6.

22 Farrah Tomazin, 'Exposed: Bracks' secret deals', *Age*, 3 November 2006, accessed at www.theage.com.au/news/victoria-votes/exposed-bracks-secret-deals/2006/11/02/1162339985892.html, 9 May 2010; Kenneth Davidson, 'Bracks owes taxpayers PPP probe', *Age*, 6 November, 2006, accessed at www.theage.com.au/news/business/bracks-owes-taxpayers-ppp-probe/2006/11/05/1162661553538.html, 9 May 2010.

23 Paul Austin, 'Bracks Urges Radical National Reform', *Age*, 15 August 2005.

24 *Queensland Health Systems Review: Final Report* (*Forster Review*), September 2005, accessed at www.istaysafe.com/health_sys_review/final/qhsr_final_report.pdf, 26 March 2010; *Commission for Children and Young People and Child Guardian, Annual Report 2008–09*, Chapter 10: 'National child death statistics: An inter-state comparison, 2007 calendar year', accessed at www.ccypcg.qld.gov.au/pdf/publications/reports/annual_report_dcyp_2008–2009/AllDeathsReport09-Chapter-10.pdf, 9 May 2010; Geoff Masters, 'Improving Literacy, Numeracy and Science Learning: Preliminary Advice', Australian Council for Educational Research, Melbourne, January 2009, accessed at http://education.qld.gov.au/publication/production/reports/pdfs/preliminary-report-masters.pdf, 9 May 2010.

25 Andrew Fraser, '$3.3 bn lost on luring companies', *Australian*, 7 November 2002, p. 5.

26 George Megalogenis, *The Longest Decade*, updated and revised edition, Scribe, Melbourne, 2008, pp. 280, 287.

27 Barry York, 'Australia and Refugees, 1901–2002: An annotated chronology based on official sources', Social Policy Group, Parliamentary Library, Parliament of Australia, accessed at www.aph.gov.au/library/pubs/online/Refugees_s1.htm#from, 27 December 2009, Table 8, pp. 154, 156, 158–9.

28 *House of Representatives Hansard*, 28 June 1999: 7599, cited in Ashley Lavelle, 'In the Wilderness: Federal Labor in Opposition', PhD thesis, Faculty of International Business and Politics, Griffith University, Brisbane, 2004, p. 234.

29 David Marr and Marian Wilkinson, *Dark Victory*, Allen & Unwin, Sydney, p. 91.

30 Ibid, pp. 75–88, 94–5.

31 Grewcock, *Border Crimes*, p. 168.

32 Marr and Wilkinson, p. 87.

33 Grewcock, *Border Crimes*, p. 169.

34 Lavelle, 'In the Wilderness', p. 240.

35 Tony Kevin, *A Certain Maritime Incident: The sinking of SIEV X*, Scribe, Melbourne, 2004.

36 Xandra Faulkner, 'The spirit of accommodation: The influence of the ALP's national factions on party policy, 1996–2004', PhD thesis, Griffith Business School, Griffith University, Brisbane, 2006, p. 171.

37 Robert Manne, 'Why do we not care?', *Age*, 13 December 1999, p. 15.

38 For accounts of the Your Rights at Work campaign, see Bramble, *Trade Unionism in Australia*, Chapter 8, and Kathie Muir, *Worth Fighting For: Inside the Your Rights at Work Campaign*, UNSW Press, Sydney, 2010.

39 Kim Beazley, 'Opposition Leader's Statement – Workplace Relations', Parliament House, 7 June 2005.

40 Kevin Rudd and Julia Gillard, *Forward with Fairness: Policy Implementation Plan*, Australian Labor Party, Canberra, August 2007.

41 Paul Kelly and Denis Shanahan, 'Leader prepared to fight unions', *Australian*, 23 November 2007, p. 1.

42 Kevin Rudd, 'New Labor leader outlines plan', *7.30 Report*, ABC TV, transcript, 4 December 2006, at www.abc.net.au/7.30/content/2006/s1804034.htm, accessed 30 April 2010.

43 'Labor to decide position on Iraq attack', *Lateline*, ABC TV, transcript, 24 September 2002, accessed at www.abc.net.au/lateline/stories/s685074.htm, 15 March 2010.

44 'Rupert Murdoch backs Rudd as future PM', *Age*, 21 April 2007. At the November election, the *Australian* backed Labor; see 'Time to think about the future', *Australian*, 24 November 2007.

45 Kevin Rudd, 'Faith in politics', *The Monthly*, October 2006.

46 Kevin Rudd, 'Time to restore the balance of strength and fairness', *Australian*, 5 December 2006, p. 5.

47 Sarah Maddison, 'Indigenous autonomy matters: what's wrong with the Australian Government's "Intervention" in Aboriginal communities', *Australian Journal of Human Rights*, 14(1), p. 44.

48 Tony Wright and Brendan Nicholson, 'Outrage at Rudd's same-sex marriage stance', *Age*, 24 October 2007.

49 Megalogenis, *The Longest Decade*, p. 358.

50 Gerard McManus, 'Rudd steering a new direction', *Herald Sun*, 7 April 2007.

51 Janet Albrechtsen, 'Pass Baton to Costello', *Australian*, 7 September 2007, p. 16.

Chapter 9: The Rudd–Gillard government

1 Wayne Swan, 2008–9 Budget, speech to the National Press Club, Canberra, 14 May 2008, accessed at www.treasurer.gov.au/DisplayDocs.aspx?pageID=005&doc=../content/speeches/2008/011.htm&min=wms, 31 August 2009.

2 Kevin Rudd, 'Building a modern Australia for the 21st Century', address to the ALP Victorian Branch state conference, 24 May 2008, accessed at www.pm.gov.au/media/speech/2008/speech_0268.cfm, 19 January 2009.

3 'Tax cuts, big surplus and spending cuts key to budget', *Herald Sun*, 8 May 2008.

4 Rudd, 'The global financial crisis', *The Monthly*, February 2009, pp. 21, 29.

5 Ibid.

6 Australian Bureau of Statistics, *Australian National Accounts: National Income, Expenditure and Product, September 2009*, cat. no. 5206.0, pp. 19–20.

7 Steve Keen, 'Have we dodged the iceberg?', *Debtwatch*, 40, accessed at www.debtdeflation.com/blogs/2009/11/02/debtwatch-no-40-november-2009-have-we-dodged-the-iceberg/, 21 March 2010.

8 Nick Gardner, 'Our new record debt', *Sunday Telegraph*, 27 December 2009, p. 9.

9 See Ben Hillier, 'Australia's resilience during the global crisis', *Marxist Interventions*, 2, 2010, accessed at www.anu.edu.au/polsci/mi/2/2.htm, 1 July 2010.

10 Kevin Rudd, 'Pain on the road to recovery', *Sydney Morning Herald*, 25 July 2009.

11 Wayne Swan, 'Australia to 2050: future challenges', launch of the 2010 *Intergenerational Report*, National Press Club, Canberra, 1 February 2010, accessed at www.treasurer.gov.au/DisplayDocs.aspx?doc=speeches/2010/001.htm&pageID=005&min=wms&Year=&DocType=1, 26 March 2010; Dennis Shanahan, 'Election urgency high, budget expectations low', *Australian*, 8 May 2010, p. 11.

12 Jane Cadzow, 'Outrageous fortune', *Sydney Morning Herald*, 17 February 2010, p. 14.

13 Eric Johnston, 'Strong rise in profits expected', *Sydney Morning Herald*, Business Day, 29 March 2010, p. 5; 'Treasurer Wayne Swan says Westpac "serial offender" in taking customers for a ride', *Advertiser*, accessed at www.adelaidenow.com.au/business/treasurer-wayne-swan-says-westpac-serial-offender-in-taking-customers-for-a-ride/story-e6frede3-1225844192889, 30 March 2010.

14 John Sutton, 'PM all talk and no action dealing with fat cats', *Australian*, 5 January 2010.

15 Ari Sharp, 'New $43 b network will be privatised', *Sydney Morning Herald*, Business Day, 25 February 2010, p. 4.

16 Andrew Fraser, 'Shadows of Thatcher in the Sunshine State', *Weekend Australian* (Inquirer section), 12–13 December 2009, p. 6.

17 Speech delivered to National Climate Change Summit, 31 March 2007, accessed at www.youtube.com/watch?v=CqZvpRjGtGM, 29 March 2010.

18 Friends of the Earth (UK), *A Dangerous Obsession: The Evidence Against Carbon Trading and for Real Solutions to Avoid a Climate Crunch*, 2009, accessed at www.foe.co.uk/resource/reports/dangerous_obsession.pdf, 2009; Adam Vaughan, 'James Lovelock labels Europe's carbon trading scheme a "scam"', *Guardian*, 10 June 2010.

19 Chris Williams, 'The people vs. the polluters', *Socialist Worker* (Chicago) online, 11 December 2009, accessed at http://socialistworker.org/2009/12/11/people-vs-polluters, 21 March 2010.

20 Peter Hartcher, 'Carbon plan fuels meltdown', *Sydney Morning Herald*, 20 December 2008.

21 Nicola Berkovic, 'Business begs Abbott to rethink opposition to market-based emissions trading scheme', *Australian*, 3 December 2009.

22 John Daley and Tristan Edis, *Restructuring the Australian Economy to Emit Less Carbon: Main Report*, Grattan Institute, Melbourne, accessed at www.grattan.edu.au/publications/026_energy_report_22_april_2010.pdf, 30 April 2010.

23 Tom Arup, 'Emissions put on back burner', *Age*, 27 April 2010, p. 2.

24 Australian Tax Office. Figures from 2010 suggest that negative gearing on investment properties alone costs Treasury $4 billion annually.

25 Kevin Rudd and Wayne Swan, 'Stronger, fairer, simpler: a tax plan for our future', media release, 2 May 2010, accessed at www.pm.gov.au/node/6741, 12 May 2010; Ian Verrender, 'Miners stand on their dig: No raps for super profits tax', *Sydney Morning Herald Weekend Business*, 8–9 May 2010, p. 5; Patrick Durkin, 'Resource tax finds broad support', *Australian Financial Review*, 24 May 2010, pp. 1, 6.

26 Dan Harrison, 'First cash penalties for truancy', *Sydney Morning Herald*, 29 March 2010, p. 6.

27 Ibid.

28 Julia Gillard, Kevin Rudd and Kate Ellis, 'COAG secures a compact with young Australians', media release, 30 April 2009, accessed at www.deewr.gov.au/Ministers/Gillard/Media/Releases/Pages/Article_090430_154925.aspx, 1 September 2009.

29 Jim McMorrow, 'Updating the evidence: The Rudd government's intentions for schools', December 2008, p. 21, accessed at www.aeufederal.org.au/Publications/2009/JMcMorrowpaper2009.pdf, 29 March 2010.

30 Phillip Coorey, 'Tell off deficient teachers: Gillard', *Sydney Morning Herald*, 26 January 2010, p. 1.

31 Tess Lee-Ack, 'Teachers' union is right to oppose school league tables', *Socialist Alternative*, March 2010, p. 18.

32 AAP, 'Gillard stands by strike-breaking plan', *Age*, 11 April 2010; Anna Patty, Rick Feneley and Dan Harrison, 'How Gillard gave truculent teachers a caning', *Sydney Morning Herald*, 8–9 May 2010, p. 6.

33 Katharine Murphy and Dan Harrison, 'Gillard buys peace with private schools', *Age*, 5 August 2010, p. 6; Michelle Grattan, 'Election 2010 – the debate', *Age*, 26 July 2010, p. 6.

34 John Deeble, 'Hospital plan is a vague prescription', *Sydney Morning Herald*, 14 April 2010, p. 15.

35 Madeline Simons, 'Rudd's health care takeover plan won't solve anything', *Socialist Alternative*, April 2010, p. 7.

36 Office of the Australian Building and Construction Commissioner, *Report on the Exercise of Compliance Powers by the ABCC, 1 October 2005 to 30 September 2008*, Commonwealth of Australia, 2008, accessed at www.abcc.gov.au/NR/rdonlyres/36149C0F-B6C9-4AC7-B2C2–34379BA26C2E/0/CPowersReportSep08.pdf, 10 June 2010.

37 Brian Boyd, 'The tide has turned', Victorian Trades Hall Council, 13 October 2008, accessed at www.vthc.org.au/latest-news/archives/2008-archives/the-tide-has-turned/index.cfm, 25 March 2010.

38 Brad Norington and Ewin Hannan, 'ACTU rails against Work Choices "lite"', *Australian*, 23 September 2008.

39 Ben Schneiders, 'Gillard at risk of contempt', *Age*, 5 June 2009.

40 Julia Gillard, press conference Melbourne, transcript, 7 July 2009, accessed at www.deewr.gov.au/Ministers/Gillard/Media/Transcripts/Pages/Article_090708_081917.aspx, 3 September 2009.

41 Julia Gillard, address to the National Press Club, 24 February 2010, accessed at www.deewr.gov.au/Ministers/Gillard/Media/Speeches/Pages/Article_100224_143429.aspx, 9 August 2010.

42 SA Unions, 'Remembering the killed and injured vital for safer workplaces', media release, 28 April 2010, accessed at www.utlc.org.au/media_releases/IWMD_Apr_10.php, 9 May 2010.

43 Natasha Bita, 'Childcare staff facing pay cuts under new award', *Weekend Australian*, 5–6 December 2009, p. 5.

44 Jeff Lawrence, 'Turning the tide on workers' rights', 17 November 2008, accessed at www.actu.org.au/Media/Speechesandopinion/JeffLawrenceTurningthetideonworkersrights.aspx, 5 June 2010.

45 ACTU, 'One year on, Fair Work laws have restored protections lost under Work-Choices', ACTU media release, 27 March 2010.

46 ACTU, 'Jobs growth welcome but it would be dangerous to prematurely wind back stimulus spending', media release, 10 December 2009; 'Investment in skills and infrastructure crucial to boost Australian productivity', media release, 19 January 2010.

47 Commonwealth of Australia, *Australia's Paid Parental Leave Scheme: Supporting working Australian families*, Canberra, 2009, accessed at www.fahcsia.gov.au/about/publicationsarticles/corp/BudgetPAES/budget09_10/parental_leave/Documents/paid_parental_leave/PPL.pdf, 3 September 2009.

48 Productivity Commission, *Paid Parental Leave: Support for Parents with Newborn Children*, Productivity Commission Inquiry Report 47, 28 February 2009, accessed at www.pc.gov.au/__data/assets/pdf_file/0003/86232/parental-support.pdf, 3 September 2009; Adele Horin, 'Let's not throw Abbott's baby leave out with the bathwater', *Sydney Morning Herald*, 13–14 March 2010, p. 9.

49 Matthew Franklin, 'PM bursts Abbott's thought-bubble', *Australian*, 10 March 2010, p. 4; Paul Kelly, 'Rudd must seize on once-in-generation tax review', *Australian*, 10 March 2010, p. 12.

50 'Victorian ALP supports gay marriages', *Sydney Morning Herald*, 21 November 2009.

51 Galaxy Research, 'Same sex marriage report', June 2009, accessed at www.australianmarriageequality.com/Galaxy200906.pdf, 28 March 2010; 'MP toes line', *Courier Mail*, 26 July 2010, p. 6.

52 Gary Foley, 'Duplicity and deceit: Rudd's apology to the stolen generations', *Melbourne Historical Journal*, vol. 36, December 2008.

53 *AM*, ABC Radio National, 'Rudd rules out compensation fund for stolen generations', 2 February 2008, at www.abc.net.au/am/content/2008/s2152790.htm, accessed 5 June 2010.

54 Amy McQuire and Chris Graham, 'A Labor of love?', *National Indigenous Times*, 178, 28 May 2009.

55 Natasha Robinson, 'Former deputy quits Labor', *Australian*, 5 June 2009, p. 2.

56 Chris Graham, 'A racist policy for racist times', *National Indigenous Times*, 178, 28 May 2009.

57 Yuko Narushima, 'Indigenous figures better but there's a long way to go', *Sydney Morning Herald*, 12 February 2010, p. 11.

58 Larissa Behrendt and Irene Fisher, 'Intervention is hurting health', *Sydney Morning Herald*, 31 March 2009.

59 'NT action more harm than good, say Aboriginal doctors', *Sydney Morning Herald*, 12 March 2010, p. 6.

60 Chris Graham, 'The grass is always greener', *National Indigenous Times*, 197, March 2010, www.nit.com.au/News/story.aspx?id=19546, accessed 9 May 2010.

61 Tara Ravens, 'Tangentyere urges Rudd government not to walk away from table', *National Indigenous Times*, 178, 28 May 2009.

62 Lindsay Murdoch, 'A community with its own intervention', *Sydney Morning Herald*, 13–14 February 2010, p. 9.

63 Jerome Small, 'Tour builds solidarity for Aboriginal walk-off', *Socialist Alternative*, November 2009, p. 8.

64 Marie Bout, 'Donated house officially handed over at walk-off camp', 21 February, ABC Alice Springs, accessed at www.abc.net.au/local/stories/2010/02/20/2825577.htm, 9 May 2010.

65 Michael Grewcock, *Border Crimes: Australia's War on Illicit Migrants*, Sydney Institute of Criminology, University of Sydney, Sydney, 2009, pp. 280–1.

66 Jewel Topsfield, 'Labor breaks detention promise', *Age*, 20 January 2009, p. 4.

67 Emma Rodgers, 'Rudd wants people smugglers to "rot in hell"', ABC *News*, 17 April 2009, accessed at www.abc.net.au/news/stories/2009/04/17/2545748.htm 9 August 2010.

68 Cited in David Marr, 'The Indian Ocean Solution', *The Monthly*, September 2009, accessed at www.themonthly.com.au/monthly-essays-david-marr-indian-ocean-solution-christmas-island-1940, 9 May 2010.

69 Grewcock, *Border Crimes*, p. 281.

70 Ibid, p. 282.

71 Yuko Narushima, 'Legal and diplomatic headache for Rudd', *Sydney Morning Herald*, 14 April 2010, p. 7.

72 Cited in Marr, 'The Indian Ocean solution'.

73 Senator Chris Evans, 'New directions in detention – restoring integrity to Australia's immigration system', speech given at Australian National University, Canberra, Tuesday 29 July 2008, accessed at http://www.minister.immi.gov.au/media/speeches/2008/ce080729.htm, 3 July 2010.

74 Ibid.

75 P. Hudson and L. Dodson, 'Security my duty too, says Beazley', *Age*, 9 October 2001, p. 5.

76 *The World Today*, ABC Radio National, 'Australian government considers returning troops to Afghanistan', 12 July 2005, accessed at www.abc.net.au/worldtoday/content/2005/s1412620.htm, 12 March 2010.

77 Denis Shanahan, 'Kevin Rudd in Bucharest for NATO summit on Afghanistan', *Australian*, 3 April 2008.

78 Emma Rogers, ABC *News Online*, 'Rudd confirms Afghanistan troop boost', 29 April 2009, accessed at www.abc.net.au/news/stories/2009/04/29/2555859.htm, 29 March 2010; Patrick Walters, 'Afghanistan war funding to double', *Australian*, 13 May 2009, p. 10.

79 Motion extracted from *Hansard*, accessed at www.1948.com.au/2008events/national/PDFnat/RUDDsMOTION12Mar08.pdf, 29 March 2010.

80 Stockholm International Peace Research Institute, 'Recent trends in military expenditure', accessed at www.sipri.org/research/armaments/milex/resultoutput/trends, 29 March 2010.

81 Hillier, 'Australia's resilience during the global crisis'.

82 Jennifer Hewett, 'An uneasy union', *Australian*, 10 November 2009, p. 15.

83 Cameron Stewart and David Uren, 'Leadership forged in the financial fire', *Weekend Australian*, 23–24 January 2010.

84 Bernard Keane 'Heather Ridout, the 21st member of Rudd's Cabinet', *Crikey*, 12 May 2008, accessed at www.crikey.com.au/2008/05/12/heather-ridout-the-21st-member-of-rudds-cabinet, 9 May 2010.

85 Jamie Duncan 'Tributes flow in for Richard Pratt', *Sydney Morning Herald*, accessed at http://news.smh.com.au/breaking-news-national/tributes-flow-in-for-richard-pratt-20090428-am4v.html, 28 April 2009, 3 May 2010.

86 Cameron Stewart, 'The nation is grateful, PM tells dying Pratt', *Australian*, 25 April 2009.

87 Paul Kelly, 'Smart, casual Kevin', *Weekend Australian Magazine*, 27–28 October 2007, p. 16.

88 Lindsay Tanner, address to the National Press Club, 6 February 2008, accessed at www.financeminister.gov.au/transcripts/2008/tr_20080206_npc.html, 5 June 2010.

89 Ewin Hannan, 'Ferguson lashes out at unions', *Weekend Australian*, 6–7 June 2009, p. 1.

90 Kevin Rudd and Kim Carr, 'A new car plan for a greener future', media release, 10 November 2008, accessed at http://minister.innovation.gov.au/Carr/Pages/ANEWCARPLANFORAGREENERFUTURE.aspx, 29 March 2010.

91 Laura Tinge, 'Whispers of discontent reach PM', *Australian Financial Review*, 9 June 2010, p. 8; Janet Albrechtsen, 'Rudd's easier for Abbott to knock out than Gillard', *Australian*, 24 March 2010, p. 12; Dennis Shanahan, 'Coalition holds edge on Labor – Gillard closes Newspoll gap on Rudd', *Australian*, 17 May 2010, pp. 1, 4.

92 Pamela Williams, 'Kill Kevin: the untold story of a coup', *Australian Financial Review*, 16 July 2010, pp. 1, 54–57.

93 Geoff Winestock, 'Due respect for market's central role', *Australian Financial Review*, 25 June 2010, p. 16; Cosima Marriner, 'Bid To Water Down Refugee Detention Policies Gets Sunk', *Sydney Morning Herald*, 31 January 2004, p. 10; 'Gillard defends ban on asylum claims', 11 April 2010, Australian Associated Press; Jacob Saulwick, 'The rise of a pragmatic negotiator, not a political purist', *Sydney Morning Herald*, 25 June 2010, p. 5.

94 Ross Gittins, 'Battle over tax leaves Labor with bloody nose', *Sydney Morning Herald* (Weekend Business), 3–4 July 2010, p.5; Simon Kearney, 'PM moves to end boat crisis: I'm not "PC", says Gillard' *Sunday Telegraph*, 4 July 2010, pp. 1–5; Julia Gillard, 'Moving Australia forward', speech to the Lowy Institute, Sydney, 6 July 2010, accessed at www.pm.gov.au/node/6876, 6 July 2010; Peter Hartcher, 'Her hair may be red, but she's no bleeding heart', *Sydney Morning Herald*, 10 July 2010, p. 9.

95 James Grubel, 'New mining tax deal: PM Gillard set for election win', Reuters, 2 July 2010, accessed at http://graphics.thomsonreuters.com/10/miningtax0207.pdf, 5 July 2010.

96 Peter Martin, 'Lack of big choices suits both parties', *Sydney Morning Herald*, 23 July 2010, p. 6.
97 Phillip Coorey, 'Labor attacks "big tax" Tony', *Sydney Morning Herald*, 27 July 2010, p. 1.
98 Julia Gillard, 'We will stay strong in Afghanistan', *Sydney Morning Herald*, 12 July 2010, p. 13.
99 Yuko Narushima, 'Parties row in the same direction over boat arrivals', *Sydney Morning Herald*, 10 August 2010, p. 8.
100 ACTU, 'Labor's strong record on jobs and the economy contrasts with the Coalition's return to WorkChoices', media release, 14 July 2010, accessed at www.actu.org.au/Media/Mediareleases/Laborsstrongrecordonjobs andtheeconomycontrastswiththeCoalitionsreturntoWorkChoices.aspx, 10 August 2010; Kirsty Needham, 'Howard-era laws invoked against striking workers', *Sydney Morning Herald*, 16 July 2010, p. 7.
101 Ewin Hannan and Simon Canning, 'ACTU ad blitz to counter business "vultures"', *Australian*, 7 August 2010, p. 10; Ewin Hannan, 'No new policy pressure on Labor', *Australian*, 5 August 2010, p. 10.
102 'Week 2', *Sydney Morning Herald*, 31 July 2010, p. 10.
103 Peter Hartcher, 'Lodge there for taking if Abbott keeps his head', *Sydney Morning Herald* ('News Review'), 7–8 August, p. 9.
104 Phillip Coorey, 'Rudd rallies for "underdog" PM', *Sydney Morning Herald*, 5 August 2010, p. 1.
105 Julia Gillard, 'Australia's New Political Landscape', speech, National Press Club, Canberra, 31 August 2010, accessed at http://www.alp.org.au/federal-government/news/speech–julia-gillard,—australia-s-new-political/, 1 September 2010.
106 Julia Gillard, 'Australia's New Political Landscape', speech, National Press Club, Canberra, 31 August 2010, accessed at http://www.alp.org.au/federal-government/news/speech–julia-gillard,—australia-s-new-political/, 1 September 2010.

Chapter 10: The Labor Party today: what's left

1 This is spelt out in much greater detail in Tom Bramble, *Trade Unionism in Australia: A History from Flood to Ebb Tide*, Cambridge University Press, Melbourne, 2008, Part 3.
2 Information in, or calculated from, statistics in Nicholas Horne, 'The *Members of Parliament (Staff) Act 1984* framework and employment issues', Parliamentary Library Research Paper 26, Parliament of Australia, Canberra, 3 April 2009, p. 15.
3 *Commonwealth Parliamentary Handbook*, 2005.
4 See 'Staffers as Pollies: The List', *Crikey*, 26 April 2005, accessed at www.crikey.com. au/2005/04/26/staffers-as-pollies-the-list/, 6 April 2010.
5 Tom Bramble, 'Leadership representativeness in the Australian union movement', *Australian Bulletin of Labour*, 26 (4), 2000, pp. 216–42.
6 *Commonwealth Parliamentary Handbook*, 2005.
7 Peter Wilson, 'UK Deals Windfall for Rein Enterprise', *Australian*, 11 March 2009, p. 1.

8   Remuneration Tribunal, 'Parliamentarians' Allowances and Entitlements', accessed at www.remtribunal.gov.au/federalParliamentarians, 15 April 2010; Remuneration Tribunal, 'Report Number 1 of 2009: Report on Ministers of State–Salaries Additional to the Basic Parliamentary Salary', Canberra, 2009; Australian Bureau of Statistics, 'Average Weekly Earnings, Australia, November 2009', cat. no. 6302.0.

9   See Andrew Leigh's calculations, 2010, accessed at http://people.anu.edu.au/andrew.leigh/pdf/TopIncomesAustralia.xls, 9 April 2010.

10 Peter van Onselen, 'Women the life of the party', *Australian*, 28–29 March 2009, p. 17.

11 Ian McAllister et al., *Australian Election Study, 2007*, accessed at http://assda-nesstar.anu.edu.au/webview, 6 June 2010.

12 Rodney Cavalier, 'Could Chifley win Labor preselection today?', *Sydney Morning Herald*, 21 April 2005.

13 John Button, 'Beyond belief: What future for Labor?', *Quarterly Essays*, 6, 2002.

14 Andrew Fraser, 'Kelly parachutes into Eden-Monaro', *Canberra Times*, 30 April 2007, p. 5; Phillip Coorey, 'Rudd's men seize control of preselections', *Sydney Morning Herald*, 12 June 2009, p. 1; Michael Stedman, 'Harkins Senate snub: Rudd blamed as preselection fails', *Hobart Mercury*, 10 April 2010, p. 7; Simon Benson, 'Labor bans conferences: executive moves to protect state premiers', *Courier Mail*, 1 March 2010, p. 10.

15 The figure of 50 000 members comes from the ALP national executive's claim to have sent out 50 000 copies of the national conference agenda to members in 2009. Mark Skulley and Laura Tingle, 'Battle lines drawn over ALP platform', *Australian Financial Review*, 30 March 2009, p. 3. Data from the earlier years are drawn from Andrew Scott, 'Fading Loyalties: Working-Class Participation in, and Electoral Support for, the Australian Labor Party since World War Two', BA honours thesis in History, University of Melbourne, Melbourne, 1990, Appendix 3.

16 Collingwood Football Club, 'Membership', accessed at http://membership.collingwoodfc.com.au, 12 April 2010.

17 The figure for the late 1940s is from Andrew Scott, *Fading Loyalties: The Australian Labor Party and the Working Class*, Pluto Press, Sydney, 1991, p. 30.

18 Ibid. pp. 37, 46.

19 Button, 'Beyond belief'.

20 Michael Bachelard, 'Labor tribes go to war', *Australian*, 23 May 2005, p. 8; *Challenge* (publication of the New South Wales Socialist Left faction), Spring 2009, p. 7.

21 Cavalier, 'Could Chifley win Labor preselection today?'

22 Personal communications with Labor Party members.

23 Michael Hogan, *Local Labor: A History of the Labor Party in Glebe 1891–2003*, The Federation Press, Sydney, 2004, p. 204.

24 Cavalier, 'Could Chifley win Labor preselection today?'; Lindsay Tanner, 'The ALP, a renovator's nightmare', *Age*, 22 March 2002; see also, Bob Gould, 'The texture, flavour and sociology of the Labor conference, 2004', *Marxmail*, 3 February 2004, accessed at http://archives.econ.utah.edu/archives/marxism/2004w05/msg00045.htm, 14 March 2009.

25 Ian Ward, 'Cartel parties and election campaigns in Australia', in Ian Marsh (ed.), *Political Parties in Transition?*, The Federation Press, Sydney, 2006, pp. 73–7; Ian

Ward, 'The changing organisational nature of Australia's political parties', *Commonwealth and Comparative Politics*, 29 (2), 1991, pp. 153–74.

26 Australian Government and Politics Database, accessed at http://elections.uwa.edu.au/partysearch3.lasso, 29 November 2009. The combined federal and New South Wales Labor Party vote in 1931 was 37.7 per cent.

27 McAllister, *Australian Election Study*.

28 Bob Birrell, 'Birthplace: the new political divide', *People and Place*, 10 (4), 2002, pp. 38–49.

29 Chi square tests indicate that the pattern of parties' votes coming from the working class is a strong one and that this result has a high degree of statistical significance.

30 Scott Steel (aka Possum Comitatus), 'Class, voting and broad left demography', *Pollytics blog*, accessed at http://blogs.crikey.com.au/pollytics/2010/04/15/class-voting-and-broad-left-demography/?utm_source=feedburner&utm_medium=feed&utm_campaign=Feed%3A+CrikeyBlogs%2Fpollytics+%28Pollytics%29, 15 April 2010.

31 See Adam Carr, 'New South Wales election of 24 March 2007', accessed at http://psephos.adam-carr.net/countries/a/australia/states/nsw/nswmapsindex.shtml, 3 May 2010.

32 Cited in Verity Burgmann, *In Our Time: Socialism and the Rise of Labor, 1885–1905*, Allen & Unwin, Sydney, 1985, p. 198.

33 Ibid., p. 197.

34 Richard Crossman, 'Introduction', in W. Bagehot, *The English Constitution*, Fontana, London, 1963, pp. 41–2.

35 John Cain, *John Cain's Years*, Melbourne University Press, Melbourne, 1995.

36 Possum Comitatus, 'Class, voting and broad left demography'.

37 Figures provided by Sydney University doctoral student, Stewart Jackson, private correspondence, 8 April 2010.

38 Bob Brown, 'A warm-hearted Australia', National Press Club speech, 8 September 2004, accessed at http://parlinfo.aph.gov.au/parlInfo/download/media/pressrel/K3YD6/upload_binary/k3yd62.pdf;fileType=application%2Fpdf#search=%22BROWN,%20SEN%20BOB%20yes%22, 1 May 2010.

39 Tad Tietze, 'The Greens, the crisis and the left', *Overland*, 199, Winter 2010, p. 34; emphasis in the original.

40 Bob Brown, 'Howard wrong on ground troops', The Greens, media release, 17 October 2001, accessed at www.greensmps.org.au/content/media-release/howard-wrong-on-ground-troops, 1 May 2010.

41 The Greens, '300 SAS troops should remain in our region–Greens', media release, 10 April 2007, accessed at http://greensmps.org.au/content/media-release/300-sas-troops-should-remain-our-region-%C2%96-greens, 1 May 2010.

42 Emma Chalmers, 'Greens say population is too high', *Courier Mail*, 15 March 2010, p. 3.

43 Lenore Taylor, 'Greens join the mainstream', *Sydney Morning Herald*, 10–11 April 2010, News Review, p. 2.

44 Bob Brown, 'Democracy in Tasmania in 2010 – some lateral thinking is required', accessed at http://greensmps.org.au/blog/democracy-tasmania-2010-%E2%80%93-some-lateral-thinking-required, 1 May 2010.

45 Farrah Tomazin, 'Greens wining and dining', *Age*, 3 April 2010.

46 Chip le Grand, 'Novice Bandt learns ropes on how to toe the party line', *Australian*, 23 August 2010, p. 5.

47 Fausto Bertinotti, 'Refounding further', *International Socialism*, 102, 2004, pp. 87–108.

48 Megan Trudell, 'Rifondazione votes for war', *International Socialism*, 113, 2007, pp. 33–48.

49 Oliver Nachtwey, 'Die Linke and the crisis of class representation', *International Socialism*, 124, pp. 24–8.

50 Stefan Bornost, 'Opposition and opportunity in Germany', *International Socialism*, 123, 2010, p. 24.

51 Lecio Morais and Alfredo Saad-Filho, 'Lula and the continuity of neoliberalism in Brazil: strategic choice, economic imperative or political schizophrenia?', *Historical Materialism*, 13, 1, 2005, p. 23.

INDEX

ABCC *see* Australian Building and
　　Construction Commission
Aboriginal and Torres Strait Islander
　　Commission (ATSIC) 112, 127
Aboriginal Land Rights (Northern
　　Territory) Act 1976 (Clth) 114
Aboriginal people 113
　　Aboriginal policy 154–7
　　deaths in custody 114–15
　　dispossession 111–15
　　genocide 113, 154–7
　　government land grab 141
　　'hub towns' 155
　　land rights 90, 111–15, 127, 182
　　National Aboriginal Consultative
　　　　Committee 91
　　Native Title Bill 114
　　Northern Territory Emergency
　　　　Response/Intervention 141, 163
　　and racist policies 116
　　Stolen Generations apology 154, 156
Accord, the 105–10
ACTU *see* Australian Council of Trade
　　Unions
Afghanistan occupation 159–60
age pension 149
ALP *see* Australian Labor Party
AMWU *see* Australian Metal Workers
　　Union
ARU *see* Australian Railways Union
Asia Pacific Economic Cooperation
　　Process (APEC) 117
ASIO *see* Australian Security Intelligence
　　Organisation
ASL *see* Australian Socialist League

asylum seekers 115–17, 182
　　Tamil asylum seekers 158–9
ATSIC *see* Aboriginal and Torres Strait
　　Islander Commission
Australia, New Zealand and United States
　　(ANZUS) agreement 58
Australian Building and Construction
　　Commission (ABCC) 152
Australian Council of Trade Unions
　　(ACTU) 102–3, 106, 108, 153
　　ACTU Congress 124
　　Your Rights at Work campaign 136–9,
　　　　169, 180
Australian Industry Group 162
Australian Labor Party (ALP) 169–71
　　1940s to 1960s 65–8
　　ALP Industrial Groups 65–6
　　ALP–unions relationship 70–1
　　break with tradition 21
　　and capitalist development 60–3
　　a capitalist party? 6–11, 182–6
　　class and power 67–8, 86–7
　　commitment to British empire 36–7
　　conflict with working class militancy
　　　　37
　　early record in office 33–7
　　economic policy 129–32, 183–4
　　the Egerton machine 75
　　electoral organisation 31
　　formal structures 74–5, 176
　　formation 27–33
　　Forward with Fairness – industrial
　　　　relations platform 138–9
　　funding 31
　　and gender 174

Australian Labor Party (ALP) (*cont.*)
  and the Great Depression 46–54
  influence on world order 119–20
  Inner Group 52
  Kevin 07 139–42, 161–5
  Keynesian economics 54, 59, 66,
    95–6, 143–6
  Labor against labour 58–61
  Labor in the wilderness 126–42
  left drifts right 120–2, 162
  legitimacy 109–10
  loyalty of 182
  male domination of 73
  material constitution 14–18, 87–8
  members, branches and voters 76–80,
    177–82
  and military expansion 36–7
  national factions 175–6
  nature of 41–2
  and the oppressed 153–4
  parliamentary Labor caucuses 72
  party machines 74–6, 174–7
  pre-formation years 25–7
  radical left assessment 19–20
  recent changes 19–24
  reforms 32–3, 44–5, 88–94, 100–1,
    187–8
  revolutionary alternative 192–3
  Roman Catholic and Irish associations
    73, 77
  shake up of banking industry
    108–9
  the Split 63–6, 68, 69, 75–6, 77–8
  'standing army' 176
  union officials' power 70–1, 169–71
  vote-winning focus 20
  and war 37–41
  a workers' party? 11–14
Australian Metal Workers Union
  (AMWU) 102
Australian Railways Union (ARU) 44–5
Australian Security Intelligence
  Organisation (ASIO) 58
Australian Socialist League (ASL) 30
Australian Workers Union (AWU)
  29–30, 39–40, 44–5

Banking Act 63
Basics Card 155
BCA *see* Business Council of Australia
bicentennial 112
Blackburn Declaration 44
blue collar unions 69
Bougainville Copper 118
British empire 36–7
Builders' Labourers' Federation (BLF)
  84, 106
Building Workers Industrial Union
  (BWIU) 102
Business Council of Australia (BCA) 107,
  162

campaigns 31, 84
  electronic media and political
    campaigning 172
  against invasion of Iraq 132
  Your Rights at Work campaign 136–9,
    169, 180
Campbell Report 101
canvassing 78
capitalism 26, 34, 47, 50–3, 58–61, 63, 64
  ALP – a capitalist party 6–11, 182–6
  Australian capitalism 66, 67–8, 106,
    168
  capitalist accumulation 144
  capitalist hostility and recession 95
  capitalist state 100
  development – 1940s 60–3
  'extreme capitalism' 162
  means of ruling 8–9
  and the Whitlam government 89
carbon pollution reduction scheme
  (CPRS) 147–8
cartel parties 22
caucuses 72, 173
CFMEU *see* Construction, Forestry,
  Mining and Energy Union
class
  ALP and 1940s–1960s period 67–8
  ALP reactions to class and social
    struggles 86–7
  class bias 180–1
  class distinctions 25–7

class relations of capitalism 6–11
    see also working class
climate change 163
coal industry 61, 64
    see also mining industry
Coalition government 66, 122–3, 126,
    128–9
Cold War 57, 64–5, 68
Colombo Plan 91
Combined Unions' and Branches'
    Steering Committee 75
Commonwealth Bank 63
Commonwealth Employment Service 62
Communist Party of Australia (CPA)
    9–10, 52–3, 58, 60–1, 64–5, 68, 108,
    175
conscription 39–40, 58, 67, 86, 93–4
conservatism 10
Construction, Forestry, Mining and
    Energy Union (CFMEU) 152
CPRS *see* carbon pollution reduction
    scheme

democracy 22, 65, 190–2
Democratic Labor Party 65
Depression *see* Great Depression
Die Linke (German Left Party) 190, 191

economics
    capitalist development – 1940s 60–3
    Coalition ascendancy 128–9
    colonial government and economic
        development 34–5
    economic crisis 94–100
    economic rationalism 104–25
    economic recovery 106
    Economic Summit 105–6
    Economic Warfare 15, 16
    economy during war 38–9
    Keynesian economics 54, 59, 66,
        95–6, 143–6
    Labor responses to the Depression
        46–53
    Labor's economic policy 129–32,
        183–4
    May 1983 Economic Summit 105–6

and tariffs 88
    world economic downturn 95–6
education 149–50, 173
electronic media 172
emissions trading scheme (ETS) 147–8
employment 62, 106, 124, 171
enterprise bargaining 107, 124
environment 140–1, 142, 147–8
ETS *see* emissions trading scheme
exploitation 12, 13

Fair Work Australia Bill 152
fascism 50, 53, 59–60
federal executive/conference 75–6
Federated Ironworkers' Association 60–1
Fightback 122–3
*Force 2030: Defending Australia in the Asia
    Pacific Century* 161
foreign policy 93–4, 132–6, 159–61
foreign trade 88, 109
Forward with Fairness 138–9

General Agreement on Trade and Tariffs
    57
global financial crisis 143–6, 183
global warming 142, 147–8
goods and services tax (GST) 130
government
    and capitalist class 9–10
    Chifley government 55–65, 68
    Coalition government 66, 122–3, 126,
        128–9
    colonial government and economic
        development 34–5
    Curtin government 56–7, 58–61, 63–5
    government land grab 141
    government services 47
    Hawke government 104–25
    Hun Sen government–Khmer Rouge
        conflict 118
    Keating government 104–25
    Lang government 45–6, 48–50, 52–4
    Menzies government 56, 64, 66
    Rudd government 139–42, 143–65
    Suharto's New Order 119
    Whitlam government 83–103

Great Depression 28, 29, 46–53
Green Bans campaign 84
Greens, the 188–90
   left stances 188–9
   political limits 189–90
GST *see* goods and services tax

health system 62–3
Henry Review 148
High Court 63, 113

IMF *see* International Monetary Fund
immigration 62, 91–3, 115
incentive payments 61
income
   CEO salaries 146
   income taxation 62–3, 67
   inequalities 10
   median incomes 130
   Prices and Income Accord 101, 169
   and profit 8
industrial awards 124
Industrial Groups (Groupers) 65–6
Industrial Workers of the World (IWW or
   Wobblies) 37, 39, 59–60
inflation 59–60, 94–5, 96
interest rates 131, 145
International Monetary Fund (IMF) 57
intervention 155, 156–7, 163
IWW *see* Industrial Workers of the World

Joint Coal Board 61

Kerr coup 98–100
Keynesianism 54, 59, 66, 95–6, 143–6

Labor Party *see* Australian Labor Party
land rights 90, 111–15, 127, 182
land tax 35
Lang Plan 48–50
Left faction 120–2
   reasons for capitulation 121
legislative reform 32–3
Liberal–Country Party 67
Liberal Party 64, 65
loans scandal 96–7

lobbying 71
Lyne Tariff 32

Mabo decision 113
Maritime Union of Australia (MUA) 126,
   169
Marxism 7, 14
media
   attitude to Rudd 140
   electronic media and political
     campaigning 172
   media coverage 78–9
Medibank 89–90
Medicare 105, 110, 145, 150–1
Melbourne Agreement 47
migrants 62, 84, 115, 174
   assimilation of migrants – 1973 riot
     92
Migration Legislation Amendment Act
   115
Migration Reform Act 115
militancy 37, 38, 43–6, 64, 106, 170
   see also strike action
militarism 117–20
military expansion 36–7, 160
mining industry 61, 64, 118
monetarism 95
monetary policy 36
moratorium marches 85
MUA *see* Maritime Union of Australia
multiculturalism 91–3, 182
My School [website] 149

National Assessment Program Literacy
   and Numeracy (NAPLAN) tests 149
national broadband network 146
National Economic Plan 58
national executive (NE) 176
nationalisation 59, 63, 68
nationalism 34, 92, 182
neoliberalism 21–2, 122, 143–6

occupational health and safety (OHS)
   legislation 153
Oceanic Viking 158–9
One Nation Party 127

oppression 153–4
Organisation of Economic Cooperation and Development (OECD) 89

paid parental leave 153
parliament/parliamentarians 17, 27–33, 72–4, 172
see also politics
Partido dos Trabalhadores (PT, the Workers Party) 191
pastoral leases 44
Patrick Stevedores 126
Payne Report 51–2
people smugglers 157
policy
    Aboriginal policy 154–7
    ALP influences on government policy 32–3
    cartel party policy 22
    foreign policy 93–4, 132–6, 159–61
    Labor's economic policy 129–32, 183–4
    monetary policy 36
    and parliamentary Labor caucuses 72
    racist policies 116
    refugee policies 132–6
    social policy 110–11
    technocratic policies 19
    White Australia policy 32, 36, 91–3, 182
populism 13, 29–30
power 67–8, 70–1, 74–6, 159–61, 169–71, 174–7
Prices and Income Accord 101, 169
private sector 9
privatisation 109, 124, 146–8, 171
profit 8, 58, 89

racism 36, 57, 62, 91–3, 116, 127, 182
radicalisation 43–6, 85, 86
rank and file membership 69, 70, 79–80
recession 95
Redfern speech 112–13
referenda 38, 39–40
refugees 132–6, 157–9, 163
    see also asylum seekers

religious sectarianism 77
Rifondazione Comunista (RC, Communist Refoundation) 190
Royal Commission into Black Deaths in Custody 114–15

same sex marriage 154
SEATO *see* South East Asia Treaty Organisation
security 58
social democracy 22
    left social democratic parties 190–2
social fascism 53
social policy 110–11
social security 34, 62–3
Socialisation Units 47, 50–3
socialism 13–14, 17, 30, 47, 51–2, 59, 61, 105–6, 175
    and the ALP 185, 187–8
    socialisation of industry 43–6
    socialist alternative to ALP 192–3
South East Asia Treaty Organisation (SEATO) 58
state sector 9–10, 36, 58
strike action 26–7, 38, 43–6, 59–60, 97, 98–100, 126
    ALP identification of strikes with communism 68
    industrial action 84–5
    miners' strike 64
    New South Wales general strike 40–1
    suppression 106
    and white collar workers 84
    wildcat strikes 38
student movement 85

tariff 35, 47, 88
    General Agreement on Trade and Tariffs 57
    Lyne Tariff 32
taxation 109
    accelerated tax depreciation rate 61
    income taxation 62–3, 67
    land tax 35
    regressive tax 148

terrorism 159–61
Theodore Plan 47–9

UAP *see* United Australia Party
unemployment 66, 106, 124, 129, 145
unions/unionism 12–13, 16–17, 23,
    25–7, 33–4, 41–2, 43–6, 67, 69–72,
    73, 101–3, 122–3, 126, 170, 173
  the Accord 105–10
  and ALP pre-formation years 25–7
  ALP–unions relationship 70–1
  blue collar unions 69
  Combined Unions' and Branches'
    Steering Committee 75
  and the Great Depression 46
  membership 69, 70
  parliamentarians and union officials
    17
  political representation of unions 26,
    27–33
  'red rules' 46
  suppression of militant unionism 106
  trade unions 12–13, 16–17, 25–7,
    69–72, 126, 170, 173
  transformation in politics 108
  union confidence 85
  union funding 186
  union officials 17, 69–71, 72, 169–71
  and wage control 94–5
  waterfront battle 137
  and the Whitlam government 87
United Australia Party (UAP) 47,
    62–3
United Nations 57, 118

Vietnam War 67, 85, 93–4

wages 47, 48–50
  basic wage hearings 54
  centralised wage fixing 106
  equal pay for women 90
  wage control 94–5
  wage cuts and casualisation 46
  wage gains 64

wage indexation 96
wage pegging 59–60, 67
war 37–41, 55–68, 132, 159–61
  Advisory War Council 56
  anti-war sentiment 39, 56–7, 67, 85
  Cold War 57, 64–5, 68
  Japanese invasion scare 56–7
  peace initiatives 58
  resources for 58
  Vietnam War 67, 85, 93–4
  see also conscription
welfare 62–3, 66, 110–11, 141, 149
  quarantining 155
White Australia 32, 36, 91–3, 182
white racial unity 30
Whitlam era 83–103
Wik people 113
Wobblies, the *see* Industrial Workers of
  the World
WorkChoices 136–9, 180
  WorkChoices to WorkChoices Lite
    151–3, 163
workforce
  equal pay and childcare access
    concessions 90
  and health system 62
  white collar workers and strike action
    84
working class 8, 11–14, 25–8, 67
  the 40 hour week 59–60
  ALP membership 79
  discipline of 184
  dissatisfaction and industrial dispute
    40–1, 43–6
  and the Great Depression 46
  and Lang government 48–50
  militancy 37, 38, 43–6, 64, 106, 170
  radicalisation 43–6, 85, 86
  working class voters 163, 178–82
world economic downturn 95–6

yellow peril 58, 116
Your Rights at Work campaign 136–9,
    169, 180